Scaling Up

Scaling Up

The revised, expanded edition
of the classic book *Snakeman*

Zai Whitaker

Illustrations by
Bruce Peck

juggernaut

JUGGERNAUT BOOKS
C-I-128, First Floor, Sangam Vihar, Near Holi Chowk,
New Delhi 110080, India

Originally published as *Snakeman* in 1989 by India Magazine Books (or Banyan Books), a division of Business India Publications Ltd

This revised and expanded edition published by
Juggernaut Books 2024

10 9 8 7 6 5 4 3 2 1

P-ISBN: 9789353456658
E-ISBN: 9789353457532

Typeset in Adobe Caslon Pro by R. Ajith Kumar, Noida

Printed at Thomson Press India Ltd

For Shama

Contents

Introduction

I grew up in one of the most beautiful homes in Bombay: the best that good taste and empty pockets can create. The empty pockets were important, and resulted in innovation, careful spending and spare aesthetics that left guests wide-eyed with admiration. My mother, Laeeq, puts it well in her book *Gardening:* 'Perhaps it was an advantage that we had a house before we had an income, for the need to organize the land without any money was good training.' And earlier in the same book, in a backhanded compliment to my father, she writes: 'The influence of (my) conservationist husband Zafar Futehally, has persuaded (me) to avoid creating gardens which make unreasonable demands on scarce resources (including money), and to search for environmentally inexpensive ways of making a piece of land beautiful.' As for the good taste, it was a combination of genetic luck and twenty years in Kobe, Japan, where she was born and grew up. Her careers were writing and garden design; her projects included the Powai and Vihar public gardens in Bombay (now Mumbai) and the campuses of Larsen and Toubro and Bharat Electronics in Bangalore (now Bengaluru). Her writing and editing skills were put to good use as Literary Editor of *Quest* magazine and elsewhere.

My ornithologist father, Baba, wore several hats in those halcyon days of conservation in India and laid the foundation for many research initiatives, projects and Protected Areas. Encouraged by my granduncle Sálim Ali, he started the *Newsletter for Birdwatchers* in 1959 and remained its editor for forty-five years, until 2004. Initially cyclostyled at Dynacraft – the company of which he and brother Nazar were owners – it created a fantastic network of birdwatchers throughout the country. He was honorary secretary of the Bombay Natural History Society (BNHS) from 1961 to 1973 (and a co-editor of the *Journal of the Bombay Natural History Society* or *JBNHS*); executive board member of the International Union for the Conservation of Nature (IUCN) for a year, then its vice president for six years. In this last capacity, he organized the tenth General Assembly of the IUCN in 1969, which marked the advent of conservation in the country.

He went on to start the Indian chapter of the WWF (World Wildlife Fund, now World Wide Fund for Nature). He was one of the two non-official members of the steering committee of Project Tiger, part of wildlife protection committees in many states and the Centre, served on the Maharashtra State Wildlife Advisory Board, wrote prolifically on conservation, democracy and ornithology, accompanied Sálim Mamoo on bird surveys, and helped kick-start important wildlife studies – among others, on the Gir lion, the barasingha, Nilgiri tahr and great Indian bustard. And there were the environment assessment committees he was part of, such as for Rashtriya Chemicals and Fertilizers, which invariably ended with the committee's recommendations being ignored. Additionally, there were horses and riding, at a level where his horsemanship was praised by an equerry at Buckingham Palace, where Baba spotted a stallion he wanted to ride, mounted it in spite of the palace team's discomfort and astounded them with his horsemanship. A conservationist friend who was related to the royals and knew of his passion for horses had arranged that memorable ride for Baba.

Over the years, our dining table in Andheri hosted several of the world's conservation pioneers: gorilla–tiger–panda biologist Dr George Schaller, Sir Peter Scott of the Slimbridge Wildlife Trust, Gerald Durrell's curators from Jersey Zoo, Sir Hugh Elliot of the IUCN, Dr Dillon Ripley, Sálim Mamoo's friend and colleague from the Smithsonian Institution, and Richard and Maisie Fitter of the Fauna and Flora Preservation Society. The Indian contingent included M. Krishnan, Anne Wright, Vasant Rajyadhaksha, Duleep Matthai and, of course, Sálim Mamoo, who was a regular visitor.

As must be obvious by now, gentle reader, Dynacraft

was not a priority for my father. Birdwatching, conservation and horses left him little time for the trivial task of making money.

Both my parents were products of interesting DNA. There was Laeeq's uncle Sálim and Zafar's grandfather Badruddin Tyabji, who lived and died (in 1906) during the British period, also a legend – he was Chief Justice of Bombay, and later president of the Indian National Congress. Other family members included A.A.A. Fyzee, the Islamic scholar and India's ambassador to several countries, who went on to become vice chancellor of Aligarh University; Atiya Begum, who started and ran one of the literary and cultural hubs of Bombay; Danial Latifi, the lawyer, and spiritual leader and renowned singer Raihana Tyabji, an associate of Gandhiji. The family's UIDs were humour, integrity and patriotism; many were a strong force in the freedom struggle, and very few chose to move to Pakistan after Independence. They were also a modern-thinking, liberal bunch. Spouses of many different religions and countries were absorbed into the '*khandaan*'. One of these would be my future husband, Breezy/Rom/Romulus.

The conservation bug bit us three kids as well . . . after all, we'd heard about wildlife protection, Ramsar sites and habitat loss practically since the day we were born; maybe even before, because Amma was helping Sálim Mamoo write popular bird articles and books while she was pregnant with me. Words like ecosystem, ecology and biodiversity were to clamber into common use later. My sister Shama spent six months – the gap between school and college – working at the IUCN in Morges, Switzerland. From this experience, as well as having been Baba's unpaid typist from an early age, she had absorbed a good understanding of conservation issues and needs. On her return and while studying for a BA at St Xavier's College, she helped out at the WWF-India office. Together, and then with very limited resources, the father–daughter team managed to get an organization going that was to be at the core of the conservation movement of the 1970s. Her achievements were remarkable for one so young; she once lurked outside Sálim Mamoo's office until he seemed to be in a good mood, then handed him a letter she'd drafted for him to sign, urging Prime Minister Indira Gandhi to scrap the hydel project on the Kuntipuzha River in Kerala that would submerge the major part of the Silent Valley forests. She felt his signature would make a big difference to the campaign to save Silent Valley because of his stature as well as his personal friendship with Mrs Gandhi. He did, and she was right. His support on a conservation cause worked magic.

Around the same time, the WWF newsletter carried an article on Silent Valley by one Romulus Whitaker, an American herpetologist living in Madras (now Chennai) who was becoming well known in conservation circles. Along with the article came a request for five thousand rupees for his snake park. My father and other members of the Executive Committee admired Rom's work and knew it was important to draw reptiles into the ambit of conservation. In its infancy, with limited funds, WWF managed to give the Snake Park that vital donation, not a sniffy sum in those days.

So, when our paths crossed (to be described later), it was a perfect conservation partnership: the desk babu (me) and the hands-on herpetologist and jungle wanderer (Rom). Thanks to this combination of skills and interests, we were able to work together and set up the first herpetological organization in the country and put reptiles on the Indian conservation map. Our teamwork included campaigns and pestering of bureaucrats, raising funds and networking with other conservationists and organizations, all while carrying out the collection, breeding and rewilding of endangered species. Of course, there were often overlaps, such as writing and editing reports together, or me collecting mugger eggs or helping Rom dissect and skin a saltie (saltwater crocodile).

This is the story of that partnership, one that also delivered a result that we are particularly proud of – the creation of a new generation of conservationists, thanks to the volunteers, interns and researchers who worked with us at the Snake Park, Croc Bank, field projects and field stations. It is a story with highs and lows, and many twists and turns as our conservation journey scaled up.

The title of the book comes from a conversation with Sálim Mamoo, who visited me in Madras soon after I got married and asked how I was getting on. I gave him a pompous reply about how satisfying it was to work for this neglected group of animals. 'Birds and mammals get all the attention,' said I, 'but reptiles are equally important . . .' He looked a bit taken aback, did his famous head-bobbing, and said 'Oh, so you're SCALING them up, are you?' A great example of his quick repartee and impatience with pomposity! And makes a great title – thanks!

How do I thank publisher–editor–writer Anita Mani? For suggesting this project in the first place, then for her fine editor's eye, and most importantly, for convincing me that my own story was also worth telling, resulting in a self-belief far more valuable to me than the book.

Hello, Hippiss!

Rom grew up in Hoosick, upstate New York, where he lived from birth (1943) to 1947 with his mother, Doris Norden, and sister, Gail, in his Aunt Elly's Dutch mansion which had adjoining gardens and a beautiful lake. This idealistic childhood saw the beginning of his lifelong fascination for snakes. There were plenty of harmless garters and milk snakes in the surrounding countryside during the summer months, but more importantly, his mother encouraged this hobby and interest in every possible way. His alphabet songs did not follow the usual pattern of A for apple, B for bat; it was A for amphibian, B for brontosaurus, C for coral snake. Doris even stoutly defended him when one of his pets, a DeKay's snake, showed up in the glove compartment of a neighbour's car. When it was time to think about school, it was St Luke's in New York City, very different from the free, liberal atmosphere of Hoosick. It was not a happy fit, and his mother later told me how his teacher ended up installing a punching bag for his exclusive use.

Within two years, there was another move, this time further afield, to Bombay. Doris had married Rama Chattopadhyaya, son of the freedom fighter Kamaladevi, who became the main force behind the movement to revive our traditional handicrafts. Aged eight and twelve, the two children, Rom and Gail, were sent to boarding school, at first to Lovedale in the Nilgiris and a year later to Kodaikanal International School in the Palani Hills. There, the evergreen shola forests provided plenty of diversion from boring studies and Rom began a systematic collection of snakes, lizards and bugs. Many of these lived under his bed and enjoyed the time and attention that his studies were deprived of. His association with the sholas of Kodai spelt the beginning of a deep interest in tropical rainforests, and thirty years later, he helped form the Palani Hills Conservation Council to protect the unique environment of these hills.

At Kodai International, children were encouraged in outdoor activities and this suited Rom just fine. You could go off and camp for the weekend at Gundar Falls, Neptune's Pool, Berijam Lake and other beautiful, forested spots within hiking distance. At age twelve, Rom made a jump into the world of venomous snakes. A Russell's viper swimming in the cold Berijam Lake at an elevation of 2,000 metres caught his attention while on a camp. It was carefully picked up in a butterfly net and deposited in his lunch box. It lived with him for a few days, until some of his older friends wisely advised him to get rid of it. After reading, in the only snake book

The Thalaiyar Falls are the most prominent landmark as you ascend the ghats up to Kodaikanal. In peak season, they are an impressive sight, but deforestation has reduced them to a mere trickle for most of the year.

in the library, that it was 'one of the most virulent snakes in all of British India and causes many deaths among natives', Rom's first dangerous snake was reluctantly taken back to the wild and released.

It wasn't long before schoolkids and community people started bringing the occasional snake to him, usually the burrowing uropeltids or shieldtail snakes that were then common in the hills, and sometimes the mildly venomous green pit viper, locally known as the banana viper. Once a friend's eagerness to bring him a snake ended badly. Bill Brannen returned from a hike with a severely swollen and painful hand and related how he had tried to stuff a fat pit viper into his water canteen! Understandably, it turned and bit him on the finger. One of the boy scout friends with him decided to try incising the bite with a hunting knife and this treatment ended up causing more problems than the bite.

Probably the main reason Rom gained a certain dubious notoriety at Kodai School was his pet python. Bought from an animal dealer at Crawford Market in Bombay, this 2-metre snake became a gentle, much-handled pet. Technically, of course, no pets were allowed at school. But the python somehow slipped by for several years, as part of the empty luggage under the dormitory beds.

Some of the things Rom and his friends did in school make me wonder how they survived their youth. In the spear and bow-and-arrow phase, they discovered the local blacksmith who turned out superb spearheads and arrowheads, based on designs copied from Tarzan comics and pictures of native Americans in history books. There were only a couple of casualties during this period. But the fireworks, bomb and rocket phase was to give a few of them burns to remember and some really close calls. They made pipe cannons to shoot marbles way out into the lake, waterproof bombs to blast fish and, eventually, rockets that actually went up. They experimented with Molotov cocktails, thanks to Rom's discovery of a World War II pamphlet called *Bomber's Handbook*, and produced everything short of nitroglycerine in the chemistry lab.

During holidays in Bombay, he visited BNHS to read up on the snakes of Palani Hills and to make contact with naturalists and taxidermists. It was here that he first met Baba and Sálim Mamoo. Rom was impressed by the fact that their interest in nature had developed into their careers. At BNHS, he learnt about bird collection and skin mounting, which was becoming a favourite activity. As it had with both Sálim Mamoo and Baba, BNHS was to play a big role in encouraging his interest in ecology. And in Kodai, the Fathers at the Sacred Heart College at Shenbaganur helped him hone his taxidermy skills and occasionally let him use their old black powder guns.

When Rom graduated from Kodai School, he was sixteen. By then, there were two more children in the family, Neel and Nina. Both were friends of mine at the Bombay International School (BIS), of which Doris as well as my parents were founders. Neel was in my class; more interested in music than homework (or even classwork). His ready wit and charming smile got him out of many tight spots with teachers and the principal. The two families, Rom's and mine, were coming together, through the BNHS, BIS and the wider natural history network of the city.

Rom didn't feel ready for college on the other side of

the world, and Kamaladevi arranged for him to work as an apprentice with a taxidermist in Mysore. He moved to Vani Vilas Mohalla there, learning from and helping out at V. Pradaniah and Sons. They prepared and mounted a wide range of animals, from king cobras to tiger cubs. An airgun and other school possessions were sold in order to buy a 1941 Triumph motorbike, a 350cc single with mechanical forks and very little spring, but the kidneys are tough at that age. This mobility enabled Rom to make frequent trips to the forests near Gundlupet and Chamarajanagar at times when there was not much work at the taxidermist. His patron here was his namesake, Brother Romulus of Guntapuram, a jolly Franciscan priest, who later started a well-known boys' town.

He loved being at Brother Romulus's farm, where he had several tasks. One was crop protection. Surrounded by forest, anything grown in the fields was quickly devoured by wild boar, deer, porcupine or elephant. He and a few others kept these animals off the crops with the help of a black Labrador and Brother Romulus's two rifles and shotgun; in the process, they ended up being the main suppliers of fresh meat to the farm and its neighbours. Luckily, Rom never shot an elephant and missed the one leopard he sat up for. But plenty of spotted deer, sambar and blackbuck fell, and the gratitude of the farmers always balanced any twinge of remorse.

Those early days with Brother Romulus greatly increased Rom's confidence and skills in the forest. The watchers had numerous encounters with elephants, both by day and night, which taught him the right measure of caution. Meetings with bear, tiger and leopard helped develop a balanced, careful curiosity for the jungle. It was in the forests of Thalavadi and Guntapuram, now almost gone, that he found his first wild python. He was by himself and the snake was too big to tackle. Rom regretfully watched it disappear slowly into the network of caves and crevices that were its home.

In Mysore, he started spending as much time at the Mysore Zoo as he did at the taxidermist and got to know a lot of the animals well. He made friends with Dieter Rinkel, a young zoo keeper from Hamburg Zoo, and helped him feed and care for the seven young elephants he was taking back to Germany. But the forest trips continued and knapsack on back, Rom would go off camping on his own for several days at a time. Unlike most mothers, Doris realized the importance of restraining her fears and anxiety. It was probably this one year's total freedom among forests and wildlife that created the conservationist he was to become.

Meanwhile, my family's journey in this area was also unfolding. No one was catching pythons or camping in the rainforest, but my parents were now recognized pioneers in the world of conservation, which was becoming a common word in the Indian lexicon. Baba was often away on bird surveys with Sálim Mamoo, and the *Newsletter for Birdwatchers* had become a springboard for many birders who evolved into important players in the conservation scene and, today, speak of the vital role the *Newsletter* played in their lives. A combination of science and popular articles, it was accessible to many levels of ornithologists, from amateurs to serious 'listers'.

I would hear from Neel – mostly during maths class, which was Greek to us both – about his brother Breezy's visits. With his long blond hair, jeans and khadi kurta, Rom attracted catcalls and greetings on the Bombay sidewalks, usually 'Hello, Hippy!' When Neel was old enough to join him on his jaunts, the call became plural: 'Hello, Hippiss!'

But now it was time for college in the States, to say goodbye to the family and head off on his own to the University of Wyoming. A tough call at eighteen, but with the consolation that there was a bunch of interesting rattlesnakes waiting for him, including the prairie rattler. While at school, Rom had written to some of the big names in American herpetology and received encouraging replies, even from the snake guru Raymond Ditmars himself. Catching and selling snakes was becoming a business among the snake community in the States, which was growing apace. Non-venomous species like milk snakes and DeKay's were easily tamed and sold to the pet trade and venomous snakes were sold to laboratories for antivenom production and medical research. Not a bad pastime to look forward to, during holidays and after (and even during!) classes.

Rattlesnakes and Moccasins

By 1961, Rom was back in the States to try his hand at college. It didn't work. He used his brief brush with academics at the University of Wyoming to check out the trout fishing in high mountain streams and investigate the Western rattlesnakes. For the next two years, he attempted a variety of careers: truck driver, travelling salesman (unsuccessfully displaying table silverware), ship's messman in the merchant marines, palaeontologist's assistant, a waiter at a café patronized by typists – catcalls at every turn – and lab technician. But the big break came at last. In 1963, he got a job at the Miami Serpentarium, a venom production centre and reptile park owned and run by the legendary snake man Bill Haast. Haast produced and sold snake venom for medical research as well as the production of antivenom. For someone interested in snakes, it was a fantastic opportunity working with the most daring and expert snake handler in the world. Rom is a great storyteller; ten years later, when he was wooing a young Bombay girl (me), she listened with rapt attention as he related his adventures in Florida and later – after being conscripted – in Arizona. There were wonderful Scheherazade moments when we would sit on the stone bridge of our garden pond, and he'd relate his snake-catching adventures in the States. My unspoken responses swung wildly from 'Silly fool!' to 'My brave hero!' The other assistant at the Serpentarium, he told me, was Heyward Clamp, a taciturn snake hunter from South Carolina who became a good friend. Their day began with cleaning the cages and clearing the compound of various missiles thrown at the reptiles by visitors: tin cans, belt buckles, sticks, stones, cigarette butts. The most challenging enclosure to clean was that of the 4.5-metre-long Nile crocodile, Cookie. Sometimes, during this routine, they played at getting the large croc to snap at them, jumping out of reach in time. Fifteen years later, Cookie had to be shot after he killed a child who fell into the enclosure.

Heyward Clamp lowers a rattlesnake into a snakepit.

The big day at the Serpentarium was Sunday when Bill

Haast used to take out one of the large Thai king cobras for venom extraction. He'd spar with the deadly 4–5-metre snake as it sat up, hood spread in a magnificent defence display. Along the edges of the well-tended 'king cobra lawn', cameras clicked on all sides as Haast and the snake watched each other, tense and alert. Knees bent, Haast would close in and jerk his right hand to divert the snake's attention. With a carefully timed move, his left hand would flash in to grab the king cobra's neck. There were always gasps as the golden drops of venom trickled down the venom glass. Heyward or Rom would then help him feed the snake with a high protein formula through a feeding gun, which ensured that the snake would both survive as well as produce high quality venom.

Some three decades later, I was with Rom during one of his big life moments; we were going to meet Bill Haast, whom he hadn't met since the time he had to leave the job when Uncle Sam beckoned. We'd travelled to the Miami Serpentarium on one of the venom extraction days and stood in the crowd watching the gripping spectacle of Haast slowly moving in to capture the snake. After the operation was over – the golden drops safely in the venom glass, snake returned to its holding box – Rom stepped forward towards his mentor saying, 'Mr Haast, may I help you?' There was instant recognition, and we were lucky enough to spend an hour or so with the great herpetologist. Today, we work with his daughter Naia, who raises funds for our king cobra conservation work through the King Cobra Conservancy. (More of that later.)

At the time Rom worked for him, Haast had been bitten over a hundred times by venomous snakes and was the only person known to have survived a king cobra bite. Heyward Clamp had been assisting him the day it happened, and there was a big crowd. When Haast moved his right hand to get the snake's attention, it unexpectedly struck at his left, which Haast jerked aside. The irate snake turned to his right hand and caught him off guard; the deadly jaws clamped in with such force that a fang came away with the bite. While tourists screamed in panic and blood dripped down his immaculate white shoes, Haast calmly went through with the capture and finished the extraction and force-feeding schedules before calling the ambulance.

Haast had not been just lucky with the king cobra bite. He had systematically immunized his system against neurotoxic venoms by injecting himself with increasing doses and ended up being a walking antivenom kit. In fact, his blood was used several times as an antidote to treat people bitten by snakes for which there was no antivenom. A particularly dramatic instance was in 1966 when a boy in a Peruvian jungle was bitten by a deadly coral snake. At that time, there was no antivenom for this species and a severe bite was fatal. The Peruvian government acted quickly. Haast was contacted and arrangements were made for his instant departure. The busy highway in front of the Serpentarium, the South Dixie

Highway, was closed to traffic and a US Air Force helicopter landed on the pavement. Haast was flown to the nearby Homestead Air Force Base where a fighter jet was warmed up and waiting. He flew to Peru and another chopper took him to the jungle clearing where the boy lay, now close to death. Attending doctors cross-matched the blood, found group and type compatible, and were able to give the boy a direct transfusion of Haast's blood. Within a few hours, he was out of danger and Haast returned to Miami.

In later years, he further increased his medical fame with his 'venom cocktail', made of krait and moccasin venom, which he administered to patients with multiple sclerosis, a paradoxical treatment where venom brought relief.

During Rom's two years at the Serpentarium, most off-duty hours were spent looking for snakes with Heyward and other local snake catchers like Attila Beke and Gary Maas; the latter was to become a stuntman in the movies. Then, in the early 1960s, Florida's environment was still relatively intact and very different from the endless suburbia of today. The swamp forest where Rom and Heyward diligently hunted for snakes was later turned into housing estates and industrial complexes. But at that time, they could walk in almost any direction from the outskirts of Miami and get to undisturbed patches of tall, flooded grass dotted with hummocks of cypress trees. Hung with air plants and strings of lichen or Spanish moss, these looked like wild, abandoned Christmas trees.

It was a fifteen-minute drive to the Everglades on Rom's decrepit BSA 500 single or in Heyward's 1961 Ford. On early winter mornings, the fog would be low as they walked from hummock to hummock looking for snakes. During the dry season, the water receded into the canals and formed pools in the hummocks, in which they found swarms of water moccasins, watersnakes and fish crowding into pitiful mud holes for coolness. The fish would soon die, their backs out of the water, and this meant a feast for snakes, birds, otters, raccoons and other predators.

The snake hunts with Miami friends taught Rom invaluable tricks about looking in the right places at the right time. General rules about snake habits became the main guidelines. For example, in an area of complete wetness, head for the high and dry spots, and vice versa. Another rule: extreme weather conditions like droughts and floods increase the odds of finding snakes. In Miami, hurricanes brought a happy hunting season in their wake. One September evening in 1964, Rom and Heyward waited impatiently for Hurricane Dora to end before they started checking the roads. The destruction and high water brought by big winds had all sorts of creatures on the move, looking for shelter. And best of all, the stormy conditions kept other motorists off the road! Twelve water moccasins and twenty-five pigmy rattlers were the venomous snakes caught that night, plus a couple of sacks full of watersnakes. These would be sold to animal dealers who specialized in snakes.

One of the legendary snake catchers of South Florida was Schubert Lee, who shared a house with Rom and Heyward at Coconut Grove, Miami. He caught and sold snakes for a living, often water moccasins, the only venomous freshwater snakes in the United States. Schubert knew all the good snake places on the edge of the Great Cypress Swamp near an old canal running along the abandoned Loop Road. They would drive 3–4 kilometres up the road, get down and slosh into the water, avoiding the thorns and poison ivy. Often, they'd see a bunch of harmless watersnakes and among them a few black moccasins slipping warily away through the grass and hyacinth. Each of them would have a couple of cotton snake bags tucked in his belt; Rom carried a fairly elegant snake hook fashioned from a golf club and Schubert, the professional, a short stick as they waded into the waist-deep, squelchy mud. It was tough going, forging through the warm sludge and thick vegetation, but worth it because every few metres they would come across a moccasin, often a large one that would sell for four or five dollars. Sometimes, they came upon one at face level and this would be tricky; one had to tread slippery mud while the irate snake vibrated its tail and reared back, mouth open, ready for a strike. It is this spectacular defence display that gives them the name 'cottonmouth' or 'trap jaw'.

One memorable day both Rom and Schubert 'got bit', one after the other. They'd slithered down to a small ledge and there, behold, were three moccasins about to slip into the water: an opportunity not to be missed by a sane snake catcher! Rom pinned the head of one and bagged it while Schubert started to pull out another by its tail from the tangle of exposed roots on the edge of the canal. You never know where the head might be, and sure enough, it popped out and bit Schubert on the top of his hand.

'This might mess up our day' was his calm comment as Rom stared numbly at him. They sat down for a smoke on the edge of the canal to wait for the swelling and pain and debated which hospital they'd go to. But there was no reaction; it was a dry bite, with no venom injected, fortunately a common phenomenon. So, back to work.

By noon they were getting deeper into the Everglades hummocks and the loot was over forty moccasins. Making a brief stop to blame each other for not having brought along edibles, they waded towards the next hummock. Soon after, Rom saw some brightly coloured baby moccasins, which were well below the commercial size but would be ideal to rear at home. One had just fed and was fat and healthy. Muttering the usual 'Hang on there, snake', he descended to pin it against the floating log that it was resting on. The log went under, the snake hook slipped and the snake bit him. He lifted it carefully, dropped it into a snake bag and walked over to Schubert.

'It bit me!' he said weakly.

'They'll do that, sometimes' was Schubert's response.

The pain started soon after and Rom had to sit down as his hand began to throb and swell. They walked back to the car and drove to Miami to ask Haast's advice. He said that though a 'good' bite, it would just be troublesome and that antivenom was not needed. Sleeping was difficult for a few days, but soon there were no traces of the bite except that even today the bitten finger becomes numb in cool weather.

That was one of Rom's last snake hunts with Schubert. One night Rom and Heyward were out and Schubert was alone at their home, which also housed a collection of exotic and dangerous snakes. A little before midnight, Schubert's girlfriend, Florence, had a premonition that something was wrong with him and drove the 20 kilometres to Coconut Grove to see him. She found him lying on the floor, almost totally paralysed. He was still barely conscious, however, and able to respond to questions. Florence knew at once that it was a snakebite and asked him if it was a water moccasin. He shook his head. No. 'Cobra?' Yes, affirmative. He had got one of their big black Pakistani cobras to bite him repeatedly on the wrist in a suicide attempt.

Florence was a diminutive woman and Schubert tall and hefty, but she managed to get him into her station wagon and drive to the nearest hospital. Haast was called and the doctors pumped Schubert with a pint of his blood and 500ccs of antivenom, but Schubert's breathing stopped and after seventy-two hours on a respirator, he died. Heyward and Rom, pallbearers at the funeral, were stricken; remorse reinforced grief. They had always known that Schubert had financial and other problems but had never attempted to break the barrier of his reticence. If only they had made him talk, if only they'd stayed home that one night or made him come along too. If only. They moved out of the Coconut Grove house, now haunted by Schubert Lee's ghost.

Rom and Heyward would often go to the Everglades in the evening after work since neither was inclined to socialize. Occasionally they were met with the bright red reflecting eyes of an alligator, which was always a welcome addition to the Serpentarium's collection. One night Heyward spotted a gator, which, judging from the gap between its eyes, seemed to be about a metre long. Clamping his headlight on his forehead with the beam directed at the eyes, he picked up a noose tied to the end of a stick, rope dragging behind, and walked slowly towards his prey.

The gator was on the edge of a large pool, head resting on a grass bank, and dumbly allowed the swivel noose to drop over his head. As Heyward tightened the noose, the alligator turned and headed for deep water. He was quite a bit bigger than Heyward had anticipated, and Rom watched anxiously as his friend disappeared into deeper and deeper water. Then there was a yell – 'Hey, it's big!' – at which point Rom jumped into the water and grabbed the trailing rope. But Heyward had gone under, his hat afloat, and every now and then his head would bob up. Rom knew that alligators were the gentlest of the crocodilians and that Heyward wasn't about to get eaten up. But he was afraid that his friend might have got a hand or leg tangled in the rope. If that happened, the alligator might drag him under the thick weeds. After a struggle, the captor and captive made it to the shallows and the struggling animal was trussed up. It turned out to be over 2 metres long and Heyward, pronouncing himself 'shook', said it was important to 'judge them eyes right'. Sometimes, an animal dealer's interest in a particular snake would take them much farther afield, and Haast would grant a few days of leave. Attila had an old Plymouth '55 and on one such occasion, he and Rom rode north for a rattlesnake hunt. The Highway Patrol showed considerable interest in the two scruffy snake hunters but always let them go in a hurry when they saw the cargo. They unloaded whatever southern snakes they had with them at an animal dealer's place in New York City before heading inland towards timber rattlesnake country.

They had an order from an animal dealer for fifty of these snakes, and Attila was pretty sure he knew where to find them. It was spring. The rattlers, having spent the winter months deep in caves and crevices and grouped together in dens, would now begin to emerge and disperse. The destination for this trip was a ridge of rock-faced hills around Binghamton, New York. A chat with locals at a roadside tavern gave Rom and Attila a fair idea of where rattlesnakes were seen each year. Leaving the Plymouth, they hiked up through the cedar and poplar trees, flushing grouse and startling a white-tailed deer.

Attila's usual canniness brought them to the south face of the rocky slopes and very suddenly, the first rattler appeared. 'Great going, hombre,' said Attila as the handsome timber rattler was lifted and bagged. But then it seemed as if their eyes were playing tricks. In every direction from that spot, there were rattlers basking in the shafts of sunlight filtering down through the trees. They just walked over to the bigger

The eastern diamondback, which looks similar to the timber rattler, is the most venomous snake of the south-eastern United States. When spotted, it curls into a tight defensive coil, rattling ominously.

ones and methodically caught and bagged them. Most of them were still close to the den openings in the shale-covered slope and some were alert enough to zip back into the safety of their holes.

Rom saw the coil of a fat, black phase timber rattlesnake protruding from under a slab of shale and lifted it. Beneath was a pile of rattlers several deep and already starting to move. Together, he and Attila flipped the big ones out into the open, letting the small ones get away – there must have been thirty or more in that pile! A biggy was getting away into a cave, so Attila quickly grabbed its tail and was just as quickly nailed by the snake on the top of his hand. He broke into appropriate language and they waited for symptoms. But once more it was a dry bite, and they thanked whoever it is who watches over snake hunters. The day's haul was over fifty timber rattlers. Rom also caught a few particularly good-looking juveniles, to rear at home.

While working for Haast, a hotel owner from what was then Rhodesia (Zimbabwe today) offered Rom the manager's job at his small snake park outside of Salisbury. But as Rom was preparing to leave, the dreaded 'Greetings from the President' letter arrived. Uncle Sam had got him; it was off to the United States army for two years, helping in a conflict – the Vietnam War – that he felt bitterly opposed to. It was a difficult time, which he tries to forget. Sadistic corporals kicked you in the backside when you fell, exhausted, before the finish of the mile run, or made you clean less than sparkling shoes with your nose at inspection time. But there were some good snake hunting days too thanks to Uncle Sam, mostly off duty. The two months basic training at Fort Gordon, Georgia, in 1965 and then duty at El Paso, Texas, provided an opportunity to see many reptiles he'd not met with before – snakes like the black-tailed and giant Mojave rattlesnakes. There were always other soldiers willing to come along on snake hunts, mostly the rabble-rousers. Rom remembers, 'One of them, Ponzo, would come back to the barracks at night drunk out of his head and piss on someone, starting a brawl. One night, he favoured my friend Jim, and Jim flew at him with a growl and tied him up with the wires of his stereo set. They all went to sleep leaving Ponzo in a peaceful inebriated slumber.' At El Paso, Rom was a lab technician at the army's William Beaumont General Hospital and his work consisted of routine medical tests, not very exciting except the weekly blood sample schedule at Ward 30, the psychiatric ward. He soon got used to wide-eyed patients begging him to take more blood, or whacking him as he went by. But these minor disadvantages were offset by the lab facilities and equipment, good for experiments with snake venoms and for making slides of blood and frozen sections of snake scales and fangs. And every evening, he was off to the desert to look for snakes, often foraying into the Chihuahuan Desert across the border in Mexico to fulfil orders from animal dealers and venom laboratories on the East Coast. The income from this parallel snake-catching occupation – fifty cents for a fence lizard and ten to fifteen dollars for a rattler, depending on the species and size – was useful in boosting the meagre army pay.

But it was tricky keeping snakes in the barracks. The wall lockers had to be clear of any suspicious belongings on inspection days. Rattlesnakes were a special problem, you didn't want some wise guy reporting strange sounds from Number 133's locker. In view of this contingency, Rom started binding their rattles with Scotch tape. Later the captain of the local fire brigade, M.K. Dick, offered to house his collection. 'MK' and his vivacious wife had a gun repair business and three pretty daughters. Rom visited them whenever he could sneak past the dopey desk sergeant.

One evening he was bitten by a prairie rattler. The pain was a deep, persistent burn and his arm swelled up like a balloon by the time he reported to the emergency room. The team of doctors, happy to have something unusual to do at last, led him off into intensive care and started an experiment by submerging Rom's arm in ice for seventy-two hours. More painful – and dangerous – than the bite; it was twenty days before he recovered from the treatment. Now, over fifty years later, the finger periodically swells up and exudes a clear, yellow liquid. The nerves in his finger never grew back and

Rom hoped that this loss of his trigger finger would exclude him from any active war duty.

All of Rom's leave was spent in neighbouring Arizona and he got to know the beautiful Huachuca and Chiricahua mountains well. Claire, the secretary in the pathology lab, shared his interest in roaming the hills and often went along. They wandered around the shale slopes, often running into coatimundis, deer and bear.

One day's snake hunt took Rom down the Montezuma trail, a steep path leading to Mexico from Miller Peak, at 2,800 metres, the highest in the Huachucas. It had rained in the morning and a mist was rising from the ground, ethereally illuminated by the early sun. A movement on the path ahead made him stop short. It was a burly brown bear tearing open a rotten log and noisily devouring beetles, grubs and ant eggs. It must have snuffed an ant up its nose because it suddenly sneezed loudly and seemed to startle itself. There was only this one route across the steep hillside and Rom had to gently encourage the bear to go away. He flapped his arms and cleared his throat. The bear quickly stopped eating and looked up suspiciously. Fortunately, it did what was required and with one backward glance, ambled uphill away from the path.

There are over a dozen species of rattlesnakes and numerous other reptilian inhabitants in these mountains of southern Arizona, and the periodic ten-day leave would fly past like a dream. Rom's most vivid memory, though, is of getting bitten by the rare and much-sought-after green rock rattlesnake. It happened when he was at 2,000 metres in the Huachucas before the sun was up, watching coatimundis looking for ripe fruit. Coatis reminded Rom of Indian civet cats, with their feline features and insatiable curiosity.

Picking his way up the old mining trail into Ramsay Canyon, Rom paused to listen to the distant roar of an avalanche. The Huachucas have many unstable cliffs, which dramatically collapse to form vast, steep, triangular slides of broken boulders. Perhaps these rumblings were the basis for the Indian name Huachuca, Thunder Mountains. About mid-morning, just as the sun was reaching down into the canyon – the very time when snakes start emerging for an early morning bask – Rom gingerly climbed a rock slide composed of loose rock. Suddenly from under a boulder came the welcome, high-pitched buzz of a green rock rattler. Carefully removing stones around the source of the buzzing, he reached down to shift a large rock. There was a moment's hesitation to find his balance, and in that instant, a little grey head darted out and caught his thumb. 'Yipes, I'm nailed!' he yelled to the forest. It was a bad bite, a deep two-fanger. To add insult to injury, the snake disappeared.

Determined to stay away from doctors this time, Rom walked down the canyon to Nell Brown's home. Nell was caretaker for a doctor's country house and apple orchard and was locally famous for her clairvoyant powers. The house had old, crudely made glass windowpanes in which she claimed to see future events like accidents, assassinations, marriages, deaths. By the time Rom got to Nell's, a burning, pounding pain was making him moan and swear, and a bloody fluid flowed from the fang punctures. The thumb was a large purplish blob and the hand so swollen and shiny that it looked – and felt – like it wanted to split open. Soon an allergic reaction began; twenty sneezes a minute and intense itching all over. This was the first indication of a venom allergy, which in later years prevented him from working with venoms altogether.

By midday, the pain was a lot worse and the evening passed in a semi-delirium under the trees in Nell's orchard. She insisted that he sleep in her barn, and the good meal she provided, complete with strong coffee, helped enormously. But when getting up at night to click on the light, Rom's eyes suddenly went dim. He was clear-headed and conscious but blind. Losing his equilibrium, he collapsed. He crawled back across the room to his bed and lay down shivering and blinking, afraid to touch his eyes but hoping to somehow blink sight back. It was several long minutes, perhaps ten, before a grey light filtered through.

A few days later, he felt normal and it was back to business. Venom experts confirmed that though rattlesnakes are pit vipers and so have essentially haemotoxic (blood-affecting) venoms, they get more neurotoxic (nerve-affecting) as you reach the Mexican border. And this frightening blindness was indeed a neurotoxic symptom.

After six months in El Paso, Rom was sent to Japan to work in US military bases in Honshu, Hokkaido and Kyushu. This was the peak of the Vietnam War and young GIs were confronted with the horrifying efficiency of the war machine. Rom was part of the fifteen-member mobile blood team of the 406th medical lab at Camp Zama, and their job was to collect and ship fresh blood to the Nam. This was the first war in which fresh, whole blood was available at the front.

There were all kinds of soldiers. Some couldn't wait to get back and kill, others wet their beds and cried for their mothers in their sleep. Hardened war regulars talked excitedly about shooting up a bunch of 'gooks' in the Nam. Camp Zama was overflowing with wounded and convalescing soldiers. There were slot machines at the club and a happy hour at the bar each evening when all drinks were ten cents, and down the road was a skivvy show, which featured stage skits with naked girls of all shapes and sizes.

Six months later, it was back to El Paso and the William Beaumont General Hospital. Night duty hours, alone among the long halls of the pathology lab, was a good time for Rom to think about the future when he stopped being a number and became a person again. Working for someone else, particularly Uncle Sam, was becoming a drag, and he didn't have the qualifications to choose his career.

One night, while attending to the blood needs of victims of a local shootout, Rom decided he would move back to

Bombay, and try to make a career from his interest in reptiles. A venom production unit, he decided, as he assured the army doc that there were two more bottles of A negative in the blood fridge. Flights to India were beyond his budget; he'd have to travel 'surface', probably a freight ship, which was still a price beyond his bank balance. But there were ways around this. On his release from the army in 1967, Specialist Romulus Whitaker managed to catch five hundred dollars worth of rattlesnakes on a final snake hunt and get on board the old Greek freighter *The Hellenic Leader* that was bound for Bombay.

Gaimukh Bundar

The war-torn Suez Canal was closed and it was a long journey; fifty days from New York to the Cape of Good Hope, another five to Port Sudan. Masawa, Djibouti . . . and another two weeks to Bombay. They'd just anchored and were yet to clear health and customs when, with typical impatience, Rom talked his way aboard the pilot boat and was soon ashore with his rattlesnakes, moccasins and a few personal belongings. Looking out of a familiar black and yellow taxi, it seemed to him that Bombay had changed a lot in the six years he'd been away; it was much more crowded and dirty. He'd also changed; so much had happened in his life. Had he made the right decision? From a distance, coming penniless to India to seek a niche had seemed a romantic adventure. But now he realized it would be a difficult one as well.

Arriving at Chateau Marine, his grandmother Kamaladevi Chattopadhyaya's apartment on Marine Drive, which had been the family home for many years, he took the lift upstairs and everyone screamed in joy and surprise at the unannounced arrival. Nina and Neel, children when last seen, were now good-looking, bead-wearing teenagers, Nina fair and blonde and Neel the 'dark sheep of the family', as he called himself! Neel had been playing the guitar for several years and it was obvious he had that special gift which brings an instrument to life. The stack of records Rom had brought was quickly unpacked and the house resounded with the latest Beatles, Dylan, Zappa and Hendrix sounds. A year later, Neel was to form one of Bombay's first 'beat groups', as small rock bands were called.

Doris, divorced from Rama, had remained a close friend of his mother Kamaladevi and often travelled with her on crafts-related projects. She was also, along with my parents, a founder of the Bombay International School (BIS), where all of us kids, my sister Shama and I and Nina and Neel, were students; Neel and I were classmates until he decided there were better things in life and left school to devote his time to music. But before that his handsome American brother visited BIS and all us teenage girls were smitten good and proper. (We were disappointed when we realized that he had a very pretty girlfriend, Linda, who had flown out to join him.)

With the help of family and friends, Rom and Linda found a beautifully located little house at Gaimukh, on the northernmost point of the island chain that makes up Bombay. It was on the tip of Gorbunder Road, which protrudes into the Bassein Creek and the story was that a

German biologist had built it before the war. The termites had indulged in a thirty-year feast on the doors and windows, and the roof was about to cave in. There was no electricity and no running water, just an open well a hundred metres from the house.

Rom and Linda made appropriate alterations and repairs to the house, to accommodate themselves as well as their snakes. Their quiet life revolved around looking after the snake collection, writing magazine articles to make a bit of extra money, and doing their shopping on his 250cc Jawa in Borivali village, 12 kilometres away. Closer by, there was a very small village with a tea shop, which serviced the labourers from a nearby quarry. It must have been lonely sometimes for Linda, but she adapted admirably to this rural environment, pulling water from the well and learning Marathi from the neighbours. Soon the *saamp wallah*, snake man, and Lindabai became popular local figures. The family turned up now and then with brownies and other goodies baked by Doris.

There was a market for the venoms of the cobra, krait, Russell's viper and saw-scaled viper, the four common dangerous snakes of India – which Rom dubbed the Big Four – in the United States, primarily for medical research. Cobra venom was being used to control intractable pain, while some venom enzymes had been found to kill cancer cells in mice, and viper venoms were a source of potent blood clotting factors used to control bleeding in haemophilia and surgery. The project had seemed a cinch, but the initial bureaucratic runaround almost made him give up; he'd been out of India too long, and the reserves of patience and self-control needed to face the loops of red tape had dried up. An official in the Department of Commerce said that venom export was banned and that Rom would have to get a special licence. But attempts to get one proved futile. 'Why do you want a licence,' the export people asked kindly, 'when no ban is available on venom export?'

Again, family and friends came to the rescue, notably Rajni Zaveri with his many government contacts, who also helped Rom source equipment for the venom unit. Saturday and Sunday were venom extraction days, and Doris would drive out from Bombay to stand by in the event of a bite and take back the venom to store in her freezer at home. At first, snakes were kept in large wooden cages and later in cement pits, round enclosures with smooth walls from which they sometimes escaped. The menagerie usually included fifty cobras, thirty or forty Russell's vipers and several hundred saw-scaled vipers, which looked like heaps of live spaghetti. Kraits were not easy to come by in that area and Rom would make periodic trips to Madras to buy them from the Irular snake catchers who worked for the snakeskin industry. He had been introduced to them by Harry Miller, a 'stayed on' British photojournalist who worked for the *Indian Express* newspaper. This unique community was to play a key role in Rom's future.

West Bengal snake catchers often play with banded kraits knowing that they rarely bite but aware that they are venomous.

He also made several visits to the 24 Parganas district in West Bengal to meet the snake catchers of Baruipur, whose specialities were banded kraits and monocellate cobras. During a winter snake hunt, one of them found a dozen banded kraits in one termite mound! The same man was bitten on his wrist by a cobra that year. He treated the bite by incising it but in his panic, sliced several tendons and within a year, his arm was shrivelled and useless. Most traditional snake catcher communities didn't believe in antivenom treatment, but they were certainly the best repositories of knowledge about reptile ecology and behaviour.

At Gaimukh, a lot of Rom's time was spent tramping about the countryside looking for snakes. Finally, and quite legitimately, he was doing what he liked best, although venom orders were few and far between and the financial outlook was bleak. The hillsides behind the house were then covered with forest, the tail end of what is now the Borivali National Park. There was forest across the 150-metre-wide creek too; cultivated areas started only towards Thane, about 5 kilometres up the road. That was good snake country, paddy fields bordered with thickly vegetated bunds, and Russell's vipers were especially common, lurking in cactus hedges waiting for an unwary bird or rat.

Identifying the common, widely distributed species was not a problem; Rom had been learning about them since his childhood. But there was no updated or comprehensive work on the taxonomy or natural history of Indian snakes; he would be the one to make herpetology a popular subject in India. There were a few reptile 'watchers' around Bombay, and he kept in touch with them as much as he could. They shared their observations through postcards and inland letter forms, and he made occasional visits to the BNHS. People there – such as J.C. Daniel, Robert Grubh, my uncles Shamoon and Humayun Abdulali – encouraged him to turn his daily logbook notes into occasional papers for the society's journal. These became an important part of his book *Common Indian Snakes*, and the habit of meticulous note-taking proved invaluable. He still scribbles notes, often an interesting titbit of reptile information or a reminder to himself, during meetings and conversations. It's a habit I've plagiarized from him, and it has proved very useful.

The one important reference book then used by those interested in snakes was Malcolm Smith's *Fauna of British India Volume III*, which gives accurate descriptions of the different species but very little about their ecology and habits. Further, since the book's publication in 1943, there had been no attempts to improve or extend it. This gap was partly filled by studies done by herpetologists in neighbouring countries such as Dr Sherman Minton's report on the reptiles and amphibians of Pakistan and the late Dr Edward Taylor's classic volumes on the amphibians, snakes and lizards of Thailand.

Rom enjoyed delving into old snake books, which have now become collectors' items, such as Fayrer's *Thanatophidia of India*, 1874, and Patrick Russell's *An Account of Indian Serpents on the Coast of Coromandel*, 1796. Russell, after whom the Russell's viper is named, produced this two-volume work, adorned with hand-painted colour plates of the common snakes of the area he mainly worked in, coastal Andhra Pradesh. His book's opening words are just as applicable today, nearly two hundred years after its publication: 'The terror occasioned by these numerous reptiles is immediately aggravated by the indiscriminate apprehension of all being poisonous. To distinguish, therefore, those that are really so, from such (by far the greatest number) as are harmless, becomes a matter next in importance to the discovery of a remedy against their poison.'[1]

The remedy – antivenom – had been discovered and was available by the early 1900s. But in Gaimukh in the 1960s, Rom found that it was yet to reach the rural poor, the most common victims of snakebite, and no effort was being made through schools or the media to tell people which snakes to watch out for or even that an effective treatment existed. His 1972 surveys on snakebite with Dr Yoshio Sawai of the Japan Snake Institute highlighted the shocker that 90 per cent of fatal cases of snakebite never even got to a hospital and were treated with mantras, herbal preparations and other 'cures' that kept quacks in business. Snakebite mitigation, with a focus on prevention, was to become his lifelong mission and morph into a major conservation project in the coming years.

At the Gaimukh venom centre orders started to trickle in, and Rom and Linda put out the word for large numbers of snakes. At first there was an incredulous silence – then the deluge. Almost every day someone would come running down the road, shouting *saamp, saamp*! Anything from a worm snake onward was called a *naag saamp* (cobra) and every snake was 'as thick as my arm' and 'Arre baba, very poisonous'. People were terrified of every snake; there were reports of deaths from panic and fright from non-venomous snakebites. And most often, a snake was assumed to be venomous and killed on sight. Surrounded by this ignorance-generated fear, Rom began to understand how important a snake park would be as an education centre. Snake parks and serpentariums were a part of the tourist trails in the States, but unknown in India at that time. It was only the animal dealers who had snake collections, and these were kept in dismal conditions with high mortalities.

Linda and Rom were also the local dumping ground for anything alive, and Linda became proficient in rearing injured foxes, fledgling kites, baby jackals, civets, mongooses and other smaller creatures. And during the monsoon, when reptiles are most active, there would be constant summons from nearby houses to come and catch snakes. One night a desperate man came in to say his wife had not been in the kitchen for three days. 'She saw a snake on the roof, Sahib, and since then there's been no food for me.' Every snake-catching visit would end up with an impromptu lecture on snakes and snakebite treatment, but the traditional beliefs and legends were not easy to dispel. Especially entrenched were the convictions about mantras and herbal medicines, and Rom had to compromise: 'Okay, take herbal medicines, but only on the way to hospital!'

One day a few months after moving to Gaimukh, Linda and Rom were summoned to a nearby field. The farmers had been in the process of uprooting a tree until they came to a snake's tail sticking out of a hole. The inevitable crowd had gathered. Holding the tail, Rom started to pull, expecting it to slide out backwards. But this didn't happen. It was a large cobra which, like Winnie the Pooh, was firmly stuck. He started to dig with a crowbar and scooped out enough earth so that some of the snake's body became visible. It took a lot more digging and pulling before they were finally able to get it out. A big bulge soon told the story; the snake had eaten a large rat before entering the hole and suffered for it. But the real culprit of the traffic jam was yet to come. Rom had the cobra in his left hand and was just about to bag it when a large monitor lizard charged out of the hole and ran into the crowd. Some of the men tried to kill it with a crowbar and indeed got the tail, but Rom yelled, 'Wait!' and jumped forward, cobra in hand, to grab it. Soon both animals were off on their first motorbike ride, in Doris's pillowcases.

The *dhaman* or rat snake was the most common large terrestrial snake of the Maharashtra countryside and people often mistook it for the cobra, an all-India tendency. Rom's diary for 1968 shows that he caught thirty-five *dhaman*s, most of them 1.5–2 metres long. The largest, 2.5 metres, 'was in the act of stalking a hare which was crouched motionless, watching the snake, seemingly transfixed with interest or fear – but definitely not hypnotized as it was quick to recognize us as intruders and made off, the snake being detained by means of a leap and a grab'. Rom's notes continue:

> All dhamans are excitable and many bite – somewhat clumsily at first – but most will become tame if handled regularly. Six of those caught emitted a fairly loud 'growl' from deep in the throat when grabbed. When approached

> in a corner or cage they will expand their throat, arch the neck and body and make spastic lunges with partly open mouth. When encountered in thick bushes they often get away, having the advantage in thorny and rocky places. They may be captured by either jumping on them before they escape (although their superficial resemblance to cobras makes this a dubious practice), or a helper could try to head the snake off and drive it towards you. I have also dug them out of rat tunnels, from under the roots of trees, from rock piles, rubbish dumps and from out of the hollows of trees. Color varies from deep olive – almost black – to very light brown and the young in this area are a 'medium' greenish brown. Most specimens feed well in captivity, killing prey by pressure from body and mouth rather than by constriction. They even take long-dead rats. Frogs are swallowed alive, sometimes beeping in protest all the way down into the snake's gut. On July 13, a 1.8 meter female laid 14 eggs, and 13 hatched on September 16th and 17th; average length of hatchlings was 285 mm.

Being called to catch a snake or monitor, the latter often considered poisonous, was always exciting and educative and brought Rom closer to local farmers, many of whom became friends. But summons to treat snakebite victims were mostly grim; hospital and antivenom were always a last resort and several of the patients brought to him were too far gone to receive any help. However, sometimes seemingly hopeless cases came round with antivenom, such as a fourteen-year-old boy bitten by a krait and carried in totally paralysed. There was no time to get the doctor and Rom gave him two ampoules of antivenom intravenously. The boy recovered in an hour.

Apart from extracting and selling venom, Rom was also collecting snakes for the Haffkine Institute, then, as now, a major producer of antivenom in India. He went on several snake-buying exercises on Haffkine's behalf to other parts of the country and one of these took him to Ratnagiri district, south of Bombay. Here, saw-scaled vipers or *phoorsi*s are common during the rains, then disappear like magic for the rest of the year. More hazardous than catching these vipers was the overnight bus journey from Bombay to the small town of

During his 'snake travels', Rom also encountered the monocellate cobra of north-eastern India.

Deogadh. The bus swung along the steep ghats like a roller coaster, and Rom noted anxiously that the steering wheel spun like a top and the gearbox was held together with rope. When it was time to change gears, the bus conductor leapt on to it and tugged gallantly along with the driver.

Anyway, in spite of this team effort or perhaps because of it, the bus did get to Deogadh. The Ratnagiri landscape is spectacular, red laterite tableland with steep cliffs plunging into the Arabian Sea and small patches of jungle dotting the stark expanse. But the moonscape tableland is the most prevalent and the boulders scattered all over provide ideal habitat for the saw-scaled viper. Its prey, mice and scorpions, are correspondingly abundant. A local Adivasi group, the Mahrs, are the traditional snake catchers in this area and Rom contacted them through a friend, Mr Doshi. They agreed to take him along on their *phoorsi* hunts over the next few days.

It rained every day, some days without ceasing, on others in short dynamic cloudbursts. The air was always hazy with moisture, the rocks always slippery. The twenty Mahrs and Rom split up into groups of two or three, and each had four basic pieces of equipment; an umbrella, a pair of tongs, a stone turner and a snake container. The Mahr stone turner was a short bamboo pole with a long iron spike at the end; the tongs were improvised with strips of bamboo bound about 10 centimetres up one end, forming a metre-long pincer clamp. The container for the *phoorsis* was a cow dung plastered conical basket with a weighted coconut-shell cover.

Rom and his two Mahr companions would start early, walking fast and covering 15–18 kilometres, occasionally coming across the other catchers. It took Rom a couple of days to learn the art of walking on the slippery terrain without falling every few steps (with a clatter of umbrella and snake hook), at which there would be a healthy roar of joy from his new friends. Barefoot was best but he didn't have the leathery soles of the others and suffered. Their job was simply to walk through the great fields of boulders, turning over every likely rock. They averaged about a hundred rocks turned for each snake – but sometimes Rom would see veteran catcher Jamsandekar in the distance, huddled under his umbrella, stooping and straightening, bending and unbending with a snake almost every time.

One afternoon they walked south along the rugged coastline, crossing the many creeks and skirting the cliff edges. The surf boomed below and the air was thick with humidity; walking was like treading water. They headed inland towards Lindahl and began the zigzag walk that would take them back to Deogadh, turning over rocks as they went along. A family of crows followed them for a long time, cleaning up the crabs, scorpions, earwigs, earthworms and chameleons that scrambled out as their homes suddenly vanished. After a while, Jamsandekar's loud laugh rang out. 'They are good snake hunters!' he shouted, pointing to the crows that were now turning over the smaller stones themselves.

That night after a bath, Rom had stretched out in one of the long-armed rest house chairs, watching the rain sweep down in sheets. It was pitch dark when a man came tearing in holding a kerosene lamp, soaked and panting. '*Saamp*, Sahib, *saamp*!' 'Where?' A big cobra had been found in Mr Doshi's house, so Rom jogged the wet kilometre to the village and through a crowd in front of the house. Several men had long poles; one had a double-barreled shotgun. Everyone gave an account of how the snake had come into the house out of the hard rain, crawling right past several people and ending up in a storage bin. 'It's as thick as my arm,' said poor Mrs Doshi, but her neighbour corrected her. 'No, it's as thick as my leg.' And sure enough, it was a good-sized cobra, 1.5 metres long, full of beans and furious when Rom hauled it out of its comfortable dark bin.

The next evening there was a repeat performance, only this time it was a Russell's viper in Mr Doshi's secretary's house. This sort of open visitation by snakes was not that

The Russell's viper is a difficult snake to handle. It is strong and agile, and reacts violently to being picked up.

common, but it had rained exceptionally heavily on both days, and snakes were seeking dry refuge after being flooded out of their holes. By the end of the week, Rom had 2,000 of the small but deadly saw-scaled vipers carefully packed for the trip back to Bombay.

Soon after, Rom and Linda went with the Madras-based journalist Harry Miller to Battis Shirala near Sangli, Maharashtra. Harry was at that time writing an article for the *National Geographic* on cobras and gathering information on cobra worship during the harvest festival of Naag Panchami. In Battis Shirala, the festival is celebrated by worshipping cobras caught in the wild with their fangs intact, unlike most places where defanged cobras are used. The local people here believe that many years ago a guru granted them immunity from snakebite. Farmers, field labourers and merchants set out to catch cobras a few days before the festival, keeping them in mud pots and releasing them back into the fields after the celebrations are over.

Harry, Rom and Linda arrived at the small town to see processions of bullock carts with raised platforms; on these sat men with one or more cobras. Intrigued, Rom asked to examine the snakes and gently prised open their mouths to find the fangs intact. There were people walking down the street with a rat snake or banded racer round their necks, and children shuffling along, draped with two or three racers or rat snakes.

In the evening, the cobras were arranged on the pavement and entertained with small pots half filled with pebbles, which a snake charmer shook back and forth. There were white spots on the pot and this combination of the startling spots and the pebbles' vibrations made the snakes spread their hoods and sit up; the defence display is universally called the cobra 'dance'. Apparently, these tricks of the trade had been passed on to the people by the guru, along with the immunity to snakebite. Monitor lizards also played a part in the festivities; hundreds were trussed to poles and marched up and down like some bizarre parody of a crucifixion.

When there was a lull in the procession or time out for a tea break, the monitors were stacked against a wall like so many broomsticks. At the end of the day, the cobras were brought to a central area, where there were tens of thousands of people, and the shouting and revelling made a loud background roar. Finally, over 200 cobras were lined up, hoods spread in a sort of swaying inspection parade, and women stepped forward to worship them with ghee, red kumkum powder and flowers.

A large venom order was just coming through from the United States when the Indian government banned its export. Since the Indian market was very limited, it was the end of the road for the venom centre. Rom was bitterly disappointed. It had been the perfect job for him. Now he was back to square one and felt that a year's effort had gone down the drain. He also needed a physical change of scene and decided to move to the epicentre of snake-hunting activity, Tamil Nadu, in a sense his home state where Kodaikanal International School is located. There was another upside; for someone who had failed to find like-minded friends, Tamil Nadu was a goldmine with a community of over a thousand Irular doing nothing but catching snakes. He'd already been organizing consignments of snakes from them to Haffkine Institute and had become friends with several Irular. Also, his Tamil had been improving, the language barrier closing. Based in Madras, near Irular settlements, it would be that much easier to collect, pack and ship snakes to customers.

He and Linda found a small house on Chamiers Road in Madras for four hundred rupees a month, with plenty of storage space for crates of cobras, vipers and kraits. They only had to make sure the landlord didn't find out what they were up to.

India's Pioneer Snake Park

Thirty kraits, fifteen cobras, five Russell's vipers. *Suratai pambu* (saw-scaled vipers)? Let's see . . . two, four, six, eight. Like a dhobi counting clothes to be washed, Arjun and the other Irular totalled up their catch for Rom. He was on one of his periodic visits to their village on the outskirts of Madras on his Jawa motorbike, to buy and take away the snakes they'd caught for him to send to the Haffkine Institute in Bombay. Ten rupees per cobra, fifteen for a krait or Russell's viper. Saw-scaled vipers came wholesale, in bunches; fifty paise per snake. Fortnightly consignments were sent to Haffkine packed in thin muslin bags that kept a local tailor busy. He'd become a professional snake bag maker. 'Sixty krait bags' would be the order, and he knew what size, which type of cloth. He'd run his sewing machine up and down the seams, determined that no snake should escape from one of his bags. Apart from the danger of their escaping, cannibalistic species such as kraits had to be packed in separate bags, otherwise

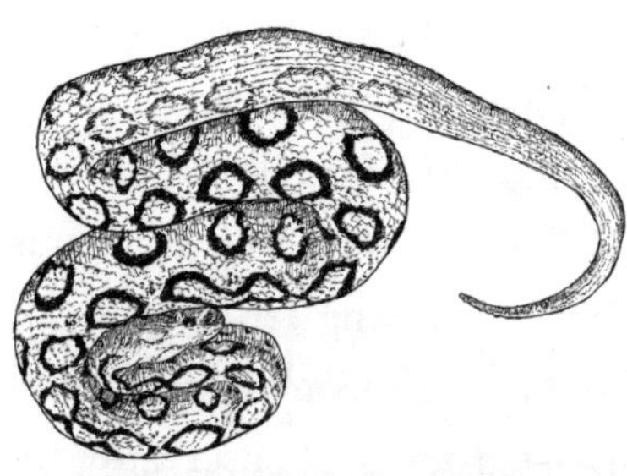

The Russell's viper and common krait (image on next page), two of the Big Four venomous snakes of India, were among the species sent to the Haffkine Institute for antivenom production.

their numbers could be much reduced by the time they got to Bombay!

With this deadly cargo strapped to the pillion of his bike, Rom sputtered to Central Station and booked it on the Bombay-bound Dadar Express. At first the railway officials were understandably reluctant to receive the snake boxes, with their sinister skull and crossbones signs. 'I am sorry, but we cannot accept. We cannot book. It is beyond the scope of Indian Railways.' 'That's nonsense!' replied Rom, and very nearly terminated his career then and there. The official was furious. 'Nonsense! You are calling me nonsense? Okay, let us see.' Soon, people appeared from all sides to participate, encourage, discourage, threaten. But luckily it was sorted out after ten minutes of wrangling, and as often happens in the sudden heated flare-ups of India, everyone parted on excellent terms. There was never any problem after that, and the kraits, cobras and vipers chugged to Bombay in comfort, to be collected by Haffkine staff at the end of the journey.

Sending consignments to the Haffkine Institute was on the whole a sweaty, underpaid job and Rom felt he deserved a better fate than weaving in and out of traffic with crates of snakes, especially after one bad fall with bags of cobras flying in all directions. He began thinking seriously about setting up a snake park that would teach people about snakes and snakebites, and also campaign for the conservation of reptiles. He had visited several such places in the States, but it would be a new thing in India. He discussed the idea with his Irular friend Natesan, known by now as Sureman because of the 'Sure, man!' expression he'd picked up from Rom. He lit a beedi and peered through thick, matted hair as Rom explained his idea. He cocked his head to one side questioningly and rubbed his thumb and forefinger together to make the sign for money. 'Visitors,' said Rom, and Sureman threw back his head and laughed till the betel nut juice bubbled at the sides of his mouth. But Rom was sure his plan would work. To the Irular, snakes were just a part of life; but for others, they were a source of wonder, fascination and fear, and thousands would come to see and learn about the different species.

And in terms of snake conservation, it seemed the right thing to do; countering the wealth of myths about snakes in urban and rural India with hard facts would help people as well as snakes: it would reduce deaths from snakebite and stop people from needlessly killing all snakes. Also, it wouldn't take much to prove to people that conserving rat-eating snakes saves their fields from the depredations of rodents. A small education and conservation centre for reptiles, Rom decided, tying on his last consignment of wriggling cargo. It would mean investing at least a few thousand rupees, which is a lot of money when you don't have it. He often thought wistfully of his thousand-dollar salary in the merchant marines and wondered why he hadn't saved any of it.

Ignoring this small glitch, however, he took the plunge and became a reptile missionary. 'Third time lucky,' encouraged Neel, referring to the two previous adventures in trying to earn a snake-centric living in India. It had been an exciting but also intensely frustrating period and now in 1969, two years after his arrival, Rom knew that if this project didn't succeed, he would have to return Stateside to get a job. He made up his mind to give it all he had. And this included most of his remaining assets – two good camera lenses and a pile of gramophone records – which he sold to raise money for the new project. Good luck and coincidence came to the rescue at this critical stage, including a small cottage with an acre of land advertised for rent near Selaiyur village on the

Velachery road. It was a forty-five-minute drive from Madras city. The rent was only a hundred rupees per month but even more incredible, there was an unfinished house foundation in the compound which provided nine ready-made snakepits... perfect for a snake park! Rom grabbed it, and Neel and Nina came from Bombay by the Dadar Express to help in the crucial initial stages.

The first big job was to clear the debris from the foundation, and armies of the local village children arrived every morning to work. They soon learnt that employment did not necessarily mean instant pay but worked hard and willingly anyway. One of these *thambi*s (young lads) was M. Mani, who is now in his sixties and continues to work at the Snake Park. Finally, Rom had to pawn his last possession of any value, a gold chain, to pay their wages. To keep the venture going, he boldly applied to Citibank for a loan of ten thousand rupees and much to his amazement, got it. With this money, the inside walls of the pits were plastered smooth to prevent snakes from getting out, and a few signboards were made, which were carefully removed every night, being the only assets of the Park besides the snakes. (Signboards were sometimes pinched at night to reinforce leaky roofs and walls of huts.) And his Irular friends started bringing in the local species of snakes for display, and rats and frogs to feed them.

There were so few visitors that each one got a lion's share of attention from the staff. Every time someone came in, a holler went up from the entrance gate to pit 1 and around the Park until all four or five attendants were in readiness to receive and educate the tourist soundly. There were rehearsed speeches in Tamil and English about identifying the Big Four dangerous snakes, the treatment of snakebite and a little on the natural history of snakes. On some days, there were demonstrations of how snake venom is extracted, with gasps as the golden drops trickled down the side of the glass container. And when tired visitors finally wiped their brows and headed towards freedom they were told – and reminded – never to buy snakeskin wallets and belts, or allow their friends to do so.

Rom had been corresponding with Baba, who was impressed with his dedication to the cause of reptiles, a neglected area in the mammal-centred conservation spaces in India at that time. He asked Rom to be the Southern Regional Representative for WWF and for the next seven or eight years, the Snake Park was the headquarters of the organization in the south. As a fundraising unit, the Madras office wasn't a great success. But in the sphere of educating children about wildlife and conservation, it made a marked contribution right from the beginning, through talks at schools and colleges, snake shows and organized outings. Rom publicized WWF by wearing a large panda badge on his lab coat, and word spread in the village that he was a policeman for bears and snakes. By this time, Linda had decided to return to her home in the States, but naturalist friends such as David Hayles and entomologist Chris Pruett often stayed at the Park to help with the increasing workload, typing, filing, buying snakes, and showing visitors around as needed, wearing their signature panda T-shirts and badges.

The long-haired American hippy who lived with snakes and swore in Tamil was a natural magnet for the press. I was, by then, helping out my father and sister at the WWF-India office and regularly chanced upon headlines in newspapers and magazines about him and his snake park: 'Hippy adores snakes', 'Plucky American starts venomous venture', and so forth. Selaiyur village was too far from the city for the Park to make ends meet – the twenty-five paise tickets rarely covered salaries and maintenance costs – but it certainly did become well known, and quickly.

Rom spent much time in local snake habitats with the Irular, often in the rocky scrub hills of Chengalpattu district with Sureman, who could answer all his questions about the snakes of this area, which the academics and local naturalists had no answers to. Rom's Tamil improved under Sureman's exacting tutorship, and the latter invented an English dialect of his own, mostly a combination of swear words and American jargon. Both were tall, spry, sharp-featured, with shoulder-length hair; one white, the other dark. They'd drive along small roads bordered by scrub forest, park the bike, and spend hours in their quest for snakes for the park. Along the way, Sureman would point out medicinal plants, describe the monitor lizard's breeding habits and more; the Irular snakeman was a Pandora's box of natural history information that Rom felt privileged to receive. Together, they also travelled further afield to places such as Nilambur Valley, with its little-known and rare snakes including many pit vipers. A series of camps in Silent Valley, Kerala, helped lay the foundation of what was to become the biggest environmental battle fought – and won – on the subcontinent.

There was often a crisis when Rom was away; that was when things went wrong if they were about to. One evening, an ascending pre-monsoon thunderhead blocked out the sun and the sky exploded with thunder and lightning. The rain swept in and continued for several hours, swirling and crashing over south Madras. Fortunately, Rom's brother Neel decided to check the snakepits. A partial palm leaf roof prevented the snakes from being flooded out but a fallen branch or pole could easily provide an escape route, and they always seemed to be stimulated to unwanted activity during heavy rains.

Huddled in a torn raincoat, Neel checked the cobras with a wavering torch beam. All okay, a few crawling around in the enclosure while the others lay in heaps at the corners. Kraits and Russell's vipers similarly occupied. 'But man, I freaked out when I saw the *surtais*,' he recalls. Swimming joyfully up the wet walls were twenty or thirty saw-scaled vipers, thin

The deep, still waters of the Kuntipuzha River in Silent Valley

and light enough to adhere to the smooth, soaked wall. Some had made it to the top and three were crawling around in the wet mud inches from Neel's bare feet. He began searching for the ones that had managed to get out and flipped them back with a snake hook. Then he scraped the eager wall climbers back in . . . only to find they promptly crawled up again. He knocked them down repeatedly, but they seemed to think it was some kind of game, and it only spurred them on. There was only one thing to do; transfer them to a closed container. So he charged back to the house in the rain and returned with an empty 200-litre drum. Just right for truant vipers. Nina joined him and the two somewhat unwilling snake keepers spent the next hour rounding up over a hundred saw-scaled vipers.

It was becoming obvious to Rom that to be financially viable the Snake Park would have to move closer to the city. He had been in touch with the enlightened Chief Conservator of Forests, K.A. Bhoja Shetty, and spoken to him about the challenges of being so far from the city. A place in the beautiful Guindy Deer Sanctuary in the heart of Madras would be perfect. The Tamil Nadu Forest Department agreed to lease Rom an acre of land in the sanctuary. It was a beautiful plot, an evergreen coastal scrub forest with several large old trees and a monsoon pond just behind it.

Building snake pens in the new location and moving the animals and operations there was going to be expensive, and Rom wrote to Baba at WWF-India for a grant for this. He came to Bombay to collect the grant and, my family suspected, to have a few more 'meetings' with me as well (after the early meetings in school when he was Neel's 'hippy' brother, we had reconnected over WWF outreach projects but more on this later). I certainly had trouble focusing on my typewriter when he was in the office over those three or four days of discussions with Baba about conservation issues in the south. I remember Baba coming home very amused one evening, and very taken with the 'snake fellow'. Apparently, while they were both on their way out of the WWF office at Hornbill House after the Snake Park grant had been approved, Rom said, 'Uh Zafar, could you lend me fifty rupees?' My father took out his wallet and gave him a note. A few steps ahead, Rom turned magnanimously to him and invited him to lunch. How we roared over the story!

The Park's move to the centre of Madras city was a vital step in its growth in every way; from then on, there was no looking back, except perhaps to the peace and calm of preceding years. In a short time, the Madras Snake Park became a famous tourist attraction, with over a million visitors a year and regular coverage in the press. The Irular complained of the long bus ride to town with their muslin bags bursting with snakes, but this was the only drawback. The early 1970s were teething years and much time was spent in designing, building, demolishing and rebuilding reptile exhibits, which both suited the hot Madras climate as well as satisfied the visitors' curiosity. Rom's frequent jungle trips were teaching him about reptile requirements in their natural habitats and he was transferring this knowledge to the Park.

An awareness of a reptile's temperature and humidity needs, in other words the microclimate that it is dependent on, was the main key to keeping it alive and healthy. For example, observing pit vipers drinking the rainwater dropping on their rough heads and saw-scaled vipers collecting tiny morning dewdrops to quench their thirst taught Rom that a regular water spray, and not a water dish, is what these snakes require. Soon, many species were breeding, and the annual births of pythons, water monitors, crocodiles and finally, the king cobra received plenty of press coverage.

The greatest attraction, a 50-metre circumference open enclosure with about a hundred snakes turned out to be a failure in the long run. Not enough attention could be given to individual feeding idiosyncrasies, and the vibrant, diurnal species were constantly disturbing the more quiet, crepuscular ones. Chameleons and vine snakes proved to be fragile captives, while watersnakes and rat snakes were winners: nothing seemed to faze them. Of course, visitors loved this exhibit, with its knots of rat snakes in the branches, bronzeback tree snakes zipping in and out of bushes, and the odd cobra briefly flashing its hood as a chameleon or watersnake went boldly over it. Some years later, the centre pit was turned over to a group of water monitor lizards and another more successful exhibit developed with fewer animals and hourly lectures on snakes and snakebite treatment in English, Hindi and Tamil.

A South American tarantula was Rom's special pet and lived in a cage adjoining the office for several years, feeding on mice and geckos. One morning, while he was holding it on his palm, a gust of wind from the rotating fan knocked the tarantula to the ground, killing it. A college student with him at the time incredulously noted and publicized the fact that Rom's eyes were blurred as he preserved the little fellow in formalin; it was probably the most loved tarantula anywhere.

The Irular hunter Annamalai was the main supplier of rats to feed the snakes at the Snake Park and his weekly visits armed with bags of gerbils, field mice and bandicoots were an education in themselves. More than once he had put his rat bags down on the floor of the bus and gone to sleep only to wake up and find a stampede in progress – the bag had hopped away, and passengers had subsequently hopped off the bus in panic. Through many such rat and snake escape adventures on buses and trains, the gentle, tolerant South Indian mentality has often protected the Irular from being beaten up or severely chastised.

At the Snake Park, Rom's day was interrupted several times by visitors who had special questions to ask and an enthusiasm that was too much for the watchman who was under instructions to keep people away from the office. The cross-section included diplomats, politicians, heads of state, doctors, journalists (always more interested in Rom's personal life than in his work: 'Do you like Indian girls?') and a variety of witch doctors and travelling mendicants who came to disprove the medical monopoly of antivenom. In 1973, while Shama and I were visiting him, a swami arrived and offered to sing his snakebite mantra in the middle of a busy morning. Closing his eyes, he launched into a crescendo, which brought people running in concern. He was not pleased when, half an hour later, we suggested he'd better shorten his mantra to ensure his patient's survival. One day, a deaf lady was brought for a 'cobra-tail treatment', believed to restore one's hearing. After many visits during which Rom failed to convince the lady and her family that she needed a doctor instead, he held a cobra tail to her ear, and they left satisfied and happy.

The Snake Park's work, its routine lectures, publications and general commotion about reptile protection had created a climate of reptile consciousness in India and popularized snakes and their value in the environment. In Madras, it was becoming usual for people to telephone the Park for a catcher to come and collect a cobra or rat snake from a house or garden instead of killing it. This was soon to become a regular organized activity of the Park for a small fee against transport. Families came again and again to learn to identify the different species and many young school and college students spent holidays there, becoming proficient in handling snakes.

By the mid-1970s, the Snake Park had become a hub of herpetological activity and a widely appreciated conservation centre, carrying out vital reptile surveys and engaging in conservation activities that sometimes made it unpopular with local wildlife officials. One of its continuing battles was about the Guindy Deer Sanctuary, the last remaining patch of coastal scrub in Madras that was being steadily depleted by wood poachers and vested interests who disregarded its precious ecological status. As a member of the Tamil Nadu Wildlife Board, Rom kept the fire stoked and suggested several measures to protect the Park permanently. But still, the Cancer Research Institute was given 7 acres of prime land within the sanctuary. In 1977 when Prime Minister Indira Gandhi visited the Snake Park, Harry Miller, Rom and others talked to her about these depredations. Within a few months of her visit, it was declared a National Park and a wall was constructed around it.

Mrs Gandhi was surprised at what she called the 'conservation furore' that the small Snake Park had managed to achieve. But it was exactly this, its compact administration, that was its greatest strength; the absence of laborious procedures made quick, effective results possible. Another favourable factor was that its doors were always open to people with academic or practical zoology interests, and so many volunteers who helped out in various ways – from licking stamps to conducting lab research – were able to use the Park as a stepping stone to involvement in projects elsewhere. This arrangement was of course mutually beneficial, giving the organization a free input of a lot of enthusiasm and energy. D. Basu, a Bengali student at the Indian Institute of Technology (IIT) Madras, worked on its first crocodile egg collection and rearing programme and went on to become one of the few qualified croc people in the country. When the combined Government of India and United Nations crocodile project was under way, he joined the Uttar Pradesh Forest Department and was soon in charge of its Gharial Rehabilitation Centre in Lucknow. In the course of his work, Basu had the honour of releasing the first gharial hatchlings reared in captivity into the Chambal River. This brought him face to face with the famous Chambal dacoits on more than one occasion, and he even exchanged words with the bandit queen Phoolan Devi. When Basu died of a tragic accident on the Brahmaputra in 2012, the croc community mourned the loss of this exceptional field biologist and conservationist.

Satish Bhaskar was another IIT dropout who came to Rom with a strong interest in marine biology and a less-than-strong interest in pursuing his engineering course. He became a field officer at the Snake Park, carrying out the initial surveys of sea turtle nesting on beaches on the mainland and offshore island coasts of India; he later became a consultant for WWF-Indonesia; but more on him later. Shekar Dattatri, a student of Loyola College, also preferred reptile studies and surveys to class and arrived at the Snake Park every morning around the time college started. He became a strong member of the team, later working on films with Rom including a documentary about snakebite. He is today an excellent wildlife filmmaker and his recent documentaries include the spectacular *Race to Save the Amur Falcon.*

One of the difficulties that Rom faced in those early years was evaluating how best the Snake Park's work could fit in with the general perspective of the conservation movement. It was the only non-governmental establishment of its kind and it was important to channel its activities into the main flow of the conservation movement but also to avoid, whenever possible, ugly confrontations with wildlife officials. It was difficult to tread the fine dividing line between meaningful conservation activities and the deterioration of relations with the powers that were. Was it really worthwhile creating tornadoes in the press about poaching in the Guindy Deer Park or the creation of a new hydel dam project at the cost of alienating the range officers and wardens he was ultimately so dependent upon for snake-collecting permits, grants and the general goodwill necessary to continue his work?

Talks with my father, with whom there was an increasing camaraderie because of the common interest in natural history and conservation, helped put matters in perspective, as did the visits of friends from abroad like Richard and Maisie Fitter of the Fauna and Flora Preservation Society, who were always ready to listen, advise and encourage. The consensus was generally unanimous – that it was worth sticking one's neck out.

With education and myth-busting as the focus at the Snake Park, it was easy for Rom to lose track of the wealth of scientific data that was coming his way, particularly since no one at the Park had the academic background conducive to conducting result-oriented science. It was Professor Carl Gans, Rom's mentor-friend, who through his gentle haranguing, put Rom on the track of serious herpetology. Carl is the guru of many herpetologists around the world and one of his passions is an unusual group of snakes found mainly in the hills of southern India. These are the shieldtail snakes or uropeltids, as significant to evolutionary herpetology as Darwin's Galapagos finches are to ornithology.

In the early 1970s, Carl was on a visit to South India to look at some of the species he'd never seen before and was travelling with a herpetologist from Palayamkottai, Dr M.V. Rajendran. Rom had arranged to meet them at Kakachi in the Ashambu Hills and providentially, just as Carl and Rajendran drove up, he stood up from an overturned log with a handful of wriggling, colourful shieldtails, a sight that must have warmed the cockles of Carl's heart.

Not only did Carl encourage the systematic collection of reptiles, but he also stressed the importance of meticulous record keeping since so little data was available on reptile ecology and taxonomy from most areas of the tropical world. About two decades earlier, for example, the herpetologist Karl Schmidt's tragic death from a boomslang bite had first demonstrated that it was a very dangerous snake. Similarly, at the Snake Park, Rom discovered that several harmless species, especially in the rear fanged category, could inflict damage. Rear fanged snakes are a large group in India, consisting of twenty tree snakes and seven brackish watersnakes. In the evolution of the venom injection systems in snakes, these are considered the most primitive. Their fangs are merely a pair of enlarged, grooved teeth in the rear of the top jaw. These enlarged teeth are also useful to hold slippery prey like frogs and lizards and to puncture the inflated bodies of frogs. Although there have been no authentic reports of serious bites from rear fanged snakes in India, some of them, like the Forsten's cat snake, grow to over 2 metres in length and could be dangerous.

Carl's advice was taken to heart, and we became more meticulous about record keeping, research projects and publications. In those threshold years of herpetology in India, there was so much to learn, so much to discover. And I was thrilled to be a part of that journey, which would turn out to be adventurous, fulfilling and, at times, just a little scary.

Honeymoon on the Rocks

By the 1970s, the panda was also becoming a big part of my life and I was spending more and more time with Baba and Shama at the WWF office in Hornbill House. Shama was organizing fundraising events, the first of which was a rock concert held at the Taj Hotel in 1970 with the help of several musicians who performed gratis. Neel was among them, and his grandfather, the poet Harindranath Chattopadhyaya, was the chief guest. College students turned up in droves, we roped in many new members, and a little money was collected . . . but the overheads were high, so the kitty maintained its status quo. Eventually, we hit upon the idea of science exhibitions at Hornbill House, which could be organized with little expense and would generate ticket money as well as create public awareness about conservation issues.

The first one was on common birds. Local newspapers kindly inserted free announcements about it, and we procured stuffed bird specimens from the Prince of Wales Museum and, with the help of our growing band of volunteers, created dioramas that were picturesque if a little scientifically uncertain; kingfishers nested in trees, and a babbler was laying its eggs in a crow's nest. There was a tremendous response from schools and Shama's hourly lecture and slide show in English and Hindi was always followed by a long question session. Some were tricky and beyond the scope of our knowledge, so one of us would sprint up to see J.C. Daniel, the BNHS curator, with a breathless 'Where do bee-eaters nest?' We leaned heavily on the goodwill and assistance of the BNHS, which never let us down. In fact, as my brother Murad said in a 2023 interview with *Sanctuary* magazine, the BNHS was something of a second home to our family.

While Shama spoke and answered questions, the rest of us focused on crowd control; the queue of students and teachers extended well beyond the BNHS campus. These were pre-internet and video days, and academic entertainment, so to speak, was scarce. But the next one, in 1972, was to be even more successful. It was a Snake Show, as we called it, and we had invited Rom – then in regular correspondence with us because of the WWF connection – to bring snakes to Bombay, set up an exhibition of the common species and the Big Four, and give talks to schoolchildren about snakes and their conservation. Entry income would be shared between WWF and the Snake Park. And this was how he reappeared on my radar.

He arrived on the Dadar Express with his Irular friend Sureman (Natesan to me), and fifty or sixty live snakes. A local carpenter, thrilled to be making snake cages of all things, had created plywood pens for the harmless species and terrariums for the venomous ones, as per Rom's instructions. The response from schools was overwhelming; for the two booking days specified on the circular to them, one of us was on the phone continuously and, predictably, the appointments went askew on a gargantuan scale. That whole week, there was a line of up to several hundred children in the hot sun, waiting for their turn at a novel experience: a chance to look at snakes, up close but safe, and watch them being handled.

Over ten thousand children came to the exhibition and learnt about the local species of snakes, how to identify the venomous ones and the proper treatment of snakebites. We ran out of tickets and information leaflets; Natesan got bitten by a green pit viper and was sick for a day; all of us became increasingly hoarse, and in the middle of it all Rom broke a tooth on a piece of sugarcane and had to go off to a dentist while a sea of hopeful children waited for his talk. The dental gap prevented him from smiling, and a group photograph shows him glaring at the camera, mouth tightly pursed.

And one afternoon, during the slide show, a small harmless watersnake escaped from its enclosure and crawled through the crowd of intent children. All hell broke loose in the darkened room. School bags and tiffin boxes were thrown aside and they burst open with a clatter, spewing chapattis and rice, as the shrieking mob rushed towards the door, which fortunately was ajar. I was at the mike, doing the Hindi translation of Rom's talk, and was almost knocked down as two frightened bodies threw themselves at me, wrapping their legs around my ankles in their bid to leave the ground as fast as possible. To add to the poor students' suffering, Rom let loose an angry tirade after the snake was caught and the children and teachers filed back into the room. 'Chickens! Cowards!' he yelled into the mike as the repentant audience looked on in fear, 'We just told you never to panic . . .'

On the fourth day, Rom looked up from a sick python he was medicating with swabs of cotton wool and asked if I would marry him. I didn't take it seriously but he persisted with all the single-mindedness of a naturalist. 'Eleven years older, and toothless,' I reminded him kindly, but he countered, solemnly, that his new tooth would be ready soon and that age was no bar where true love was concerned. I said I was impressed with his philosophy and would think about it.

Soon after this, my parents came back from a month in national parks and conservation meetings in Europe. They found me on the phone a lot, and suddenly very interested in snakes. Initially resigned but then excited, they set about getting to know Rom. He and Natesan were invited to lunch by my mother, after which event they dug up her best flower beds in a hunt for rats to take back for their python.

During lunch, Rom had inadvertently announced his bank balance, causing my mother to wince transparently. But my parents sensed the core of Rom's character and their affection and respect for him was an added incentive to my eventual decision. 'He's a good chap,' said my father; high praise indeed from him.

We met occasionally over the next two years and wrote often. My collection of love letters from Rom is mostly treatises on deworming cobras, the difficulties of feeding tokay geckos, and the interesting issue of compacted bowels in monitor lizards. At the end, there was often a small afterthought, such as this one: 'I love you and love you and love you. Could you ask your father to donate the Gir project jeep to the Snake Park?'

About a year after the snake exhibition, my parents suggested that Shama and I travel to Madras and visit Rom. Shama was to be the chaperone, a task at which she failed miserably. We were both asked to study his character, especially the categories of honesty, kindness and family feeling.

It was a fascinating and fun recce. We arrived at Central Station at the tail end of a heavy two-day storm. Large roadside trees had collapsed, whole colonies of huts were flattened and several of the major roads made inaccessible. Rom was nowhere to be seen but we found a brave taxi, willing to navigate the flooded roads and then we realized, the Snake Park would be closed and we didn't know his home address. 'Let's try the Snake Park anyway,' said Shama, 'there may be a watchman or somebody else who knows where he lives.' At this, the big taxi driver sat up at attention. 'You want *pambukaran?* [snakeman?]You want English Britishman catching snakes?' 'Yes, yes,' we said, and after elaborately skirting the flooded roads, we were deposited at a small cottage on Lattice Bridge Road, then a remote suburb bordered by paddy fields. The *pambukaran* turned up himself in his little Ford ten minutes later, having fruitlessly circled the city in an attempt to get to the station.

Rom told us that a week of great excitement had just come to an end at the Snake Park. Triggered by the rain, the biggest marsh crocodile had escaped from his enclosure, climbed over the 3-metre chain link fencing and lumbered off into the adjoining Guindy Deer Sanctuary. It had taken up residence in the Duck Pond at the Raj Bhavan, the estate of the governor of Tamil Nadu. For five days, Rom and his assistants camped on the bank of the pond to protect the crocodile from the security guards who were threatening to shoot it. At first, Rom tried sneaking around at night with a torch and noosing it, but the croc was too smart for that. Then they tried a trap made of bamboo poles, but it shot through it and into the bigger pond nearby, 3 metres deep in the middle. By this time, news of the *tamasha* had spread and a goodly crowd, complete with peanut vendors, gathered each morning to watch the progress of the exercise. Ideas deteriorated with the situation; a local football team was asked for their uniforms, which, tied to poles, were supposed to act as scarecrows to keep the croc in one area. Finally, the Fisheries Department came to the rescue with a large drag-net and the runaway was caught and brought back to his enclosure.

Shama and I spent the mornings with Rom at the Snake Park. Being Bombaywallas, we were ignorant about southern folklore and beliefs and would trail after visitors, taking in the wealth of snake myths circulating at the enclosure walls as different species were spotted and their attributes related. Listening to these 'facts' was fascinating – the eye-pecking vine snake, vengeful cobra (with a jewel in its head), leprosy-giving sand boas, breath-sucking snakes, the ones with two heads, snakes' love of milk, and more. Every now and then Rom would emerge from the office, overhear some of the comments, and vociferously counter them in his colloquial Tamil. '*Ayyo pa, adhe yelaan dhundham*!' (All this is nonsense!)

The most interesting enclosure was the central pit mentioned earlier, which had a moat running along the wall and was thickly planted with local vegetation. At first, it looked as if there was nothing inside, and people started moving away. But the foliage parted as a large Bengal monitor peered curiously through and the water rippled as a rat snake shot out after a skittering frog. Once your eyes became accustomed to this spotting game, you could spend an hour enjoying the reptile panorama. The bright green vine snakes swayed balefully from side to side if you went too close and inflated their bodies to show the black-and-white chequered inter-scale pattern, which Shama called their underwear. Rom took out one to show us, and as he explained how harmless and tame they were, it bit him right on cue, first on one hand, then the other. Bronzeback tree snakes gleamed like copper wires as they slipped over branches. In the evening, after the Park was closed to public visitation and the jackals of the Guindy Deer Sanctuary joined wildly in with the 6 p.m. siren, we watched Rajamani, one of the Irular snake catchers, deposit bags of frogs for the snakes. Each species had its own style of catching these: fast or slow, competent or blundering.

Behind the palm leaf structure of the office and laboratory were a row of cages for the Big Four dangerous snakes

A canebrake rattlesnake from the south-eastern United States was among the gifts Rom received for the Snake Park.

and species from other countries that periodically came in gift parcels from Rom's herpetological friends, such as canebrake rattlesnakes, African puff adders, and mamushis and habus from Japan. There was a large and very attractive tank for sea snakes with two common species from the Coromandel coast, the narrow-headed and banded sea snakes. Keepers would drive to the nearest beach once a week, buckets strapped to the bike, and return with fresh seawater for them.

What a beehive of activity the place was! Public education, research and conservation were at the forefront of the Park's work and no detail related to these objectives, however small, was ignored. All queries about snakes were answered, and there were hundreds every month, including barely comprehensible postcards in many languages, obviously written by village 'scribes'. 'I am afraiding too much of my wife who has killed a snake in the today. Is it true the snake will come for revenge purposes?' There were letters in Bengali, Malayalam, Marathi, Kannada, Oriya, Telugu, Gujarati . . . and we found that every effort was made to answer each one. Rom recognized the importance of this service since the 'MSPT' (Madras Snake Park Trust) was the only such organization in the country. (While we were there, he received a letter from the UK, addressed to Snake Park, India.)

It was sad to think that just a ten-minute drive from this snake conservation centre, where snakes were being looked after so well, were skin dealers' hubs where they were being mercilessly killed. Often, the skin was stripped off the living snake after nailing the head to a post, where it was then left to die. Madras had several big snakeskin markets, and thousands upon thousands of skins changed hands at the skin market every Friday.

Shama and I became deeply interested in the Irular, their knowledge of the forest, their culture, and the fact that they were among the communities that faced social discrimination on a daily basis. One evening, Rom offered us a dainty bowl of little brown fried snacks, which were delicious until we discovered they were termites. They'd been hunted by Rajamani, for whom the pre-monsoon weather in Madras was termite time. He told us that he'd just found a 'ripe' mound, one in which the termites were ready to swarm. Since there was a lull in the rains, he planned to try his luck again and invited us to come along. It turned out to be a memorable insect safari, about which we boasted shamelessly on our return to Bombay.

Eesel is the Tamil name for adult winged termites, which leave their mounds and swarm on their nuptial flight during the rains. This spontaneous fountain of protein from the ground is a universal treat for a wide range of animals that gorge themselves silly on insects: frogs, squirrels, mongooses, jackals, birds, scorpions. And in South India, the Irular join them, sometimes even squatting beside the mound and popping live *eesel* into their mouths. Rajamani once came upon a swarm in the forest and sat down to eat. Soon a jackal appeared and the two of them, man and beast, amicably shared the feast from opposite sides of the mound. Termites are eaten in many parts of the world but elsewhere, people have to wait for them to swarm. Here, the Irular have a 'trick' they use to make termites emerge early, thus ensuring that they are around to trap them.

It was a muggy night. Now and then a breeze blew, the clouds shifted and a star flashed briefly. Rom, Shama and I set off with Rajamani. 'These people are ready to come out,' he said, using the anthropomorphic Irular lingo for animals. The mound we were about to hunt turned out to be a *katta puthu*, the most common *puthu* or termite nest in the Madras region, and also the largest. Some *katta puthu*s are as tall as a human and 3 metres in circumference. This was one of the four varieties of termite mounds that the Irular classify. The others are *kavaram*, *patti* and *kerian.*

The last, which is inhabited by a species of large, black termite and which lacks the exit holes typical of the others, is ecologically the most interesting. It is in the *kerian puthu* that the monitor lizard of South India, the Bengal monitor, often lays its eggs, tunnelling into the side of the mound and leaving the eggs to the care of these aggressive termites with their optimum incubation chamber. On hatching, the baby lizards make their exit holes at the top of the mound.

The *katta puthu* Rajamani took us to was just under 2 metres high with terraced towers and balconies, like a miniature Spanish castle. With the mosquitoes out in full force, we sat down to wait as he performed his customary pre-hunt pooja with a piece of camphor. Rajamani was superstitious and, of late, he had been seeing a little midget ghost with blue hair near his home in Chitlapakkam. 'He even follows me every night, when I go out to relieve myself,' he said despairingly.

But at the moment ghosts were far from his thoughts as his wife Lakshmi tied an old sari around the periphery of the *puthu* to protect it from the wind. He readied his crowbar and dug a hole a short distance from it. Into it, he wedged a cooking oil tin so the top was flush with the ground. Over the opening he made a bridge with two twigs, placed an oil lamp on this, and lit it. Rajamani then sat down to light a beedi and a yawn escaped me. 'What are you waiting for?' I asked, unable to curb my urban impatience. 'For me – of course. You city people, you want everything to go like this,' he said, snapping his fingers. Rom translated gleefully.

Finally, the beedi was thrown down. A large brown seed was roasted over the lamp fire and ground into powder on a stone. Rajamani walked around the castle of mud, blowing the seed dust into the hundreds of tiny holes, which dotted its surface. 'This is the magic powder,' he explained. 'It tricks the termites into thinking it's raining, that it's time to come out.'

Half an hour later, my legs had gone to sleep but I dared not fidget and risk further aspersions on my city brand of impatience. Rajamani circled the mound again, sprinkling the seed powder and making a whirring sound by vibrating his lips, a sound that resembled the frenzied noise of swarming termites. At intervals he called, 'Come out, come out, it's raining, come quickly.' He peered into the little exit holes as he walked about. After a few more minutes he addressed us. 'Come here. Something is happening . . . these people have started moving.'

We applied our faces to the mud walls and squinted into the tiny peepholes. There was definitely some hasty brown activity going on in there. Lakshmi took a look. 'These are the workers,' she said. 'It is their duty to stop the *eesel* from going outside until they are sure the time is right.'

Another wait, then the first winged termite – Rajamani's prey – flew across our vision and attracted by the light, fell into the tin. '*Seri* [all right], they are coming. The *sel* [worker ants] have given them permission.' A few more emerged singly and taxied towards the light, like small aircraft before take-off. Then the deluge. They started pouring out of the holes, oozing forth in a continuous stream. They created a living road towards the light and in less than five minutes the tin was full and Lakshmi emptied it into a gunnysack. Rajamani squatted beside the sack and began to gobble live termites, periodically spitting out the wings that collected in a corner of his mouth. We hesitantly followed suit, but got our tongues bitten and decided we weren't hungry. Now the air was thick with termites, the oil tin a fluffy mass of wings once more.

Rajamani pointed to a large warty toad a few feet away. It was busy mouthing termites; soon it was too stuffed to move and just sat there, looking ill. A black scorpion and several geckos Rajamani called *puthu balli* joined the party. He generously moved aside to let them eat their fill, while Shama and I maintained a cautious distance. When we left an hour later, the gunnysack was almost full. Next morning, Lakshmi would separate the wings, fry the termites, sell some and keep the rest for her family.

Our recce accomplished, Shama and I were on our way back to Bombay and just as the train started moving forward Rom pressed a porcupine-quill necklace into my hand. 'Next June, then?' I looked hesitantly at Shama. 'Your sister is most welcome to come and live with us,' said Rom gallantly, and we were off.

We were married in June 1974, an exercise fraught with uncertainty, including the small detail of whether Rom would turn up at all. Ninth June was the date we'd decided on, and soon after, he set off on a six-week gharial survey in Corbett National Park. As it turned out, the Registrar of Marriages was only available on the seventh, so Baba booked an appointment with him but was unable to contact Rom and tell him the change of date because we had no idea which part of Corbett he was camping in. Finally, he sent a telegram to Rom c/o every Forest Department office in the park, saying, 'You getting married 7 June Bangalore stop You must repeat MUST get back in time.' Life could be exciting in those pre-mobile days! Rom got back to Madras in good time to drive Doris, Neel and Nina to Bangalore for the big day. But this was the time of a major petrol crunch, and on that day gas stations were hoarding their wares in anticipation of a favourable price hike. The marriage party was delayed by over ten hours and arrived in Bangalore in the middle of the night, well after we'd given up hope.

After the short, simple wedding, Rom borrowed some money from his new father-in-law and we went off on a honeymoon, to Nilambur Valley in the foothills of the Nilgiris. It was a beautiful day; an early morning shower had left the foliage with a wet gleam that made the forest dance and twinkle. The tree trunks and branches of the massive rainforest trees were hung with mossy creepers, epiphytes and lichen. The persistent, pulsing sounds of the cicadas and crickets were like an orchestra of tiny harps and violins – 'Here at last is the church organ,' said Rom. We'd driven into a narrow mud road that ended half a mile in, where a huge *Bombax* had fallen across it. As we collected our gear, the drizzle changed to a downpour, as if on a sudden impulse. Drops of rain trickled down my back. 'Can't we wait until it stops?' 'It won't, it rains here all the time during the monsoon,' came the answer. Reluctantly, I eased myself out of the dripping vehicle and plodded down the track hung with knapsack, sleeping bag and water canisters.

We left our gear under a rock overhang and started upstream. Rom was especially keen on finding hump-nosed and Malabar pit vipers for the Snake Park and crawled on hands and knees under the overhanging clumps of ferns and bracken. Pit vipers are often coiled in the cool tangle of the undergrowth, waiting for a frog or lizard to come along. This slow creeping along gave me an entirely new perspective of the jungle. I'd grown up looking upwards, for birds, and now realized I'd missed one stratum of the forest altogether – the intricately meshed microhabitats and small details of jungle fabric on the forest floor.

Once we tuned in to our surroundings, we were amazed at just how plentiful these statuesque little snakes were in this small tract of evergreen forest. Malabar pit vipers are partial to the edges of steep hill streams, and although they often lie in the open, they are easy to miss. The smaller ones like to hang on low plants and bushes where they blend in very well. The larger ones, some 45 centimetres in length, have lichen-patterned backs and look more like roots than snakes when you first spot them. A year earlier, Natesan and Rom had found thirty-eight of these pit vipers in one morning on a stream near Nilambur, the location of which Rom kept secret. 'It would easily be hunted out if someone suddenly got interested in pit vipers; let's hope it survives the forest clearance and agricultural development in the hills.'

We found them on the forest floor, often on or near a rock or at the base of a big tree, just sitting there, perhaps patiently waiting for prey. Later, we saw one that had swallowed a frog and another that had a gecko inside it, probably a diurnal tree gecko. Ten years later, Rom drove a group of 'herp' people to Nilambur after the IUCN Snake Group meeting in Madras and, in a few hours, they saw a dozen pit vipers; it was gratifying to know that the pit viper population at Nilambur hadn't suffered too much damage.

There are many species of pit vipers in the Western Ghats, the lower Himalayas and the Andaman and Nicobar Islands; it is one of the most easily observed forest snakes and some are quite remarkable. The large-scaled, green pit viper is common in some hilly areas such as the Palani and Ashambu hills. Its large, plate-like overlapping scales give it a primitive look. Young pit vipers usually have a light-coloured tail tip, which they hold up and wriggle to lure frogs and lizards, which are then caught as they come forward to investigate.

The Anderson's pit viper is common in the Andamans; and as more of its forest habitat is hacked away for cultivation, this snake has been causing a fair number of bites. During a trip there, Ganesh, a Forest Department assistant, told us how he was bitten in the cheek by a pit viper as he was cutting away the bamboo. 'My head swelled up like a football,' he said, 'my eyes were sealed tight by the swelling and my head pounded like a drum for one week.' A Burmese-Karen woman we met at Karmatang in the Andamans in 1975 was bitten on the hand when a pit viper fell on her from the ceiling of her hut. Some local remedies were tried, including slicing the arm with broken glass and using heated glass jars and a bamboo tube for suction. This resulted in the loss of her arm from gangrene. There is no antivenom for pit viper bite in India and the best medical treatment is probably minimal tampering with the bite and very careful management of the infection to avoid necrosis (dry gangrene), which often results from their bites.

One species of pit viper even lives at the foot of the glaciers in the Himalaya. The Himalayan pit viper has been found at over 5,000 metres above sea level and like the European adder of the Arctic Circle, is probably only active for a month or so of 'warm' weather. Does this mean that these snakes live much longer than their brethren at lower altitudes, which spend much less of their lives in hibernation? Roger Conant, the well-known American herpetologist, has taxonomically reorganized the pit vipers of the genus *Agkistrodon* which, besides the Himalayan form, include the far-flung American moccasin and the Japanese mamushi. In 1984, he asked Rom for help in collecting distribution data. Rom's Snake Park colleague Shekar Dattatri offered to help with this and travelled to Kashmir. His sojourn in Dachigam National Park was most interesting and pleasurable, thanks mainly to the Chief

Wildlife Warden, Mir Inayatullah. Shekar found several of the large heavyset Levantine vipers and a few Himalayan pit vipers. Thanks to him, Dr Conant and his wife, who visited Madras a month later, were able to see and photograph them for the first time.

But back to our honeymoon. Three or four hours later that same morning, we had crossed the stream several times and my smart new walking shoes, part of the wedding trousseau, were causing considerable anguish. Rom motioned me down to a small cave into which he jabbed a stick, and a throaty growl started immediately, like the purr of a giant cat. 'King cobra!' I shouted, caught between fright and excitement. Obviously pleased with this ignorant response, Rom reached down and pulled up a large and angry rat snake. It continued to growl and strike wildly but with mouth closed, and I started my assistant snake-bagger career by pulling out a snake bag from his knapsack and holding it open. But just then Rom saw a vine snake on a bush behind me and thrusting the rat snake into my arms, dived after it. My charge bit me twice, quick smart and was poised for a third strike. I was about to let it go when Rom returned with the vine snake and managed to bag them both. We turned back – it was late afternoon and I was exhausted and, by now, frantic about the ever-increasing procession of leeches feasting on my blood. 'Enjoying your honeymoon, sweetheart?' asked Rom as I limped down to the stream on blistered feet to wash off the blood.

We found a gently sloping rock face to sleep on, the slope ensuring that we had to wake up every hour to haul ourselves up like ungainly caterpillars lest we ended up in the stream. At my insistence Rom made a fire to keep elephants away; we'd seen too many large, fresh droppings that day for my comfort. Nevertheless, a big bull came within 10 metres of our rock, leaving his large, pancake footprints in the slushy mud of the stream bank. My diary entry for 10 June 1974 reads: 'It was not a romantic night.' And the conversation, mostly about pit vipers, was not romantic either; but it was the beginning of a strong interest in reptiles, which was to be one of the cornerstones of our marriage.

Back at the Snake Park, Rom threw himself into the usual administrative tangles that had developed during his absence and I began editing and putting together reports on the status and ecology of the mugger or marsh crocodile, for which he had gathered information over the last few years. This sort of final putting together of raw material became my special responsibility at the Park and fulfilled both a need there, as well as my own interest in writing and editing. This was familiar ground for me, not much different from the WWF work in Bombay. I started the herp newsletter *Hamadryad,* which went on to almost forty volumes and still exists as an online journal. My other Snake Park activities were correspondence, meeting and talking to visitors, and cataloguing and filing the heaps of information that was coming in from all parts of the country, about all things related to snakes.

These were useful resources when we began working on Rom's field guide to common Indian snakes (published by Macmillan) with much editing help from my mother. Incidentally, she continued to play this role in all our writing projects; my mother-in-law Doris, an artist, contributed illustrations to the *BNHS Encyclopedia of Natural History*, for which we wrote the section on reptiles. The field guide's success indicated the growing interest in snakes and their natural history and ecology. A reader from Nagpur made a flattering comparison between it and Dr Sálim Ali's bird book. 'Much smaller and less comprehensive as it is, it is having the same sort of effect on people already interested in wildlife but for whom snakes have always been taboo. People like me who had to depend largely on scanty, outdated information now have something concrete to fall back on and what pleasure it gives the amateur to be able to identify, without doubt, the species around him.'

One of Rom's favourite jungles in the south was Kalakkad Reserve in the Ashambu Hills, where he had caught two king cobras and helped his entomologist friend Chris Pruett with his butterfly and moth collections in 1971/1972. Nary had the leech bites from the honeymoon stopped itching and oozing when we were off to Kalakkad, travelling up the ghat road with Tom Struhsaker of the New York Zoological Society. He was on his way to visit Steve Green, who was studying lion-tailed macaques, one of the rarest primates in the world. Steve was staying at one of the Manjolai tea estate guest houses at Kakachi and we spent an evening with him before leaving for Sengeltheri, our destination. He had finally acclimatized the macaques to his presence, and was now able to approach those that had been rigorously hunted earlier and so took fright and fled at the approach of a human. A day before our arrival, Steve had watched a young male lion-tail catch a forest lizard and chomp it like a breadstick.

At four thirty the next morning, we started on the Sengeltheri track, a walk of about 17 kilometres. Today there is a motorable road from the plains to Sengeltheri and the forest is badly degraded compared to what we walked through that day. The thick undergrowth and hardwood buttresses were dotted with the remains of abandoned tea and cardamom estates and the animals were making a comeback. Once, a sambar stag dashed through the trees a few metres ahead of us, rearing back momentarily as he saw us, then caught his balance like a trapeze artist and flung himself forward. The leeches welcomed us hungrily; at first we kept stopping to pull them off, then gave up. They had no problems penetrating our socks and wriggling in through the shoelace holes. Then they'd begin their march upward, getting fatter and fatter as the blood feast progressed. After an hour, the cold, wet feeling behind the knees had to be investigated and the bloated leech pulled off. Over the years, we have tried all possible leech repellents, from soap to kerosene and even invented a concoction of snuff and petroleum jelly that seemed to have possibilities. But there doesn't seem to be a foolproof answer to the leech problem!

We took our time getting to Sengeltheri, investigating streams and collecting a couple of pit vipers too well fed to resist capture. The stick insects of these hills often span over a foot in length and one calmly climbed on to me while we rested under a tree. At first, I thought it was a twig but when flicked, it began to walk determinedly forward. With it still trekking down my head

A giant stick insect showers affection on me in Kalakkad during a strenuous trek.

and shoulders, we scanned the adjoining slopes and cliffs for Nilgiri tahr, the unique wild goat of the southern highlands, but with no luck. Eager to catch at least a small glimpse of the animals, we stayed on, making a fire for tea. 'Jungle tea!' shouted Rom as he gave me a warped tin mug with steaming liquid. He stirred in a leaf-full of sugar with a twig and we sat back to watch the slopes and the incredible avian panorama in front of us. Scarlet minivets flitted about in their bright red coats; velvet-fronted nuthatches crept up nearby tree trunks; sunbirds flew past with flashes of brilliant colour; a splash of yellow-gold flashed as a flame-backed woodpecker landed vertically in front of us; the strong, clear tune of the Malabar whistling thrush sounded the background score while the shama composed a song in the dense branches overhead.

With this sort of easy loafing in progress, it was dusk before we'd gone too far and Rom found another pit viper. We watched it stalk and catch a frog, moving in slow motion along a wet, ferny bank so as not to frighten it away. By the time we made it back to the original track, it was dark and we found we'd missed the turning west towards Sengeltheri. Rom went back to try and locate it while I sat on my knapsack for half an hour counting the minutes and wondering anxiously whether leopards were still prevalent in these hills. He came back with the good news that our turning was a short distance away. We could cook dinner by the stream, he said, and be in Sengeltheri after half an hour's walk by torchlight. It sounded like a good plan.

What a luxury it was, paddling in the cold stream, waiting for the rice and dal to cook. 'Let's live it up, eh,' said Rom as he extravagantly threw a potato into the mixture. Lunch had been a square-inch cube of Japanese army survival rations, so the mush tasted like a royal feast, and at nine, we washed our plates, dried them on our jeans, put on sodden shoes and hauled up our knapsacks.

Suddenly a few choice words split the silence ending with, 'Bloody torch – where's the bloody torch – I'm sure I bloody packed it.' Rom was scrabbling through the contents of his knapsack which, the embers of our fire showed, did not include the spotlight we'd been depending on. That was bad enough; visions of elephants and panthers crowded my brain. But to add fuel to the fire, Rom burst into a helpless roar of laughter. My frightened expression, he said, was so funny.

We made it to the decrepit old forest rest house with a wood torch, like a small Olympian team, and in my anxiety I stuck to Rom like a leech, tripping him up as my feet scurried in time to his steps. And at the end of that anxious walk, we found the door of the rest house locked; a stained cyclostyled sheet pasted on the pelmet proclaimed in government language the lengthy procedure for booking a room and the list of tariffs. Rom must have sensed my fatigue and anxiety working up to an explosion and took out his Swiss army knife. 'Calm down, we're staying here,' he said, proceeding to pick the lock with suspicious expertise. As the rusty hinges fell away, he ceremoniously bowed me into a room reeking of rat and bat droppings, a fitting denouement for a day short on comfort and long on drama.

King of Snakes

Kanyakumari, where sunrise meets sunset, is the southernmost tip of India. Stretching north from this point, the magic mountains of the Western Ghats wend their way to Bombay over a thousand kilometres of coastline. These giant buckets of thick foliage catch the monsoon and tip some of it over to the dry east. North of Goa, the forest cover is mostly deciduous and the greenery fades during the dry months. But south of the Goa Gap, the mountains are always green. Proceed a little further south, down through Karnataka, and you come to large stretches of wet jungle and walk under 30-metre-tall trees embraced by giant vines as thick as a human

The Malabar frog is one of the colourful denizens of the Western Ghats.

body. Walking through these jungles, there is the occasional open corridor with sunlight briefly dancing through delicate ferns . . . and then you are back again among impenetrable bushes that cling with pronged thorns and mesh with thin, tough vines that trip and hold you back.

These forests had been Rom's retreat during his teen years in the 1950s and continued to be so when he returned from the States. Apart from their striking beauty, the Western Ghats also meant king cobras. These, the largest venomous snakes in the world, would excite any herpetologist but Rom's interest was further stimulated by the exploits of the great African snake man, C.J.P. Ionides, in Thailand. This is where the king grows the largest, often reaching 5 metres in length. With Jon Leakey, son of the famous palaeontologist couple Louis and Mary Leakey, Ionides visited southern Thailand in 1966. They were taken to no less than fourteen king cobra nests in the space of a couple of weeks! The misleading stories about the aggressiveness of these snakes, supported even by naturalists like Jim Corbett – which Rom takes every opportunity to refute – were trashed by Ionides' experiences in Thailand. Even nesting females that he caught made no attempt to attack them.

Practically nothing was known about Indian king cobras at that time. All king cobras feed exclusively on snakes, and the most common prey species in India are rat snakes and spectacled cobras. Slightly less toxic than that of the common cobra, the venom of the king cobra comes wholesale. The glands can contain 6 or 7 millilitres, probably enough to dispatch an elephant. There are only a few cases of human deaths from king cobra bites and these are results of foolish behaviour (by the human). One of these was an Englishman named Slater, who placed his foot on a king cobra's head, was bitten above the knee and died some hours later. Today, many derring-do snake rescuers take idiotic risks with kings, often to multiply their 'Likes' and followers on social media, and some have come to grief because of this.

It was 22 March 1972. Rom was in Agumbe in the southern Western Ghats with Linda and their friend David Hayles, who had been helping them at the Snake Park. When they arrived at the rest house, which faced the edge of the Ghats, a smooth creamy fog was surging up from the valley below, engulfing the forest on every side.

Agumbe is the Cherrapunji of the south, with 7,500 millimetres of annual rainfall but, like it, has been decimated by deforestation and burgeoning human numbers and activities. Incredibly, Cherrapunji with its 10,000 millimetres rainfall – among the highest in India – has become a drought-prone area because the forests there have been so drastically plundered for short-term gains. A high rainfall encourages a greater diversity of plant species and Agumbe, situated on a little piece of the Ghats that juts out towards Udipi in north-western Karnataka, was a biodiversity jewel that Rom visited whenever he could get away.

In those days, one could never be dry in Agumbe; the air

was so loaded with moisture that it was like being drizzled on continuously, and towels, bed sheets and clothes were always damp. I remember my own first visit there five years later, with Rom and our friend Ranil Senanayake, the Sri Lankan herpetologist. We sat down for breakfast only to find the table had disappeared, like in a fairy story; a thick white fog blew in through the door like a genie, and we ate our bread and butter by feeling them on our plate. This climate is, of course, congenial for leeches.

On the first day of their 1972 visit, David and Linda stayed at the rest house and Rom packed a sleeping bag, pan, some *rava* (semolina) and brown sugar in his knapsack, and walked up a nearby track to find a good camping site. The forest thickened with every step; soon the trees were choked with orchids and smothered with streamers of lichen, which defied the sunlight. Recent timber felling on the periphery had left gashes like pieces of a bombed-out city. He stopped near a small stream to make a fire and cook some *rava* porridge for himself. *Rava* is a practical camping food; a little goes a long way and it cooks quickly. Not quite gourmet stuff, but highly nutritious, it 'sticks to the ribs', keeping hunger at bay for long periods.

Having eaten, Rom continued on his way. Three kilometres in, then up a westward path towards the edge of the hills. It was the still, silent transition between afternoon and evening when even the tireless crickets and cicadas seem to slow down. Halfway up, a black tail whisked into the thick bushes to the right and Rom, assuming it was a rat snake, instinctively plunged to the ground and grabbed it. But from his prone position, he saw a large, hooded snake over 3 metres long charging at him with open mouth. Taken by surprise, the king cobra growled throatily; Rom's reflexes came to life and he dropped the tail. The big snake immediately stopped its charge and shot back into the bushes.

The chance of a lifetime had slipped away, and Rom fell from the pinnacle of excitement with a heavy thud. Breaking off a stick, he followed the snake's tail and feverishly poked a brush pile, which seemed the most likely place it could be hiding in. The king cobra plummeted out and was off towards another brush pile nearby. Rom grabbed the tail again and this time, as it raised itself for a lunge, he fenced it with the stick, heart beating like a drum. It struck at it repeatedly and stood up higher, almost at eye level, its intelligent, disconcerting eyes watching Rom. For the next twenty minutes, Rom concentrated on keeping its attention and pulling it back from its efforts at getting away. It began to tire, the lunges getting less springy.

This was Rom's cue. Using the stick to keep the snake's attention away from himself, he used the other hand to pull out his sleeping bag and stretch it on the path. He propped the mouth open with dry sticks to make a cave. With the other hand, he guided the snake towards the opening, offering it an escape from the strange madman blocking its way. It struck and bit the cloth for more endless minutes, then slid into the sleeping bag, and Rom tied the heavy load with shaking hands. This was his biggest triumph so far, but the price could have been heavy. Harry Miller wrote about this adventure in the *Indian Express:* 'King cobras possess huge amounts of venom and because they are rare snakes no one in India has embarked on the complex and expensive task of producing an antidote to their venom. If Rom had been bitten, it is unlikely that he could have survived. The catching of so large and fierce a venomous snake, alone and almost literally bare handed, must surely go down in the annals of natural history as an act of almost unbelievable skill and heroism.'

The next morning, the three of them walked many zig-zagging miles looking for a campsite. 'A real five-star one,' said David as they found a small stream shaded by giant trees and marked with wild pig, jungle cat and civet tracks. They made the evening fire and brewed strong tea as the day ended with the fantastic sounds of racket-tailed drongos, hill mynahs and hornbills. The fire went cold as they slept heavily on flat rocks. In the morning, Rom was cooking *rava* porridge when a cobra went right by Linda's foot as she sat on the bank, watching David dive after watersnakes in the cold stream.

One evening a few days later, Rom was walking down a dry stream bed trying to find his way back to the camp. It was getting dark and he'd walked further than planned; a hungry stomach turned him around but the several attempts at shortcuts proved time consuming. Finally, he found the original path with his own crossed stick landmarks. And as he turned in, there again was the spine-tingling sound of a big snake in the leaves.

Looking up, he imagined the sound came from a thick cluster of bushes to the side and stepped towards it, stick and large muslin bag ready this time. A split second later, there was a movement and a low moaning growl. A 4-metre king cobra was sitting straight ahead of him in the stream bed! The camouflage had worked perfectly; if it hadn't vocalized, Rom might have walked straight into the snake! Standing up over a metre off the ground, it was facing the bushes, showing off its yellow chevron-marked hood in a striking defence display.

Once more to the tune of his heart's drumbeat, Rom stepped forward; and the snake immediately rushed into the bushes, barely giving him a chance to grab its tail. As he did so there was a louder growl from the mid-body and a sharp hiss. By this time, it was securely trapped in the tangle of bushes in the embankment, so they started a ten minute tug-of-war, the snake staring down at its opponent with mouth open. Eventually, Rom managed to free it without injury and the snake landed with a thud near his feet; he hastily stepped back. And again, the open mouth charges and another long session followed of hanging on, dodging out of range and hauling the snake back into the open as it tried to get away.

By now, it was almost sundown and the forest was

illuminated with the fantastic threads of sunset colours. The technique of propping the bag open didn't work this time because the active snake would not allow Rom to take his eyes off him for a moment. Rom threw the bag at him in desperation, hoping it would slide over its head, but the snake bit it and that was that. Retrieving the bag with his cross stick, which now shook in his fatigued arm, Rom tried once more and this time it landed clear over the snake's head and erect forebody. The king cobra slid neatly inside. Jumping gratefully on the bag, Rom clamped it closed after slapping the tail a few times to speed things up. The king cobra and he trudged back to camp in the moonlight, and over vegetable stew and chapattis, the three friends wondered at the good fortune of finding two of these magnificent snakes in the space of a week.

But cruel disappointment lay ahead. On getting off the train in Madras, Rom went home to bathe, after leaving the king cobras in the Snake Park office. He asked one of the keepers to wet down the floor for coolness. He came back to find the bags themselves had been soaked and the snakes had suffocated to death. Grieved, Rom prepared his once vibrant and plucky rivals for their ignominious end in a formalin jar, becoming even more determined to rear and breed king cobras in captivity. He was sure that if he caught them himself, without pinning the head, which is so physically traumatic for the snake, they would do well as captives; and offspring might then replace the large numbers of wild snakes that zoos went through and which the declining wild populations could not sustain. In later years, the Snake Park did breed king cobras for the very first time in India.

Soon after this encounter, Rom was back in the jungle with his friend Chris Pruett, who was then making a butterfly and moth collection in South India. Chris wanted to look at the bugs in the Ashambu Hills, south of Tirunelveli, and Rom went with him to the Singampatti tea estate at Manjolai where they were guests of John Bland and his family. Among the chota pegs and shining silverware, the two naturalists must have stood out in stark relief, with their mud-caked jeans, bloody leech bites and long stringy hair.

The incredible luck held out. On the fourth afternoon, they left the jungle at the bottom edge of the estate just before dusk; stopping for a smoke, Rom walked over to the path's edge and looked down a rocky slope just in time to see the now familiar banded form. He whistled to Poolappan, a shikar guide with him that day, and told him to keep an eye on the *kurra nagan*, as the Tamilians called the king cobra, while he ran down the slope. Descending rapidly, he heard Poolappan yell, 'Watch out, it's near your foot!' He looked down in time to move his stick between the snake's head and his bare feet. The 3-metre female king cobra saw the stick and, letting out a hiss, lunged forward, pushing her head into a hole in the rocks nearby. Rom gently lifted the tail and, gripping it firmly, made his way slowly up the steep slope towards the open path. The cross stick strategically placed protected him. Once on level ground, he allowed the snake to let off steam and played the old catch-me-if-you-can game to tire her out. Poolappan meanwhile opened up a specially modified butterfly net frame with visibly shaking hands. He attached the bag to it and held it open on a 2-metre pole as they manoeuvred the king cobra into it.

A few days later, Rom caught her mate, close to the same spot. He knew that sooner or later they would get their heads smashed in if they remained there; king cobras are regularly clubbed or shot in the tea estates, which have encroached so extensively on their habitat. Both these specimens became very tame in captivity and were star attractions at the Snake Park. Soon, word spread that the Park was interested in keeping king cobras alive, and a few of the tea estate managers sent specimens, which soon died due to the rough handling received at the time of capture. But two were caught with great aplomb and courage by Nikko Rawlley of the Mudis tea estate in the Annamalai Hills. One of them had been grabbed by labourers who thought it was a rat snake, a common identity confusion. By the time they discovered their mistake it was a tiger-by-the-tail situation, and they were too enmeshed in the snake to let it go. Nikko rescued them and the snake, by holding its neck and bagging it.

Continuing his quest for the king cobra, Rom visited the Nandankanan Biological Park in Orissa (now Odisha) and made friends with the snake keeper, a boy from the famous village of Patia near Bhubaneswar where a clan of snake catchers specialize in the art of king cobra 'charming'. Together they went to Patia and several of Das's relatives took out their snakes for Rom to photograph. Every year in the winter, these hunters went in groups to the mangrove swamps in Bhitarkanika to look for king cobras basking in the sun. They caught them with nooses, defanged them and carted them across the countryside as far as Delhi and Kashmir – eking out a day-to-day living by making the cobras 'dance' to their flutes.

Rom had seen the two chunks of king cobra habitat on mainland India, the Western Ghats and the mangrove swamps of Orissa and West Bengal. But the most enticing were the jungles of the Andaman Islands in the Bay of Bengal. His interest was further sharpened after my trip there in 1975 when I returned with stories from Saw Allen Vaughan and other Burmese-Karens about common sightings (and killings) of females at their nests. For a while, the islands were out of bounds since Rom was a foreign national and he had to satisfy himself with reading old natural history accounts of these fascinating evergreen forests. But he became an Indian citizen in 1975 and a few months later, he was in the wet, almost visibly steaming, jungles on the island of Middle Andaman. His companion was Allen's brother Brian, who claimed to have seen a big snake lying in a bamboo grove. This was the month of April, reportedly the nesting season of king cobras, the only snakes in the world to build nests. Brian's account could only mean one thing, and they were off together, not daring to waste time on too much preparation.

En route, they stumbled into thick sheets of April rain, often tripping over spiky bamboo and sliding down slopes. They had to stop frequently to remove the clusters of leeches that burrowed through socks and canvas shoes, soon to become swollen blobs on a toe or ankle; Brian had one hanging from an earlobe like a bizarre ornament. After an hour, he stopped to indicate a dark stand of overhanging bamboo. 'That's where it was,' he said.

Rom was out of breath and panting. Wiping off the sweat and raindrops from his face, his eyes cleared and focused on a thin but healthy-looking king cobra coiled over her carefully tended nest mound. They extracted the camera from layers of protective plastic and took some blurred pictures in the fading light, then sat down to watch her. When finally approached, she slid off into the bamboo without the least sign of aggression or resistance. So much for the deadly attributes of chasing people and unprovoked attacks. The

A sight to warm a herpetologist's heart –
a female king cobra on her nest

leafy mound was a metre across and as Brian remarked, you couldn't imagine it was the work of an animal with no arms and legs. The surrounding area had been cleared of leaves and humus with sweeps of the snake's body. At the bottom of the nest was a neat cup of leaves like a bird's nest, with nineteen oblong yellowish eggs. Brian said that the farmer who had discovered the nest planned to come back and destroy them, so they transferred the eggs to a cloth bag lined with leaves and brought them back to Madras.

Rom kept these eggs in our plastic bread box on a bookshelf at home, with holes in the cover for air; unnecessarily large, as it turned out, for, on hatching, the 45-centimetre-long king cobra babies climbed out and into his collection of Arthur Clarke and Isaac Asimov. It took several hours to

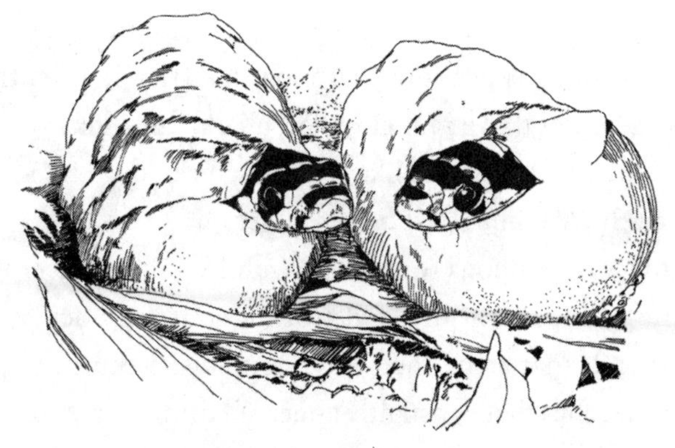

A big breakthrough at the Snake Park was the successful hatching of king cobras. These hatchlings peered out at us from the safety of their eggshells for two days before finally slipping out into the world.

collect all the deadly little truants, equipped from birth as they are with fangs, venom and the will to defend themselves by biting. Reared at the Snake Park, three of them survived and one of the females mated with a male king cobra from the Mangalore Zoo to produce the first captive clutch in the country.

A year later, in 1976, Rom was back in Middle Andaman, this time in mid-monsoon and with photographer Rajesh Bedi, to photograph and record the hatching and dispersal of king cobras from a wild nest. They were near the eastern shore of the island at a settlement known as Karmatang No. 9 and their guide, a Bihari farmer, had seen a nest several weeks earlier while cutting fence bamboo to protect his rice fields from the ravages of spotted deer and wild pig. He explained, 'My companion poked a stick into this mound of leaves and a big snake appeared and stood straight up with its neck spread out! We ran! Even left all our cut sticks behind! In Bihar, there is a snake like this, which can burn trees with its breath. We thought it better to get out.'

It was a strenuous walk that involved jumping over logs, wading through streams and trotting gratefully across any flat stretch that came their way, stopping of course to pick off the leeches that constantly appeared from every direction. And finally, they reached a thick bamboo slope where the guide stood aside to let them pass. The rain had flattened the nest and there was no sign of the female. But digging carefully into the mound, they found sixteen eggs. And here again, by a stroke of uncanny luck, they found that the eggs had all been slit and several small black noses were emerging into the world. Snakes break free of the eggshell using a temporary projection on the snout, called the egg tooth. Viviparous (live-bearing) snakes are naturally not equipped with this tool.

They had hit the right day and the right time to see one of the greatest natural phenomena of the reptile world unfold before them. From a crude shelter fashioned at the spot, Rom and Rajesh watched the hatchlings for the next twenty-four hours. These were startling to look at, with their little hoods and bright black and yellow bands. Without exception, they all headed straight up into the bamboo, as the rain beat down ever harder on the now-empty nest.

Ocean Reptile

Midnight, first week of November 1975. The early evening shower had left a damp chill, which, combined with the heavy sea spray, made us wish we'd brought sweaters along. The phosphorous-laden sand threw up gleaming, turquoise sprays as our feet kicked it; and the waves were masses of liquid silver. Even the watery half-moon seemed to glow unnaturally in this fairy world.

A few metres ahead of us, Valliappan stopped, bent down attentively, then strode ahead again leaving behind a blazing wake of phosphorous. This was the first 'turtle walk' of that winter's turtle nesting season when hundreds – formerly thousands – of olive ridleys come ashore to lay their eggs on the Madras coast. With the help of interested people like Valli, Rom had organized a conservation project for this beleaguered turtle that was rapidly declining in numbers because of the heavy, uncontrolled collection of its eggs for the market. The leathery ping-pong ball eggs sold for three or four paise each. And the efficient collectors often gathered

The Madras coast has several turtle nesting beaches where olive ridleys come ashore to lay eggs.

them as they dropped into the 50-centimetre-deep nest hole the female had laboriously dug. Rom and Valli's survey during the previous (1973–74) nesting season told a grim story, that over 90 per cent of the eggs were taken by dogs, humans and jackals.

Given natural predation levels in the sea, some scientists claim that only one in a thousand hatchlings reaches adulthood and it seemed that every effort was needed to discourage the illegal trade in eggs if the species was to continue nesting on our coast. 'It looks bad for Mrs Ridley,' said Valli as he pored over increasingly depressing data.

To arrest this depredation of eggs and to create awareness about the plight of this sea turtle on the beaches, we started a media campaign during that season (1974–75) with articles in newspapers and magazines and leaflets for distribution. We also set up a small hatchery at a beachside garden

Eggs collected on the beach at night by conservation agencies are incubated in fenced enclosures and the hatchlings are released into the ocean after they emerge.

belonging to friends, where eggs were brought and buried in simulated nests. Jean and Janine Delouche were delighted when they hatched sixty days later, and the hatchlings were released into the ocean. For four years, volunteers from the Snake Park collected an increasing number of eggs, averaging 3,000 per season. Later, the programme was adopted by the WWF branch in Tamil Nadu (by then, independent from the Snake Park), the state Forest Department and the Central Marine Fisheries Research Institute, and conducted on a much larger scale.

That particular night we hadn't planned to go turtle walking, but Valli was sure that nesting would begin earlier than it had the year before. 'I feel it in my bones, man,' he said tapping his elbow confidently. So, we'd driven south of the city and left the jeep at Thiruvanmiyur around 9 p.m., walking out briskly to cover the longest distance possible before the optimum nesting period between midnight and two in the morning. After a while, the soft sand – which gives way and strains the foot muscles – became uncomfortable, and we began walking along the water's edge where the sea soaks in to make a hard pavement. Just after midnight, we saw an egg collector coming along from the opposite direction with his thin wooden pole that was used to jab the nest area to locate the eggs. It is cruelly easy to find nests; the prominent, churned-up track of the female as she comes ashore and returns to the ocean makes a V-shaped mark and is as good as a signboard. Female ridleys lumber about 20 metres up the beach, dig a nest hole, lay their eggs and go back into the water. The nest is at the apex of the V.

The egg collector had been luckier than us; he'd already collected four nests, about five hundred eggs, and now he couldn't carry any more, so was on his way home. This, really, is the only thing the Madras ridley had to be grateful for – that a person can carry only so much and no more.

We found a stranded narrow-headed sea snake on the beach and Rom caught it by the tail and returned it to the sea. Its survival was doubtful though – it had been out of water too long and was almost too weak to move. Its breathing apparatus is not designed for extended periods out of the ocean's buoyancy. The year before, on another turtle walk, we'd found two banded sea snakes and taken them home to add to the Park's collection. We had no bag or container and the deadly venomous snakes had slithered around on the jeep floor while I hugged my knees, eyes fixed on the banded forms. During the night, they escaped from their buckets – 'They can't possibly climb out, don't worry,' Rom had assured me – and were lying on the pile of washing near the sink in the morning.

On this walk, Valli came to an abrupt halt ahead of us and jerked his thumb triumphantly. Fifteen metres ahead was a dark boulder walking ponderously out of the water. At this initial stage of the nesting sequence, sea turtles are very timid, turning back if disturbed by a strange object or sound; but once the nest excavation begins, even an earthquake might not interrupt the determined female. We stood like statues watching her progress towards the dry sand. 'Let's go,' said Valli when she stopped and began to excavate a 'body pit'. We trotted up and flopped down by her side. I got a face full of sharp dry sand as she tossed it back with her hind flippers. Once she had shifted the upper layer, the systematic digging of the nest hole began and about thirty minutes after she had left the water, the half-metre-deep cavity was ready. This strenuous terrestrial activity made great demands on the stamina of the turtle and she breathed in deep gulps punctuated by short sharp whistles. The water from the lachrymal glands, which wash the eyeballs, streamed down, giving her a tearful look.

A five-minute rest period followed, and then the eggs started appearing. By widening the rim of her nest, we obtained a clear view of the cloaca suspended over it and of the eggs dropping in. Round, white, smooth and bouncy. They came within seconds of each other, sometimes two or three at once. As the hundredth fell in, three jackals appeared from the casuarina stand bordering the beach but retreated on seeing us. Their sharp noses serve them well! A year later, in the Andaman Islands, we were to see the remains of turtle egg feasts, probably by wild pigs and water monitors.

One hundred and thirty-seven eggs in all. Valli marked the spot with a stick after the mother turtle filled it with sand, so we could find them later. And then began the most incredible phase of the whole exercise. Lying on the now closed, flattened nest, Mrs Ridley proceeded to rock her 40-kilogram body from side to side in a comic tap dance. The deep drumbeat thus produced, blended with the booming surf. Having packed in her eggs, she proceeded to make a false nest, rotating round and vaguely agitating the sand with her flippers while moving away from the nest site. Ten minutes later, she made her way back to the water's edge and we watched the domed figure enter the surf, disappear, surface again, and then she was gone, bound for an unknown destination. The only job that remained was for us to haul the eggs back to the hatchery. On some nights when we found too many eggs to carry, we would erase the ridley tracks with our feet, a simple way to protect these turtles.

Two months and many nests later, Jean Delouche was at our doorstep at the crack of dawn, looking a little worn. 'Hey! All night I've been listening to those damned turtles of yours! *Keech-keech-keech* all night long. Listen! The whole rotten bunch is hatching at once.'

We went back with him to find that indeed, half the 'rotten bunch' had hatched, and the fenced hatchery was dotted with black shapes grappling weakly with the sand. The initial twenty-four hours of a sea turtle's life are crucial, and survival requires determined efforts on its part. It has to break free of the eggshell with the help of the tiny egg tooth, then scramble frantically to get out of the nest hole. The simultaneous activity of its hundred siblings creates an upward movement towards light and freedom. In the frantic melee, some suffocate to death. This same scrambling instinct helps to carry the babies quickly past the menace of predators, first on the beach and then in the sea, and also through the powerful waves and currents.

Rom managed to popularize turtle walks among school and college students and converted them into regular programmes organized by the WWF, enthusiastically looked after by Ann Joseph, the Snake Park's secretary at the time. Walking along the beach stretches within the city limits sometimes brought added excitement, and two or three times, 'turtler' groups were held up at knifepoint and had to surrender watches, money and jewellery. We ourselves had a close encounter one night. We were out with the German filmmaker Heinz Kramer and his wife as they wanted to film the nesting sequence of the ridley. Kramer was deeply stricken by the plight of the exploited sea turtle and when we came across two egg collectors forging onward with bags of eggs, he could not control his anger. He brandished a pocket knife at them, shouting German swear words. *'Schweinhund!'* he thundered. And, turning to the other man, *'Schweinhund, Das darf man nicht! Nicht erlaubt. Schweinhund!'* (You pigs! This isn't allowed, you pigs!) The egg collectors shouted with fear and fishermen from a nearby village came running to their defence. Sensing the danger, Herr Kramer pocketed his knife; but it was difficult to convince his enemies that the little murder threat had been a mistake, and for a while, it looked tricky.

A few days after this incident we were back on the beach with the Kramers, edging along the hard sand at the water's margin in a hired jeep packed with filming equipment, including a generator for the floodlights, tripods and cameras. They did manage to film a nesting female ridley, but then the jeep gave a sudden cough and froze as the advancing tide lapped greedily at the wheels. Half an hour later, the water was considerably higher and we were just beginning to unload the equipment and consign the vehicle to the deep when the engine suddenly came to life once more. We were relieved when they returned to Germany!

Rom had been writing in all directions about the plight of sea turtles in India and, together with Valli, created a booklet on the olive ridley of the Coromandel coast that was printed and distributed by the Snake Park. All this publicity helped, and the Wildlife (Protection) Act included all five species of sea turtles which are found in Indian waters – the ridley, green, loggerhead, hawksbill and leatherback – in its first Schedule, which offers the highest level of protection for species. Penalties for collecting eggs and killing turtles could include heavy fines and even jail sentences. On paper, the sea turtles were very well off; but typically, the laws had little relevance to the reality in the field.

Turtle markets, where they were openly slaughtered, continued to flourish along the east coast; in Calcutta (now Kolkata), several thousand ridleys came to the markets every year from Orissa. On the Tamil Nadu coast, small fish markets often had a few sea turtles too, but at Tuticorin, it was a weekly affair and on Sunday mornings, fishermen brought in their week's catch of turtles to the butchers. As we wanted to verify reports of this continuing trade, I travelled there with Ann and Binod Choudhury of the government's crocodile project. We took the overnight bus to Tuticorin and walked down to the market at dawn to photograph the illegal butchering. It was a sight to turn the strongest stomach. Soon after our arrival, upturned turtles started arriving in wheelbarrows and pickups. During the two hours we were there, over thirty sea turtles – ridleys, greens and hawksbills –

were brought in. Then the butchers took over. The plastron or lower shell of the living turtle was pulled off and the insides removed as the flippers beat frantically in agony. Soon there were piles of intestines and meat, still twitching and jerking. Mouths gulped for air in non-existent lungs, eyes on severed heads blinked slowly.

When the turtles were first cut up, the blood drinkers would queue up carrying their small stainless-steel cups and bowls; mostly old people hoping to revive their waning powers through the ancient elixir. It cost a rupee per cup and the fresh blood had to be drunk quickly, in one gulp, before it congealed. We heard that the Tamil Nadu Forest Department had received a petition from the Sea Turtle Blood Drinkers' Association of Tuticorin asking permission to continue their traditional activities in the interest of their health!

A few days before our visit, Tuticorin had seen a case of poisoning from consumption of hawksbill meat, a phenomenon that occurs now and then and which had (then) not been satisfactorily explained. The Sri Lankan naturalist Deraniyagala, and others, have reported that the hawksbill is rendered poisonous after it feeds on certain algae. Fisherfolk in some areas are said to chop up its raw liver and throw it to crows; if discarded, the animal is considered poisonous.

A lucky thing that happened to sea turtles in India was Satish Bhaskar, who worked for the Snake Park for four years, surveying nesting beaches and populations on mainland India and its offshore islands. At the time we first met Satish, he was a student at IIT Madras, but his schedule did not include the classroom; every day, he'd jog to the beach 2 kilometres away, have a long swim, jog back, then pore over books on seashells and coral reefs. To break the monotony, he would sometimes have a swim in the evening too. When Rom offered him the job of mapping sea turtle nesting beaches and collecting data on their status and distribution, a slow ecstasy dawned on his sun-beaten face. 'Wow,' said he.

Knapsack on his back, Satish started walking. He covered over a thousand kilometres along the east and west coasts of India, timing his visits with the reported turtle nesting seasons in that area. Often, he slept on the beach in a boat or on the sand, in the process getting persecuted by sand flies, village dogs (one encounter resulted in him getting bitten as well) and once, by a group of thugs. He combined a burning energy in the field with accurate and readable reports and this combination made him one of the ace field biologists in India. Satish became an internationally acknowledged sea turtle biologist who went on to work in Indonesia as well, formulating a management plan for their leatherbacks.

Unfortunately, while Rom and I were away in Papua New Guinea for two years, 1978–80, Satish had an altercation with the group of trustees in charge of the Snake Park's administration and resigned. Luckily, WWF-India asked him to continue his surveys and we remained in close touch with him; wonderful Brenda Leveiro, his wife and our office manager, had moved to the Croc Bank with us and they lived in one of the cottages there. Rom continued to advise and support Satish and his work. One of the first areas Satish looked at was the cluster of Lakshadweep Islands in the Arabian Sea, west of the Kerala coast. In 1982, he spent five months on the uninhabited Suheli Island during the monsoon to record the green turtle's nesting patterns there. There was no inter-island transport in Lakshadweep during the rains and a fishing boat dropped him at the island in early May, promising to return in mid-September. But that year saw a prolonged monsoon and the boatman couldn't get permission to cross to Suheli until mid-October, a delay that caused an anxious wait for Satish. On his departure from Madras, we had seen him off with comforting possibilities of what might be in store for him – What if you break an arm, a leg? Sea snake bite? Run out of fresh water? Appendicitis? As it happened, his biggest problem turned out to be a 10-metre whale shark which washed up, dead and very rotten, on his beach and soon the entire island was enveloped with the stench. Fortunately, the sea finally carried away the smelly cargo.

By this time Satish and Brenda had a child, Nyla, born a few weeks before Satish ventured forth on his island mission. Sitting in the solitude of Suheli, he wrote Brenda several letters, sealed them in bottles and consigned these to the ocean, asking the finder to forward them to Brenda. She got one of these letters, sent on by a Sri Lankan fisherman, five weeks after it was written.

Satish's major triumph during these surveys was in the beautiful Nicobar Islands where he found a rookery or mass nesting ground of the leatherback turtle, which grows to 2 metres in length and is the largest of the world's sea turtles. His letters were full of adventure and discovery. 'Met a shell diver who has encountered sharks on numerous occasions while diving and has seen a Bengali colleague dismembered off Herbertabad. When I questioned him about sharks, the first incident he related was about a co-diver who grabbed his neck and hung on in terror when approached by a 'monster' – which was a dugong.' In another missive, he wrote:

> At Cuthbert Bay, Middle Andaman, I found another leatherback excavation and inadvertently got to within a few inches of a sea snake once again. It was in ankle deep water, probably making for nearby rocks when I disturbed it, and it made off after splashing me. Did no more shore walking that night and slept on a high rock! Soon after that, on Little Andaman, I saw my first nesting leatherback. She had finished egg laying and was camouflaging the nest area when I saw her. Tried barring her path to the sea by standing in front of her but she kept coming on and I had to step aside.

Little Andaman is the home of the Onge, a group of hunter-gatherers about whom little is known. They are fast diminishing due to the appropriation of their forests and the inevitable spread of diseases to which they have no immunity. Satish was lucky to see one of the more remote Onge camps near West Bay. He'd been walking for three and a half days without seeing people, when, as he related:

> I ran into a camp, occupants missing, and green turtle meat roasted and just begging to be eaten, which I surreptitiously did (being really famished – had eaten only biscuits and vitamins for the previous four days). I left two biscuit packets for the Onge to salve my conscience ... no, actually to reduce chances of stopping a spear if found out!

Some encounters were a little more dangerous. Relating his adventures at Trinket Island in Central Nicobar, Satish wrote:

> I'd found a hawksbill nest the previous night and tired after trekking the whole day, spread my polythene ground sheet on the beach. At 4 am I was woken by a rustling sound near my head. It was a crocodile gaping at me through the mosquito net. My enthusiasm for sleeping on sandy beaches has since suffered.

The Croc Bank was fortunate to be in contact with the sea turtle biologist Dr Jack Frazier who has collected extensive data from the Indian Ocean and published an impressive pile of papers on sea turtle distribution, ecology and conservation. In December 1984, Jack came to India for the centenary symposium of the BNHS and spent a couple of months in Madras. Jack is one of those naturalists who is open and generous with ideas and suggestions and willing to help others in the field. He managed to organize all the sea turtle nesting data for Madras from our notes, scattered over many notebooks and sheets of paper, and injected a lot of enthusiasm into the group of students associated with the Croc Bank. These interactions with him often happened while swimming in the ocean in front of our home, his metre-long beard floating in the waves. With his twinkling eyes, Jack looked like a mischievous octopus.

With Jack Frazier, Rom went to the Gahirmatha coast in Orissa during February 1985, to see the annual olive ridley mass nesting or *arribada* (Spanish for 'arrival'). In this incredible nesting orgy, thousands upon thousands of sea turtles nest on the 5-kilometre beach over a week during January–February and again in April. Along with Chandrasekhar Kar who had been studying the *arribada* since 1977, they arrived on the beach on a night when twenty thousand turtles came ashore and nested. It was one of nature's frenzies, like the mass migration across the Serengeti plains. Wave upon wave of them hobbled out of the sea to

The night after 20,000 olive ridleys laid their eggs on Gahirmatha beach, Jack Frazier and Shekar Dattatri watched one that was still at it when the sun rose.

nest and return to the ocean as if taking part in some bizarre military operation. There wasn't enough space on the beach for all the nests, so females were digging up other nests. Egg yolk and sticky sand flew in all directions. Rom wrote:

> The hours went by quickly as the flow of turtles seemed to ebb and swell with its own dynamic tide. This was a small

> *arribada* but that did not detract from the excitement as we pondered over the mechanisms and senses that caused the turtles to travel in huge flotillas which coast guard officers once described as 'islands of turtles migrating northward'. Over two million eggs were laid that night and over forty million in the season.

In late March and early April, the beach at Gahirmatha is again dark with moving shapes. Millions of tiny hatchlings crawl laboriously through a deadly gauntlet of crabs and birds. Only 15 grams in weight compared to their 40 kilogram mothers, the little turtles instinctively head towards the sea, attracted by the glow of the waves and reflection of the stars. Meanwhile, nature pulls one of its dark jokes and a new arribada of adult females starts in the midst of hatching. The care one takes not to step on the hatchlings is made a mockery of by the adults who just clamber over the babies, suffocating them by the thousands under their heavy plastrons.

In 1981, Chandrasekhar had discovered another *arribada* beach, also in Orissa, with a hundred thousand nesters on 2–3 kilometres of beach. It now appears that over half a million female ridleys use the Orissa rookeries.

Just as it is virtually impossible to count the number of turtles coming up during an *arribada,* it is even more difficult to predict how many hatchlings make it back to the sea after their fifty- to sixty-day incubation under the sand. Wild boar, hyenas, jackals, lizards, cats, crabs and birds prey on the eggs and the successive waves of nesting females destroy millions. Once in the ocean, there are other marine predators. No wonder it is estimated that a year after hatching, as few as one in a thousand may survive because of these hazards.

Jack Frazier and Rom spent a lot of time discussing the future of this massive breeding population of turtles. Will its fragile habitat, buffeted by annual cyclones, survive? Should one persist with total preservation and not acknowledge the resource potential? Can a number of turtles or eggs be safely taken to supply the massive demand in West Bengal? If so, how do we arrive at figures and a system that will prevent overexploitation? There were some ill-advised efforts at captive breeding of ridleys in India instead of concentrating research efforts and money on the wild population. Captive rearing of turtles in Orissa, which has the largest wild nesting populations of ridleys in the world and where neither the meat nor the eggs are eaten, would use up local protein in the form of shellfish, crabs, shrimp and fish, all of which are eaten by the local people.

A few days before Rom and Jack arrived at Gahirmatha, the chief minister of Orissa had landed on the beach in a helicopter to see the sea turtles. Governmental sympathy and concern for the survival of the ridleys began in 1976 when the Forest Department banned the lifting of eggs from Gahirmatha. But poaching continued unabated and Chandrasekhar used to watch poachers operating offshore, hauling the helpless animals into their boats as they returned from nesting, some with the tags that he had clipped on. The catch was transferred to trawlers and ended up at Howrah station in Calcutta. In 1982, *India Today* published photographs of the mass poaching, taken by Croc Bank's own J. Vijaya, today famously known as the Turtle Girl. This led to an outcry, highlighted by a letter campaign from the international sea turtle conservationists targeted at the Indian Prime Minister Indira Gandhi. She acted quickly and decisively, and the following year navy and coast guard ships patrolled the sea when nesting began. Helicopters, fixed-wing aircraft and patrol boats apprehended poachers as the turtles nested with a massive protection force looking on. In another enlightened move, the Orissa government banned the use, during the nesting season, of the deadly offshore trawlers in which turtles are often trapped and drowned.

The future of sea turtles in India is uncertain. The danger, as always, comes from uncontrolled trade and not from the local consumption of meat. In the Andaman and Nicobar Islands, the Adivasis and local settlers have speared turtles for generations, and this has remained a sustained source of protein for a small number of people, but when organized business interests set in, there is little chance of the populations holding out. The central government created a sea turtle specialist group – of which Rom and Satish Bhaskar were members – and later, organizations like the Dakshin Foundation carried out research and conservation measures that will have far-reaching effects on sea turtle numbers. But the recent plans for the development of Great Nicobar, which will result in massive forest felling and beach erosion, do not bode well for sea turtles, Earth citizens for millions of years before our arrival.

The Shining

By the 1970s, the plight of India's crocodilians was rapidly worsening. All three species, the mugger or marsh crocodile, the saltwater crocodile and the gharial, had valuable skins and had been hunted out in many habitats. They were listed under Schedule 1 of the Wildlife (Protection) Act of 1972, but this looked like too little, too late. The most endangered was the gharial of which fewer than 200 remained in the wild; and even this remnant number were being shot, speared, netted and their eggs robbed. Their riverine habitat was being destroyed from the heavy siltation of rivers, which follows deforestation in the hills as well as the increasing scale of sand mining for construction, an industry that has today reached huge proportions and is warping the geography of rivers like the Chambal.

Rom's gharial status surveys in 1973 had confirmed the dire situation of this species. The first of these, funded by WWF-India, took him and Rajamani, his Irular colleague at the Snake Park, to the states of Uttar Pradesh, Rajasthan,

Bihar and Orissa, where a few wild gharial reportedly survived in stretches of the Ganga, Chambal and Mahanadi rivers. Shikar tales from the turn of the century told of rivers teeming with both the mugger and the gharial, and reports of over twenty gharials on one sandbank were common. But by the 1970s, the picture was very different.

By the third month of one of these surveys, they had collected a lot of bad news and run out of money. In those times, money was transferred through the post office via a money order or MO. The Snake Park sent an MO to the main post office in Cuttack, Orissa, but the postmaster wouldn't allow Rom to collect it without an official identity card, and the local police station understandably refused to issue one. The travellers returned to the post office to plead some more. 'But how are we to know you are you,' the postmaster insisted until they gave up.

So the two herpetologists found themselves 800 kilometres from Madras, with about seven rupees between them, and no place to stay. Rom thought it would be too embarrassing to approach the Raja of Kanika, whom they had visited the day before, so they tried another strategy. Putting on khaki shirts after washing up at the railway station, they strode into the reception room of the Circuit House. 'Crocodile officers from the Madras Snake Park,' announced Rom in a deep voice and procured a room, coffee and lunch. How good that felt!

The next day, the choice was between thumbing a ride

south or attempting ticketless train travel. Rajamani favoured the former. By then, he was disgusted with the northern cold and the wheat diet, which he said was weakening his rice-accustomed system. 'The last thing we need is to get arrested by a ticket inspector,' he groaned.

So, at dawn, the two positioned themselves on the southbound highway holding a placard saying 'Madras'. As luck would have it, a truck slowed down soon after; and fifty hours later its driver Ram Singh dropped them at the gate of the Snake Park! During the journey, he supplied them with tea, food and smokes, feeling intensely sorry for the white sahib who had fallen on bad times.

A year later, the New York Zoological Society sponsored further surveys and E. Mahadev of the Snake Park was able to map in the missing links in Madhya Pradesh, Arunachal Pradesh and Assam, travelling on his motorbike with a bedroll strapped to the pillion. His conclusion was that large net fishing, shooting and the damming of rivers had accelerated the gharial's decline.

In the summer of 1974, the year we got married, Andy Ross of the Smithsonian Institution came to Corbett National Park to observe the gharial and mugger on the Ramganga River. Rom and his Snake Park colleague D. Basu decided to join him, and the three of them spent six weeks just before our wedding, watching the crocodiles of the area and interviewing local fishermen about their previous and present status. Using the nocturnal 'eye-shining' method, beaming torchlight on to the water's surface at (human) eye level, they found two pools that were frequently used by five gharials and eight mugger, and constructed rough blinds from where they could watch the activity on the river. Croc eyes have a reflective material called *Lucidium tapetum*, which reflects directly beamed light. Suddenly, the darkness is dotted with red rubies, a beautiful sight (especially when you're safely inside a big boat). Eye-shining is not an infallible census method, however, because crocs can, when they sense danger, remain underwater for several hours at a time, slowing down their heartbeat through a metabolic trick called bradycardia.

One afternoon in May, Rom was sitting in one of the blinds overlooking the gharial pool, dozing off periodically. It was hot and sticky – the rain was not far away. Just as the first sounds of thunder rolled down the valley, Basu and he decided to call it a day. They walked to the Ghairal rest house to find that Andy had seen a large 3-metre mugger from a few paces away. They went back with him and there it was, just lying on the bank, only hissing as they moved closer and closer. It was obviously very sick, its body covered with wounds, possibly from homemade bombs of black powder and plaster of Paris that local woodcutters were using to bomb fish in the deep pools.

The mugger died soon after and Andy, a keen taxonomist, decided that the skeleton must be saved for a museum collection. Whole mugger specimens are scarce, he declared, adding that since they only had a couple of days left – it would take three weeks for bones to get completely free of rotten meat and gristle underground – burying the skeleton was impossible. So, after the vultures had had a full day's feast, the three of them, Andy, Rom and Basu, worked with handkerchiefs tied over their noses and half-hourly tots of the local brew to help bear the horrible stench, working at night to avoid the flies. The skeleton they created now resides at the government's Kukkrail Crocodile Centre in Lucknow.

The trio would often walk 18 kilometres downriver to the main rest house at Dhikala. But it wasn't all slogging in the hot sun; Rom indulged in his passion for fishing using a hand line and bread dough and often returned to the rest house with hefty mahseer and bleeding cuts from the line. There were other adventures as well. On one afternoon walk, they saw a large croc slide into a side pool on a dry tributary or *sot*. Andy walked up the dry tributary and Rom sat down to wait with his camera to see if the croc would come up again. Basu, who had a bad cold, stretched out on the path adjoining the jungle's edge. After a while, Rom saw Andy coming back down and so started towards Basu who was about a 100 metres ahead around a bend. Suddenly, a tiger came out of the jungle on the other side of the tributary directly in front of him, making a fantastic orange collage against the white river stones. It coughed once and didn't see Rom until the latter whistled sharply to Andy. The tiger was heading straight towards the path where Basu was sleeping! 'Basu, tiger!' they yelled, and started racing towards him; luckily the tiger, startled, leapt up the rocks and cliffs, and disappeared over the hill.

Basu looked up and sleepily enquired what the commotion was all about. 'Nothing much, just that a tiger almost ran over you,' chuckled Andy. That wasn't Basu's lucky day; later in the afternoon, a kilometre from Dhikala, Andy and Rom who were walking ahead, saw a big tusker stride out from the forest and come towards them. They started walking swiftly to get well ahead of where he was going to cross the road, all the while looking back to get Basu's attention as quietly as possible. Basu saw the danger and started to sprint, but by now the tusker had got to the forest's edge near the road. Rom and Andy yelled for Basu to stop, which he did, slowly crouching against a tree and trying to look small. The elephant stood still, one foot raised in doubt, then crossed over slowly and disappeared into the forest.

Often bumping into elephants, the trio criss-crossed Corbett, which seemed increasingly small and vulnerable: just 6 kilometres upriver were villages and farmlands, and on the regular riverside path, tiger pugs, deer and human tracks obliterated each other. They walked the length of the Ramganga in the park by day and by night. Porcupines were some of their common companions on nocturnal walks along the river and one evening, they found the answer to the old question of how porcupines mate: with extreme care!

They would sit on a bluff overlooking Boksar, once a well-known gharial spot, and watch the water backing upriver from the Kalagarh dam, of which the last spillway had been closed. Deforestation in the lower Himalaya had already created a situation that had resulted in devastating run-off, erosion and floods down below on the plains with every monsoon. Authorities often use this argument to justify the construction of dams. But unfortunately, migratory animals like the great mahseer fish, the unique riverine gharial and the Gangetic dolphin are never considered when these developments take place.

Rom's surveys – such as the one in Corbett – turned up information on the ecology and behaviour of wild crocodiles, a subject largely unexplored except for a few fragmentary notes in journals. In 1975, for instance, he conducted a census of crocodiles in Gujarat and spent a week in the Barda Hills in Kutch. It was the worst drought in forty years and over fifty mugger were reported to have been killed while trekking overland looking for water. Rom followed one track a kilometre up into the hilly scrub forest, to find, and catch, a metre-and-a-half-long mugger sheltering under a large boulder. It was in search of water, possibly on its way to a reservoir 12 kilometres away. In later years, we were to see this same 'land croc' phenomenon in other habitats.

Another strategy that the mugger uses to tide over the hot season is to dig tunnels. These are usually from about 3–6 metres deep and a metre in diameter. They are often horizontal and sometimes horseshoe-shaped, with two entrances. Mugger that live in hill streams and in the small rivers such as the Hiran River in Gir, which often dry up leaving only large, deep, perennial pools, use tunnels all year long.

Rom had heard about Hiran Lake and sent off the plucky Ann Joseph of the Snake Park to travel there and take a look. She returned with positive mugger information, so he visited the area during the nesting season. Jeevan Nana, a Maldhari living in the Gir, helped him look for nests in Hiran. They found eighteen tunnels dug into the embankments of the then almost dry lake. He and Jeevan were on a steep cliff, so steep that you couldn't imagine a mugger climbing up; but there were clear, ascending tracks from the water and Rom peered down to investigate. As he bent over the cliff's edge, there, half a metre from his face, were the jaws of a large mugger flush with the embankment!

With about 250 animals living in nine or ten habitats scattered throughout the state, Tamil Nadu, along with Gujarat seemed to have the largest populations of crocs in the mid-1970s. In Tamil Nadu, this hardy, adaptable species was once much more common in rivers, lakes, streams and any habitat with some water and protection. But it was being increasingly hunted. In 1974, two years after the passing of the Wildlife Act, one of the Snake Park's volunteers stood by with open mouth as a mugger caught on a baited hook in the Cauvery River was tied up and carried off to be skinned. The clandestine profit from one such skin was worth several months' pay to a local fisherman or farmer, which made effective law enforcement difficult.

Sitting on top of Ram Singh's truck during his hitchhike from Orissa, Rom had written me a letter about our future plans for crocodiles. 'Tell your father about this plan. Captive breeding is the only thing that will save them, there's too much pressure on wild populations. A croc farm might even provide us with a "living", which the Snake Park certainly won't do. I would like Mrs Whitaker to have three meals a day, though it does seem slightly ambitious . . .' Baba, as always, helped with advice and funding suggestions, and I typed project proposals for a 'Crocodile Bank' on the old Smith-Corona typewriter, which needed a manual tug every time its ribbon spool reached its end. And to type through three sheets – two A4s and a carbon sheet – one needed some muscle power as well!

Apart from animals being poached for their skin and meat, mugger eggs were being collected, and in some habitats, all nests were poached; the cleared ground and nest-protection habits of the female make mugger nests easy to spot. The Smith-Corona and I requested permission from the Tamil Nadu Forest Department to collect eggs from wild nests, incubate and hatch them at the Snake Park, and hand over a percentage of the offspring to the Forest Department after rearing them for a year. These would be used for a rewilding project they were keen to start. The Chief Conservator of Forests agreed and one day, the precious 'egg permit' arrived in the post.

During the first season of egg collection, in 1975, we got to the main habitat, Amaravati, to find eleven empty nest holes baking in the sunlight. Over 500 potential hatchlings had either been turned into omelettes or gobbled up by predators.

The answer was to plant nest guards – Snake Park staff – at the major mugger habitats well ahead of the start of their nesting season (February to May). The first 'egg-guard' experiment was a success. A vanguard of egg protectors was sent off and as soon as we got telegrams from them that nesting was beginning, we got our Nissan Jonga serviced and were ready to go. With ace Irular tracker Chockalingam, or Choky, and the Snake Park's Mahadev and Solomon, we drove south to Chidambaram and on through to the Vakkaramari Waterworks, which then had a population of twenty mugger. The Jonga had its first, and one of many, tantrums just south of Chengalpattu. 'Brakes failed,' Rom announced calmly as we slid towards a ditch after narrowly missing a bullock cart. There was half a day's delay while a mechanic was found to repair the severed brake line.

First stop, Chidambaram. Natesan/Sureman, the nest guard stationed there, had good news for us. The previous day he had almost stumbled over a mugger nesting in broad daylight on one of the bunds dividing the two main tanks. 'Let's get the eggs out right now, those mongooses have been nosing about near the nest,' he advised. Sweaty and tired, we set about unpacking the plywood boxes – 50 centimetres square and 20 centimetres deep with perforations for air – in which the eggs would be safe on their journey to Madras. We lined one of them with slightly damp earth and in the orange glow of dusk, transferred the white oblong eggs to their foster nest. The female watched from the water's edge 5 metres away as the earth was scraped back and each egg lifted out carefully, without turning it. The top was marked with a cross and placed in the box in exactly the same position. Turning or jarring an egg can rupture the delicate blood vessels attaching the embryo to the shell wall. 'Handle them like nitroglycerine,' Rom advised Mahadev, 'and they'll make it.'

Each layer of eggs was covered with earth and humus to make them as shockproof as possible and the box was deposited in a corner of the Waterworks office. It would be Natesan's job to keep the eggs damp and free from ants until half the sixty-day incubation period was over when he could take them back to Madras by train with a minimum of worry about damaging the embryos, which would be stronger by then. These eggs would form the breeding nucleus of the Madras Crocodile Bank, which we were soon to start. But more – much more – about that later.

Early the next morning, we loaded up for the 375-kilometre drive to the Amaravati reservoir, now part of the Annamalai Wildlife Sanctuary, one of the last refuges of the Nilgiri tahr. The reservoir is an example of how natural fish predators like crocodiles can actually be beneficial to the fisheries industry. The mugger at Amaravati feed on catfish, cormorants, otters, turtles and a number of other creatures, which in turn hunt the commercially valuable species of fish. Of course, you can't tell a fisherman this; for him, crocs break nets and eat fish, and that's that. But the fact that Amaravati had both the highest fish catch in India, as well as the largest southern population of crocodiles, was certainly beyond coincidental.

Nesting hadn't begun at Amaravati. All we could see were faint trial nests and a lot of tracks zigzagging across the banks, which indicated that the females were active: egg-laying would start any day. There was also a lot of disturbance along the lakeshore – fishermen and cow herders with their herds of cattle looking for good grazing areas. At night, the wild creatures took over, with elephants and sambar coming down from the hills for a drink. We wondered if the increased daytime activity on the banks had disturbed the nesting schedules of the mugger – or maybe they were nesting elsewhere! A year later, walking around Amaravati with our friend Binod Choudhury of the government's crocodile project, we saw a strange phenomenon. Following tracks leading out of the water, we came upon a 3-metre female, a kilometre from the water's edge. She had clambered halfway up a small hill, over rocks and thorny bushes, and later laid her eggs in these inhospitable surroundings, but the soil was not deep enough for a nest and the eggs rolled down the dry hillside and broke.

On that first trip, however, as nesting hadn't begun, we decided to leave Solomon in Amaravati to collect the eggs before a poacher or predator got them. Ahead of departing for the next habitat, Bhavani Sagar, we spent a night out on the reservoir 'shining' for croc eyes from one of the locally popular coracles. These circular boats, about 2 metres in diameter, are made from buffalo hides stitched together with leather. The frame is bamboo, woven like a basket. Twenty pairs of gleaming orange eyes answered our spotlight beam. Without quite knowing what he was doing, the boatman got us pretty close to the grandaddy, a 4-metre mugger lying on a slab of rock facing us. The flimsy coracle oared silently up to the dreaming giant, with all of us expecting him to retreat like a normal croc; but he didn't, and we realized how vulnerable the coracle or parachal could be. When we were practically on it there was a massive splash and the boat rocked wildly as it dived under us and shot away. We could feel his bumpy back scrape the underside of the coracle.

Apart from being fishing boats and transport, coracles also provide effective storm shelter. Once, at Sathanur Dam, a sudden squall blew up on the reservoir. The intensity of the wind whipping up the waves was frightening, and our fisherman friend Kalimuthu glanced apprehensively at the water sloshing over the sides of the boat. Rom bailed with a coconut shell and Kalimuthu took us towards the shore with strong paddle strokes. Knowing how difficult it is to keep one of these coracles going in a straight line even in calm waters, I was amazed at this fisherman's skill. We reached the shore just in time because a huge storm was following at the heels of the wind and hailstones suddenly started falling. But Kalimuthu was prepared for any weather. He hauled the coracle up on the pebbly bank and turned it over, bottom facing the wind. We all crawled underneath, dry and with a nice view of the storm on the lake.

But to return to the Amaravati story, we left the next morning for Bhavani Sagar Dam, which is flanked by the Nilgiris. At the dam itself, there was just one trial nest hole; but the rest house cook at Bhavani town told us of a small group of mugger living in the Kedarhalla stream 400 metres up in the foothills, on the Kerala border. This was exciting news indeed; it was the first report of the mugger still surviving in a wild, unaltered habitat in Tamil Nadu. So far, all the mugger we had seen were in artificial environments like reservoirs and tanks. The best time to survey the stream would be at night, and we decided to go the next day and camp on the bank. Mahadev and I went off to Bhavani town and bought provisions – rice, dal, tea, sugar – and tried to find a guide to take us up to the stream. But this last proved impossible; the Kedarhalla area was believed to be haunted and no one was prepared to come along as a guide, certainly not for the night. We finally set off on our own and hired the watchman of the Electricity Board at Gejeleti village on the banks of the Moyar River at an exorbitant price. The next day, halfway up the hill, he doubled his fee with cunning presence of mind.

The morning of the expedition, the sun rose like a chunk of red-hot coal; the gentle interval between night and day had been done away with, and this was summer in earnest. The track, which led to Gejeleti village below the croc pools, was an obstacle course, and the Jonga bulldozed its way through the patches of scrub, between large boulders and down steep, dry stream beds. Further on, we stopped at a cattle camp, which had been ravaged by elephants the night before; the feeble thorn fences were torn down, banana trees stripped, two huts trampled and practically shredded. Over the last two years, three people had been killed by elephants in this area, all of which pointed to the dramatic dwindling of forest habitat in South India and the increased harassment by ivory poachers. A forest official in Bhavani had told us that elephant poachers were now hanging live wires from electric lines and the trauma and slow death of the animals was unimaginable. Forest Department officials had recovered several carcasses after the painful device finally killed them. It sounded like the South Indian tusker was on the way out.

On the drive up towards the Moyar River, we saw several small herds of elephants dotting the dusty, dry hillsides as well as their tracks on the banks. They were sticking close to the river this time of the year, but it was incongruous to see the big animals in the dry, low thorn forest. Here we almost had to turn back, not because of the jumbos but because the floodgates had been opened and the Moyar, which flows into the Bhavani Sagar Reservoir along with the Bhavani, was in spate. We decided to drive across anyway through 20 metres of white, surging water, a metre deep in some places. 'Motor no, motor no,' pleaded the guide, which perversely was an added encouragement. In the event, we almost lost the vehicle, and Rom as well. The rest of us got out to lighten the vehicle's load and crossed over. From the other bank, we watched the Jonga lurch drunkenly across the furious water, once hitting a large boulder – dong! – and almost keeling over. As it arrived with a final ponderous wobble, we set up a strangled cheer.

Across the river, there wasn't even a pretence of a track. Mahadev walked ahead, cheerfully waving us over boulders and steep slopes, and the Jonga gave of its best. We parked the vehicle on the bank of the Kedarhalla stream, opposite a small Kali temple, which, our guide explained, a tiger visited every year at Dussehra to watch the people who come to make offerings and to pray. Suddenly, in mid-story, he jerked his thumb disapprovingly at me. 'Women cannot go beyond this point. If she goes any further the *sami,* God, will get angry, and bring trouble for my family.' We tried to reason that any trouble would surely fall on me, not him, but he refused to accept this argument. Finally, the religious controversy was settled with a further sum of money, and we picked up our gear and started upstream towards the three pools the watchman at Bhavani had described.

Two kilometres along the jungle's edge, at the beginning of a steep gorge before the first pool, we found a good place to camp, with large flat 'sleeping rocks' and plenty of shade. But the still, stagnant water was filthy with slime and undrinkable. We boiled some and scraped off the green layer hoping it was okay, but two days later I was so sick with dysentery that I had to be practically carried back down to the Jonga. It was getting dark and Chockalingam and I made a small fire and cooked up a tortured mess of rice, soup cubes and dal. After nightfall, we 'shone' Pool 1 for croc eyes but saw nothing bigger than frogs and toads. We then went on towards Pool 2, hopping along the big boulders on the banks as silently as possible. A young python was enjoying the retained heat of a large rock and almost got stepped on. It was so quiet in the forest, the birds and animals seemed to be holding their breath, but as we went further up into the box canyon, there was a loud crash from overhead and all of us jumped in unison.

We 'shone' Pool 2 – nothing – and went on to Pool 3. This was the largest and deepest of the three. Chockalingam, the local guide, and I stopped 50 metres away, while Rom and

Mahadev crept forward quietly to try and take the crocs by surprise. The pools had obviously been hunted recently and the crocs were sure to be wary and shy, going underwater at the least sign of danger. As mentioned earlier, they can stay under for at least an hour, a factor which makes accurate censusing a challenge.

As Rom and Mahadev went ahead, we sat down to wait. Suddenly, an agonized scream shattered our wits. 'Hari Ram,' the guide whispered, trembling. Chockalingam and I froze, my body felt as if filled with iced water. It was several seconds before Rom came stumbling back in the dark, giving us another fright, to say it was the cry of the forest eagle owl; a call, as I later read, that was described by Samuel Baker in 1855 as a 'dull low note of indescribable pain and suffering'. Having delivered this comforting news, he ran back to Pool 3 and returned half an hour later with Mahadev to announce two pairs of eyes, which had submerged as soon as the torch was clicked on, then surfaced for a few seconds fifteen minutes later. A couple of hours later back at Pool 1, we leaned over a rock to see two orange eyes floating near the edge of the bank, adding up to a total of three crocs.

Just before dawn the next day, we collected around the breakfast pot. 'Continental menu,' Mahadev grinned, less than eagerly mixing his share of boiled ragi, alternately taking mouthfuls and flexing his muscles. Walking back to Pool 1, Chockalingam found some tracks near the bank, which led to a trial nest hole. Further on, another cavity yielded pieces of eggshell scattered on the ground and a dead hatchling on a nearby rock. Against all odds, the little mugger group of Kedarhalla had survived and was carrying out its tasks of procreation. The mother croc had carried the hatched and partly hatched young to the water, but there was no sign of them, so we decided to stay on another day to try and locate them. At this point, our guide suddenly remembered some urgent work at home and disappeared, hoping to find a cowherd who would accompany him down to the plains.

I was dealing with a *babul* (Acacia) thorn in my foot when Rom nudged me energetically, pointing to a patch of sunlight on the water below a large rock outcrop. 'See that – there. Right there – see?' I couldn't see anything. 'Where, what?' I began but by then Rom was taking off his jeans and shirt and was in the water, gesturing to Chockalingam. Only then did I spot the knot of hatchling heads floating vertically like twigs in the shade of the large rock. By now, Chockalingam was in the water too, holding a lungi. The two waded and swam as quietly as possible towards the group of tiny crocodiles, the lungi spread like a fishing net beneath the surface.

It was a successful but foolish venture. They were in 3 metres of murky, opaque water, at the mercy of a protective mother croc. After endless minutes, the lungi was spread out in slow motion under the hatchlings and lifted up slowly. Nineteen baby crocs took their cue; we held our breaths as the chorus of *wah, wah, wah* filled the air. Luckily the mother remained submerged; as often happens in heavily hunted areas, the natural defence instincts were subdued by the fear of man. The babies were transferred to a box lined with leaves and earth, watered down and left at the campsite. We moved on upstream.

Pool 2, so normal in our torch beams the night before, looked like a disaster area. Pieces of the poisonous *euphorbia* plant, which deoxygenates water and is used as the local version of dynamite fishing, floated on the surface along with hundreds of dead fish. At one corner of the pool was a trickle of fresh water from upstream and to this the surviving fish had converged, mouths open, trying to breathe. The culprit, probably a cowherd from a neighbouring *patti* (village), had destroyed hundreds of valuable fish to get a few for his family.

Rom whistled from the other side of the pool. He was standing next to a slight mound of damp earth: a mugger nest, still intact! The raised dome looked untypical of the mugger, more like the nest of a saltwater crocodile. Closer, we noticed that the surface was very wet, almost as if a bucket of water had been recently poured over it. We wondered if the female crocodile had evacuated water from her cloaca on to her nest. Rom kneeled down and tapped the earth covering with his fingers. Incredible: the unmistakable *umph, umph* of ready-to-hatch crocodiles. The faint protesting sounds are the vocal cue for the female crocodile to come and scrape the earth away, so the hatchlings can emerge. We'd arrived at exactly the right moment! Standing in for her, we dug

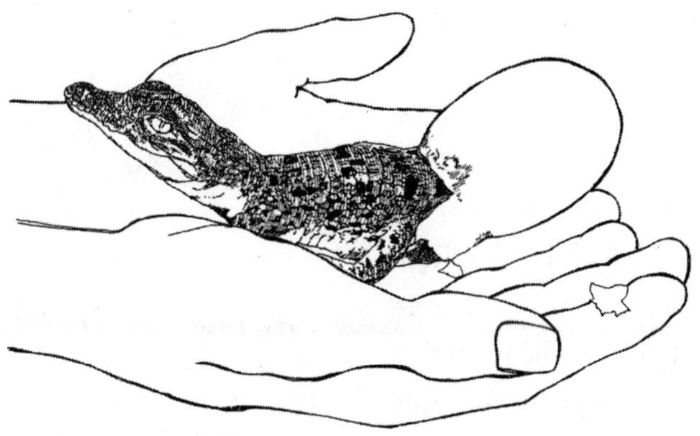

Weighing just 100 grams on their hatchday, crocodiles can grow over 7 metres long and weigh up to a 1,000 kilograms.

down to the twenty-five eggs and watched the young break free of their shells with varying degrees of energy. The first one out scrambled away from the nest hole and towards the water, with a piece of eggshell perched rakishly over its head. These animals also became a part of our nucleus group at the Croc Bank.

Crocodile management – for conservation and commercial farming – was becoming more and more popular as a perfect example of sustainable conservation. As an adviser, Rom was to travel to many parts of the world including Africa, Bangladesh, Malaysia and Papua New Guinea for organizations interested in this, such as the WWF and the Food and Agriculture Organization (FAO). I went along on some of these trips. In 1977, Rom and I undertook a survey in Sri Lanka at the invitation of its Wildlife and Nature Protection Society. Our job was to travel around the island identifying crocodile habitats, and to produce a report on the status and distribution of the two species found there, the saltwater crocodile and the mugger.

The strange forest lizard of the hills of central Sri Lanka. It opens its mouth wide when threatened and has earned the name of 'devil lizard'.

In order to be free from the uncertainties of public transport services, we took Rom's old Jawa motorcycle with us on the ferry from Rameswaram to Talaimannar in Sri Lanka; and over the two-month survey period, the old antique covered 3,000 kilometres with nary a puncture. The packing arrangements were painful, with me wedged between camera bags and knapsack at a marked slant. I'd become frozen into that position, and getting off and standing upright after a drive of several

The horned lizard is a Sri Lankan endemic.

hours was difficult. Arriving at the port town of Talaimannar on the boat, we drove down to Colombo the next day just as the first showers of the northeast monsoon hit the south-eastern corner of the island. With the help of our friend Ranil Senanayake, we made up data charts for the rivers and reservoirs, which included salinity levels, 'shining' counts, vegetation. The most productive crocodile habitat, which in our report we recommended should be declared a crocodile sanctuary, was a lake called Panama near Arugam Bay in the southeast. How well I remember weaving our way down that dirt track hung with camera and binoculars and me clutching the big green knapsack for balance, while a group of local children split their sides laughing! But the indignity was worthwhile: there in the early morning sunlight were about fifteen large mugger, basking complacently on the banks. In the depths of the forested lakeshore beyond our vision, we heard them catching fish with loud claps of their jaws.

The close approach these mugger allowed us was untypical of the species in South India. The bolting range of an animal is a useful indication of the degree of protection it enjoys in the field, and we found many instances of happy coexistence between crocodiles and people in areas which poachers had left alone. At Kataragama, pilgrims bathed in the river while mugger soaked up the sun on rocks 20 metres away. But in some areas, the animals allowed only a 300-metre approach and we found that the main culprits were nomadic fishing clans who travelled around

When we reached the lake at Panama in south-eastern Sri Lanka, it was mid-morning. The sun was warming the banks and crocodiles basked on all sides, a primeval scene that is rarely seen on the subcontinent.

the country systematically netting, hooking and trapping crocodiles, mainly for the meat.

The most interesting encounter of the survey was not with crocodiles but with old Mothalay Peter, a toothless Burgher of Dutch descent who was one of the regular croc catchers in the 1940s when it was legal. Even now, in his sixties, he would take on jobs to catch nuisance crocs for the local government agent. He and his family sat with us under coconut trees in front of his house at Batticaloa and he told us how they caught giant gourami fish by wading into abandoned croc tunnels. Peter also amazed us with his tales of catching mugger in the same way. He'd spot an active croc tunnel and then crawl into the half-submerged slimy hole with a rope but no light. Gingerly feeling around in front of him, he would contrive to slip the rope around the crocodile's body. Crocodiles, like most reptiles, are quite ticklish; and a gentle prod will make one raise its body just enough to slip the rope under. Tying a secure knot on it, Peter would back out of the tunnels resembling one-way streets, and he and his stalwarts would haul on the rope, bring the croc to the tunnel's mouth and axe it to death.

One of Peter's favourite stories was about the crocodile that didn't want a rope around itself and forced its way out of the tunnel the only way it could: over Peter. He showed us the claw marks on his back, a reminder of this adventure. People like him and our wanderings in what was then prime habitat with healthy mugger populations gave us an idea of what parts of our own country must have been like before the hunters and burgeoning human development got in on the act.

Herps in Paradise

And it was crocodiles that first took us to what became our heartthrob place, complete with (unrealistic) retirement dreams featuring two boats (one small, the other big) and our own private beach and a patch of mangrove. I'm talking, of course, about the Andamans and the Nicobars, the chain of some 600 islands and islets located in the Bay of Bengal a 1,000 kilometres east of the east coast of mainland India. This trail of dots and blobs of land runs north–south and spans 370 kilometres. They constitute one of our union territories, administered by the chief commissioner in the capital city of Port Blair. In the process of gathering distribution and status data on India's crocodilians, we planned a survey in the Islands that were, in the 1970s, one of the last two strongholds of the saltwater crocodile; the other was the Sundarbans delta. The species had paid a high price for having the most prized skin among the crocodilians and been almost wiped out in its other habitats across the country.

The Islands held other fascinations – 'hostile' indigenous communities struggling to survive, jewel-like coral reefs dotting the turquoise ocean, thick tangles of evergreen forests fringed with ice-white beaches where sea turtles nest and a species of sea snake comes ashore to lay eggs. We read whatever we could lay our hands on, including hundreds of pages of old gazette reports typed for us by the Snake Park's wonderful Brenda when we managed to borrow the precious originals from the Tamil Nadu Archives. This came about thanks to its director Gopal Gandhi; Gopal and his wife Tara, an ornithologist who had been Sálim Mamoo's student, became (and remain) wonderful friends.

The endemic fauna and flora of the archipelago include several species of herps, and Rom couldn't wait to see and study them. In 1975, a year after our marriage, we decided to visit the Islands. But access to non-Indians was restricted and Rom, then still an American citizen, was denied an 'Island Pass'. Only a handful of foreigners had been allowed there since Independence, including King Leopold II of Belgium and the Italian anthropologist Lidio Cipriani, who did a study on the Onge, one of the six indigenous tribes that were living out various levels of primitive cultures. So we decided that I would do a preliminary saltie survey, and also bring back preserved and live reptiles for the Snake Park collection. Annamalai, an Irular assistant at the Snake Park, agreed to come along. That six-week sojourn was the beginning of our rich relationship with this amazing archipelago.

There were no flights then, only a fortnightly sea cruise of three or four days, depending on the weather and the age and condition of the ship. On the deck of the INS *State of Haryana* on the way to Port Blair, I found a chair that achieved a fine balance with the help of a folded newspaper. Every now and then Annamalai would summon me to the railings, to see a school of dolphins frolicking along the ship's stern or, twice, whales on the horizon. For the three-and-a-half-day journey, I kept company with our copies of the gazette reports about the history of the Andamans, written by British officers in the nineteenth and early twentieth centuries.

What a story! I was never a wide-awake history student in school or college, but the narratives about these islands and their unique indigenous communities fascinated me. The decimation of these, through the British era and then after Independence, are examples of what we 'civilized' people have done to many ancient cultures around the world.

The colonization of these islands by the British administration in India is a tale of high drama and cruelty, ending in 1942 with the Japanese occupation, during which an unknown number of 'informers' were tortured and killed by the invading army. For thousands of years before the arrival of the British, the only inhabitants of these islands were the six groups of racially distinct tribes: the Andamanese of the Great Andaman land mass; the Onge of Little Andaman; the Jarawa, now confined to a reserve on the western coast of Middle and South Andaman; the Sentinelese on the small, isolated island of North Sentinel; and the Shompen and Nicobarese of the Nicobar group. Until the post-Independence settlements and subsequent forest encroachment, they hunted the endemic wild pig with bows and arrows or speared fish and sea turtles for food, occasionally driving away ships on their territory with a stream of arrows. Their primitive, forest-based lifestyle brought them the hostility of merchants passing through these waters and other seafarers like the slave pirates who came into contact with them. Reports about the Island people became more and more exaggerated, such as this mythical 'observation' by an Arab traveller in the ninth century: 'People on this coast eat human flesh quite raw, the complexion is black, the hair frizzled, their countenance and eyes frightful, their feet are very large, and almost a cubit in length . . .'

The British story begins in 1789 when Lieutenant Archibald Blair of the Indian navy was entrusted with surveying the Islands in order to find safe harbours 'where fleets in time of war can refit by any means . . . or to which any part or the whole army may retire in the event of a disastrous conflict with the Enemy . . .' Blair's report led to the colonization of Port Cornwallis, present-day Port Blair. The settlement was later shifted to North Andaman but abandoned due to the prevalence of cerebral malaria. During this time, contact between the outsiders and the indigenous

Jarawa and the Andamanese, who inhabited the islands of the Great Andaman group, was limited to brief 'encounters', with bows and arrows pitted against British weaponry.

At the end of the unsuccessful venture, the tribes were left in peace for sixty-five years, until the War of Independence of 1857 and the need arose to accommodate the thousands of freedom fighters sentenced to life imprisonment. To this end, the notorious penal settlement was established at Port Blair, and its effects were disastrous for the Andamanese and Jarawa. The two tribes reacted differently to the invaders of their homeland, and their future destiny was determined by the degree of their contact with them.

The British began a process of taming the Andamanese with gifts and building the Andaman Home to which 'friendly' individuals were transferred. Very quickly, the new diseases to which the tribes had no immunity began to take a heavy toll. Syphilis, measles and pneumonia killed half the Andamanese population of 4,800, and none of the 150 infants born in the Andaman Home survived beyond two years. By 1931, their numbers had dwindled to ninety and the superintendent of Census Operations, M.C.C. Bonington, noted that 'this devastating fall in the numbers of the Andamanese in less than 75 years of contact with the administration paralyses comment'.[1] At the time of my first trip in 1975 only 20 Andamanese remained, reportedly heavy opium users, a habit they indulged by trading birds' nests, ambergris and turtle shells with passing boats. The extermination of this wonderful tribe of hunter-gatherers must be laid squarely at the door of the British government.

Fortunately for the Jarawa, they kept aloof from the invaders except for occasional mischief – mainly in the form of raids on the settlement – for which they were punished out of all proportion to their crimes. A series of punitive missions against them left hundreds dead. In one such conflict, the Jarawa killed four convicts from the penal settlement; this triggered a retaliation in which thirty-seven Jarawa were shot down. In his book, *A History of Our Relations with the Andamanese* (published in 1899), M.V. Portman, one of the early administrators in the Islands, talks about the reason for the friction between these tribes and the colonists. 'On our arrival the Jarawa were quiet and inoffensive toward us, nor did they disturb us until we took to continually molesting them by

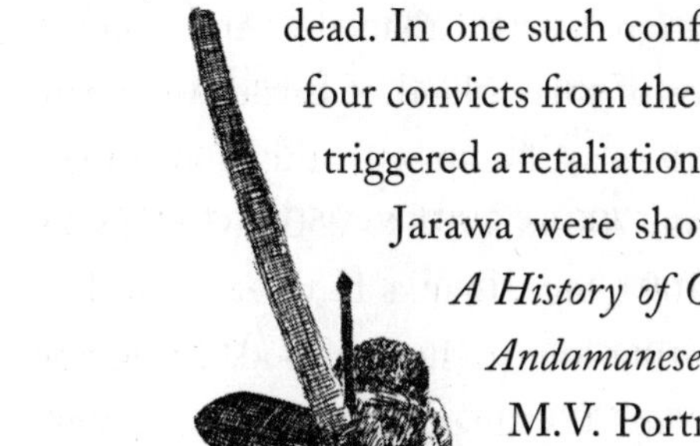

The 'hostile' Jarawa remained safe from 'civilization' until they left their forest home and habits.

inciting the coastal Andamanese against them. After a few years of this disturbance the life of the Jarawa became very hard and in retaliation they began to attack us.'[2] The British policy of divide and rule, so successful on the mainland, was applied to the fragile Andaman situation as well, where the friendly Andamanese were given rewards for their help in persecuting the Jarawa.

Initially, the Onge fared better than the Andamanese because of the distance of their island of Little Andaman. But the brutal intrusion caught up with them, and their numbers fell from about 700 in 1901 to 250 in 1931; now there are less than a 100 Onge, thanks to disease and loss of forest land for hunting and gathering food. The Onge Reserve has shrunk from 700 square kilometres to a mere 110, within which is a 'settlement' built for them at Dugong Creek, complete with wood and tin sheds for 'civilized living'.

Like the Onge, the Nicobarese and Shompen also escaped the initial crossfire of colonization and development, but the development of the Nicobars wasn't far behind. We tracked the deterioration of the indigenous Andaman–Nicobar cultures with dismay, using the accounts of our field staff as a measure. Until the mid-1980s, they spoke of having seen Shompen, Onge and Jarawa camps deep in the forest; venison and turtle meat hung up to dry; Jarawa shell-collecting on beaches and rocks; and body coverings made of bark and shells. In later years we heard about the Andaman Trunk Road, cutting right through the heart of the Jarawa

The Onge tribal reserve of Little Andaman was deforested for settlers and oil palm plantations. There is little doubt that this has spelt doom for this small, unique Negrito tribe which today is reduced to under a hundred people.

Reserve, and then about their increasing interactions with officials and tourists, who danced and cavorted with them on boats and beaches. The Onge and Shompen began to barter their nutritious jungle foods like honey for the poisons of civilization: tea, sugar, tobacco and polished rice. Their land, cultural markers and languages are disappearing. Today there are huge plans for the development of Great Nicobar, which will see the end of the forests, biodiversity and indigenous cultures of the Nicobar group.

The Sentinelese tribe proved to be the shrewdest and most successful. They resisted all attempts by the administration to befriend them, seeming to divine the fatal consequences of contact with the outside world. It is still impossible to approach the island of North Sentinel without attracting a hail of arrows. Practically nothing is known about them, not even their number; estimates vary from 50 to 150. In an article in Britain's *Sunday Times* magazine of 14 September 1975, the photographer Raghubir Singh describes his dramatic but unfruitful attempt to make contact with the Sentinelese, along with an official government team and an Onge from Little Andaman who they hoped could act as a go-between. 'Several armed Negritos emerged from the forest,' writes Singh, 'drawn bows in hand and arrows tucked in belts of bark. The Onge, holding a portable mike, shouted: "We are friends, come close, we mean no harm." The answer was the clang of an arrow against the side of our boat less than 80 yards from shore.'[3] Ironically, it is this sound – the clang of an arrow – which has been the sound of survival for the Andaman tribes.

The Sentinelese were recently in the news (2019) when the misguided American missionary John Allen Chau got himself deposited on the island by fishermen, determined to convert them . . . and convinced that Jesus would save him. Neither happened, and hopefully the Sentinelese will now be left to enjoy their independent and self-sufficient lives in peace.

To return to my journey on the pest-infested ship *State of Haryana*, by the third day, we were gliding past tiny, glistening dots of islands, with a standard geo-pattern: a thick, green mohawk of jungle, with peripheral rings of mangrove forest and stark white beaches. By dusk, we were in Port Blair harbour and it was a memorable arrival. In the general chaos of disembarking, our luggage was lost. It was finally located an hour later but by then the small band of Port Blair taxis had been engaged. Through the kindness of a local timber merchant, Annamalai and I made our way to the rest house where we'd booked ourselves, to find there was no room because some VIPs had arrived unannounced. This was before the day of hotels in Port Blair, and we circled the town for an age before being offered a room at an ashram, a room stinking of urine and crawling with cockroaches; in the corners especially, the floor seemed to be alive with them. Later in the night, the rats took charge, trotting boldly in and out. I wondered whether this or the ship cabin was worse, and decided it was a draw.

A sleepless night later, the bad luck held out. In the morning, we were waiting for a crocodile egg collection permit at the Forest Department office on Chatham Island when the clerk cannily began to question my bona fide. 'Name is Whitaker, no? Whitaker is foreigner, no? But you are Indian or foreign? Please show passport, police identity.' My protest that I was not required to carry my passport in my own country only aggravated the already shaky situation and the outcome was that we would have to get police verification of our identities in order to stay on in the Islands. 'Otherwise, madam, you will please to return to mainland with immediate effect. On same ship only. You are not possessing the necessary papers.'

They directed us to the police station but it seemed unlikely that the cops would be willing to verify the nationality of someone they hadn't set eyes on before. On the way there, we passed the Wimco factory and Fate relented; I remembered the name Fred Burn, Wimco's manager, who was a ham radio friend of my uncle's. For years they had laboriously contacted each other on the wireless and through a deafening crackle, discussed the weather since all other subjects seemed to be taboo. So I took a chance, found Fred, and greeted him with tears and my sorry tale. He dialled the police station, vouched for me and I was legal once more. He also called Uncle Saad and informed him that his niece was in good hands. Fred said we should return that afternoon so he could take us home and introduce us to his wife Jean. She offered Annamalai and myself their guest annexe, which we accepted with alacrity.

The Burns' bungalow was on the crest of a hill overlooking Port Blair harbour and how well I remember sitting out on the lawn with Jean, watching the dark sea alive with the moving lights of fishing boats. Fred and Jean Burn were to become good friends of ours, and I was to discover that the name Burn Sahib was a passport to every little hamlet or town in the Islands. When he died two years later, thousands of grieving mourners gathered at his grave to pay homage to this most generous and kind man, an Andamans legend.

Rom had mapped a croc survey route for me, starting with the island of North Andaman, reputedly the best crocodile area, but there were two days before the *Cholunga* ferry would leave on the twenty-four-hour run to Aerial Bay, our base there for the first few days. Meanwhile, we visited local areas like the edible-swiftlet caves in Chidiatapu, preserved the dead-on-road snakes we found at night and caught geckos for the vine snake Annamalai found in the Burns' garden.

Through Fred's connections with the navy, we were allowed to visit the evocative ruins of Ross, the headquarters of the British administration in the Islands. It was an island of ghosts. The chief commissioner's palatial bungalow had fallen to pieces; in the large ballroom, a banyan tree had flung out branches, which coiled around pillars and windows. In the officers' barracks, we found many geckos and nesting

Ghostly ruins of a cathedral on Ross Island

swallows. Perhaps the British statesman Lord Mayo had walked here, in this very courtyard or corridor, on the day he was murdered by a convict in 1872. And out in the bright sunshine, the loving epitaphs in the cemetery were covered with weeds and moss. I cleaned the stones with pieces of rubble . . . and tragedies sprang at me; young officers killed by the Jarawa, children dying of disease. 'Sacred to the memory of James Pratt, A.B. His Majesty's Naval Brigade, who was killed by the natives of these islands on the 28th of January 1863 aged 25 years.' On the way back to the Burns' mansion there was a dead krait on the road, which we collected and preserved the way Rom had shown us. Their storeroom was to become our interim museum for dead and live specimens to take back for the Snake Park. Incidentally, that krait turned out to be a new species.

On the way to North Andaman, the *Cholunga* stopped at Strait Island where the handful of surviving Andamanese had been 'settled' by the government and given cows and pigs to raise! The boat picked up Loka, the headman, and his granddaughter, both so youthful and lively that it was hard to believe they were the last of their race. The sea was crystal clear and we watched fish, dolphins and green sea turtles swim below us as if under glass. At Aerial Bay, we stashed our bags at the Forest Department's rest house and enquired about getting to the creeks once famous for saltwater crocodiles – Shantinagar, Shivpuri, Mugger Nullah among others. We were fortunate to meet a Bengali boy,

The view from Aerial Bay rest house in North Andaman

Bimal Roy, who owned a dungy or canoe; for the next few days he rowed us up and down the creeks adjoining the bay, often starting at sunrise and returning after dark, the oars throwing up flames of phosphorous. The schools of dolphins cavorting along the boat's side seemed to be playing with fire. Sometimes when the channels became too narrow or shallow, we'd have to moor the dungy and continue on foot, a painful exercise because of the slippery mud studded with sharp mangrove roots. But we found little evidence of the once common saltie except for the massive tracks of two wary giants who slipped into the water at our approach. As we'd been told, the poachers had done a good job.

In the notes he'd made for me about croc survey strategies, Rom had mentioned that 'talking to people in tea shops near croc habitat is a good one'. In Diglipur town, I asked the tea shop owner and his cluster of customers whether any '*bada mugger machch*' were still around. No, was the answer: all the big crocs were gone. Poaching had been an organized industry for the last ten to fifteen years, with two or three full-time hunters who sent consignments of skins to the mainland. They used nets, hooks and traps with deadly efficiency. One of these, K, proudly boasted of his achievement in killing 883 salties, and his exploits made interesting tea shop conversation. He showed us one of his trophies, a metre-long skull and gave me, with great reluctance, one of the teeth which was the size of a pig tusk. His prize catch was an almost 7-metre giant and it had taken a hook, spear and several shots to kill the beast, during which process K fell into its mouth, which it fortunately didn't close! It needed a crane to lift the crocodile on to a truck for the ride back to Diglipur.

Apart from the hunting for skins and croc parts that are used for medicine – such as the fat and gall bladder – the other factor responsible for the saltie's sad plight in the Andamans was that fresh water is a requisite and the females nest at the top of the creeks with perennial fresh water. But these are also coveted agricultural and settlement sites that are becoming more and more populated. The collection of crocodile eggs during the nesting season, May to June, was another factor. I saw people buying them in the market, for fifty to seventy-five paise each. A year later Rom found several empty nests in Middle Andaman, with the skeleton of the hapless female draped over the mounds. Since salties often come back to nest in the same spot and are conspicuous both because of the large mound nest and their own size, they are perfect targets for poachers.

When not out on the creeks, Annamalai and I went into the forests behind the rest house looking for snakes and lizards and found several. But there was a price to pay. Every log and branch was crawling with ticks, and the tangled undergrowth made it impossible to avoid touching the dry branches and twigs on which thousands of parasites waited for a juicy meal. For years after our trip, we'd remind each other of the bulging grey bodies that attached themselves to our arms, legs, backs, ears, between the toes, and there were the clever ones that remained tiny and undetected for days.

From Aerial Bay, we went back south – again on the *Cholunga* – to Mayabunder on the island of Middle Andaman, the nucleus settlement of the Burmese-Karens who had been brought to the Islands from Myanmar by the British to work in the timber industry. Although the Karen community became well educated, with men and women holding jobs in local schools and government offices, hunting and fishing remained favourite pastimes with many. They were the main suppliers of *trochus* and *turbo* shells that abound in the shallow coastal waters, used by the mother-of-pearl industry to make buttons and jewellery. In the 1970s, some of the coral reefs of the Andamans and the Nicobars were probably still one of the most ecologically undisturbed marine systems in the world. During a later trip made together, Rom and I explored some of the reefs around Port Blair with the help of our good friend Captain Dennis Beale and snorkelled through the wonder world of coral reefs, impossible to describe with justice. Resting briefly on the hard skeletons of the coral polyps, we swam up to every shape, size and colour of fish, mollusc, marine worm, echinoderm. After dark, tiny luminous organisms glowed through the silhouettes of coral gardens as we waded into the warm water for a nocturnal swim.

During our stay in Mayabunder, we were fortunate to meet and stay with a Karen family, the Vaughans. Fred introduced me to Jerry Vaughan, who was the wireless operator in Aerial Bay; he was the one who received, via Morse code, the croc egg permit that Fred had managed to get for me from the Forest Department in Port Blair (for just one egg!). One of his sons, Allen, who was later to become the first manager of the Crocodile Bank, took me to their family farm at Panighat, a short bus ride from Mayabunder. There we spent two days looking for reptiles. Allen always had his pack of hunting dogs with him; they crashed excitedly through the forest, whimpering and yapping as they caught the scent of a wild boar, monitor or spotted deer. Allen crashed along like a boar himself, slashing wildly but accurately at branches to cut us a path, with me breathlessly following. Again, ticks descended on us with radar-like precision; in the evenings, the clean floors of the Vaughan house were splattered with second-hand blood.

Much of what Allen, Annamalai and I were exploring was not primary forest but secondary growth, witness to the continuing and damaging forestry operations in the Islands. In the early settlement days, 'Elephant Bill' Williams who worked for the Bombay Burma Trading Company was sent to the Andamans to assess whether timber extraction on a large scale would be commercially feasible. He found that it would be more trouble than it was worth and recommended that the forests be left alone. Later, well-known foresters of the Indian Forest Service, like H.G. Champion, as well as ecologists expressed their hope that the forest would be left intact.

But unprofitable forestry was apparently desirable, and a massive amount of timber was being extracted. Official reports on forestry in the Andamans never mentioned soil erosion and reef siltation, but the thin topsoil of these tropical forests is quickly lost once tree cover is removed. The natural regeneration that is supposed to be rejuvenating the forests is unsuccessful in keeping up with the pace of timber removal.

Although the geographic isolation of the Andamans had provided some protection in comparison with many other tropical forest areas in the Asian region, recent 'development' fads were already devastating much of its pristine evergreen forest and waterways by the time we began visiting the Islands. By the early 1970s, authorized settlements, as well as illegal land encroachments, had had far-reaching ecological effects. Practically every perennial freshwater stream had been colonized; the population had escalated to a staggering 400,000 (it was 50,000 in 1960). In the twenty years between 1950 and 1970, millions of cubic metres of timber were extracted, over 100,000 hectares of forest cleared, and 600 kilometres of road constructed. Many of these developments were unplanned and disorganized, and very often the powers that be were unaware of the realities. Several ecological impact teams, conservationists, geologists, naturalists and other experts had questioned the wisdom of these policies but with practically no effect. The mayhem continued.

In Mayabunder, Jerry Vaughan's house on stilts was perched on a rise, with the ocean below on three sides – a view fit for a king. Annamalai and I set out one night with him and Allen in a dungy, from his own private jetty, to fish for mackerel. We were heading towards a small offshore island across a quarter-mile stretch of sea when the oar snapped and Allen, who had been rowing, crashed down at our feet from the triangular helm of the boat. In the confusion, the better part of the oar fell overboard and was gone, which quickly ended the general atmosphere of gaiety. '*Ayyo sami,*' muttered Annamalai, tightly clutching the sides of the violently rocking boat. But Jerry managed to look confident and in control, pounding the water with the foot-long oar stub while the boat raced in the wrong direction with the wind. 'We'll wait awhile,' he said when the wind died down somewhat – as if the decision were his – and we all threw in our fishing lines and caught, between us, over 5 kilograms of prime fish. In an hour, the wind and water calmed down, and we started back, mostly a metre forward and a metre back. But we finally made it and scrambled on to the sharp rocks to reach the small brightly lit house across the reef.

There were adventures on land as well. One morning, we found an Andaman cat snake, an endemic species of these islands. I was chasing a day gecko on the roof of the Vaughans' farmhouse when there it was, its thin delicate neck almost under my foot. '*Andha saamp, andha saamp* [Blind snake],' farm workers yelled and we were soon considered heroes for handling the deadly venomous snake that was even reputed to breathe fire! Confession: Initially, Annamalai and I misidentified it as a pit viper and he carefully pinned the head in order to hold it up for a photograph.

The shallow, reef-ridden waters just off the west coast of Middle Andaman are the hunting grounds of both the Karens and Jarawa and encounters between them were becoming increasingly frequent in the 1970s as both groups had to go further and further afield to find good hunting and fishing areas in the depleting waters. Exactly a year after my first trip there, a group of Karens were out diving for *kloe-suchhi* (trochus shells) and after a tiring day, camped for the night on a small uninhabited atoll, Mowar Tikri. Unfortunately, this was within the confines of the Jarawa reserve, off limits to outsiders, and as they made their evening fire, a group of Jarawa planned their attack. At dawn, there was a loud *zing*! – an arrow went through a diver's chest and everyone rushed towards the dingy anchored just offshore. The Jarawa charged and kidnapped one of the party; he has not been heard of since. On a later trip, we met one of the lucky ones, a plucky twelve-year-old who had dived between the forest of legs and escaped.

In the months following my trip with Annamalai, Rom received Indian citizenship and was soon in the Andamans, with Allen. He had a permit to collect eggs but every nest they found was either old or a fresh one with the eggs robbed. Allen had brought him a few saltie eggs from Diglipur market but they'd been moved around a lot and the chances of any hatching were minimal. Then they heard that several female crocs had been killed on nests at a new settlement called Kishorinagar near Kalighat. They got on the *Cholunga* to Mayabunder the next day and from there boarded the speedy *M-5* to Parangara, a small town on the edge of a dense mass of mangrove channels originally named Congo Bay. Once they had explained their presence at the local tea shop, run by Bengalis and complete with rasagollas, there were several offers to accompany them as guides.

The rest of that day and half of the next was spent slogging through heavy stands of grass, pandanus, cane and bamboo along the freshwater streams adjacent to the mangroves, perfect nesting places for crocodiles. It was a bit scary, considering our experiences with captive saltwater crocodiles, and Rom carried a stout stick, even though it was clumsy. The group separated in order to cover one particularly dense area, all of them moving on hands and knees through the eerie tunnels of vegetation. Minutes later, Rom almost bumped into a nest in a clearing obviously made by a female crocodile. He couldn't believe his luck and made a cooing jungle call to alert Allen and the guides. A quick answer told him they were on their way. The first thing he did was to look around carefully for the female. There was no waterhole or wallow that she could be lying in, and the nearest channel of water was 15 metres away. He looked around for a quick escape route in case she suddenly charged from the water, but it was tight vegetation all around except for the tunnel he had crawled into.

Allen arrived, followed by the guides from Parangara. 'Hah,' they said in unison, happy that they'd finally found a nest. 'Where's the female?' asked Allen. 'Did you chase it away?' 'No, I looked for it and it doesn't seem to be here,' Rom responded. They all peered doubtfully into the dark vegetation around them; the sun was almost totally blotted out and it was steamy hot. They scraped the leaves and sticks off the top of the huge nest (nearly a metre high and a metre and a half in diameter) and yelled with excitement on seeing the gleaming white eggs. Everyone posed for a photograph, crouching proudly beside the open nest. Just then Rom, now accustomed to the heavy shadows, perceived the outline of what looked to be the open, heavily toothed jaw of a crocodile under a thick pandanus nearby. He hissed a warning and as he pointed, everyone backed away, peering under the bush. 'Yes, it's the female,' said Allen, 'and we'd better be sure she doesn't attack while we're taking the eggs.' They tried to head her back towards the nearby channel but she held her ground, hissing ferociously but restraining herself from charging. When they saw that she wasn't going to move, they felt confident enough to extract and pack the fifty-one eggs, using humus and leaves from the nest to cushion them, and began the long walk back to Kalighat. Rom came back to Madras soon after and a month later thirty-seven hatchlings emerged, probably the first saltwater crocodile eggs to be wild-collected and hatched under captive conditions in India.

Rom's travels in the Islands took him to North Andaman as well, and looking back now, even the 1970s had shades of the unspoiled Eden it must have been. Just south of Aerial Bay is the stretch of bamboo where local farmers used to see king cobra nests and from where Rom wrote to me in June 1977:

> Yesterday's walk was not exactly a normal excursion through the forest, it turned out to be more interesting than usual. One of the farmers had been cutting bamboo a month ago and saw what appeared to be a nest of some sort on the ground. It sounded very interesting so we made our way toward his farm by a path that cut along the pandanus-lined beach, through the mangroves and across several large streams, the home of the saltie in this area. A big water monitor startled us, charging across our path and as we walked, we flushed out an amazing variety of birds, butterflies and lizards. It was the first sunny day that week and everything seemed to be taking advantage of it. We watched a pair of Andaman day geckos on their palm tree near the path and several day skinks, from the massive 35-centimetre Tytler's to the high-diving tree

skink. The black-striped skink slithered through the grass to the safety of the thorny cane and palm tangle, and green forest lizards of many colour variations clung to nearly every tree in some areas. As we waded across one of the deep streams, we saw a large, green tree snake and got a close look at this beautiful animal with its fantastic colours and excellent camouflage.

The old farmer was waiting for us and we set off at a good pace to a small hillock below Karmatang Hill, the second highest hill in North Andaman. Crossing a stream, we entered the uncut, unmolested rainforest and started uphill, among the abundant leeches, which were only partially discouraged with the raw tobacco smeared on our legs. We finally got into the bamboo belt and saw the king cobra nest, 30 cm high and 60 cm wide . . .

In the evening, over venison curry and rice in a wooden house in the forest, we listened to recent accounts of crocodile adventures and about islands where you cannot sleep on the ground at night for the numbers of amphibious sea snakes coming ashore to lay their eggs.

We travelled to this paradisiacal archipelago many times, singly and together, and later with our children. One of these trips was not a particularly happy one; our friend Dennis Beale's boat had dropped us at an island off Port

Blair where we planned to camp for a few days and explore the coral reefs. On the second evening, I took off my mask and snorkel in the shallows to find myself bleeding profusely; I was five months pregnant at the time and there was no way of getting to a hospital. Fortunately, it didn't develop into a great medical crisis but when we got back to Port Blair and were preparing to go south to the Nicobars, Rom began feeling ill and turned a bright yellow. The local doctor put it down to the sun. 'Please take your rest, sir, you are simply exerting too much,' but Dennis agreed it looked like jaundice. And to cap it all, I began to shiver violently on the way back to Madras: malaria. My parents took charge of us. I was packed off to hospital for ten days while Rom was fed vegetable soups at home.

West of Mayabunder, across Austin Strait, is the 20-kilometre-long Interview Island where three years later Rom was to spend several days camping with photographer Rajesh Bedi, in an effort to publicize the urgent need for protecting these island ecosystems. The ecology of Interview had been seriously affected by the introduction of elephants in the 1950s by P.C. Ray, a timber contractor. He had started an ambitious wood extraction operation there, complete with trolleys and tramways, the ruins of which are scattered through the jungle. The business went bankrupt, Ray died soon after and the mahouts and other staff, tired of waiting for their pay, left after freeing the elephants to wreak havoc in the leafy Interview forests. Rom and others found plenty of fresh signs and there were estimated to be thirty to fifty of these feral jumbos, several of which were 'nuisance animals', known killers reputed to chase people on sight, creating a tricky problem for wildlife authorities!

Appeals to the government from us and other NGOs to stop the tide of destructive development in the Islands have been largely ignored, and we now await further news on the transhipment port that is coming to fruition in spite of appeals from conservationists. The early response was that our reports were 'unduly pessimistic' and based on 'limited information', but concerted pressure from conservationists had some effect and resulted in Protected Areas in the form of marine national parks that we hope will remain as remnants of what the reefs once were.

In 1984, Rom was asked to give a talk in Cambridge on the endangered environment of the Andamans. He produced a report, which was widely circulated and published by the Department of Environment in Delhi. In 1986, the Indian National Trust for Art and Cultural Heritage (INTACH) asked him to be its convenor for the Andaman and Nicobar region. It seemed like a good platform from which to get ourselves heard and early the next year we set off, with flippers, snorkels and children, for our first visit in several years.

Our 'big brother' in the Andamans, Captain Dennis Beale was a human gem like Fred Burn, known and liked all over the territory and who probably knew the Islands better than anyone else. He was one of the post-war adventurers who helped to open up this area, with the Forest Department once totally dependent on his log-hauling boats. Subsequently, he provided tourists in the Andamans with boats to visit the charming little islands in the Labyrinth group off the southwest coast. His death in 1993 was, like that of Fred's, mourned widely.

During that fifteen-day visit, we stayed with Dennis, who generously put his fleet of inter-island boats at our service. But it was a sad time – a peep into the ongoing destruction and portent of things to come. We witnessed the navy's blasting of coral reefs and primitive rock formations for practice, heard plans for absurd developments and met people who advocated taming the indigenous tribes. Underwater, we saw acres of dead coral.

The Andamans were noticeably changed and Port Blair's already unplanned appearance had been further trashed, complete with traffic jams and garbage dumps. Although lip service had been paid to the moratorium on the cutting of virgin forests and regenerating forests, it was evident that the demand for these tropical timbers on the mainland was unrelenting. The blanks in the forest remained weed-choked, with little indication of the original forest coming back. We left the Islands feeling sad and disappointed.

It was apparent that the best thing we could do via INTACH was to organize an environmental awareness campaign with children as the target audience. During

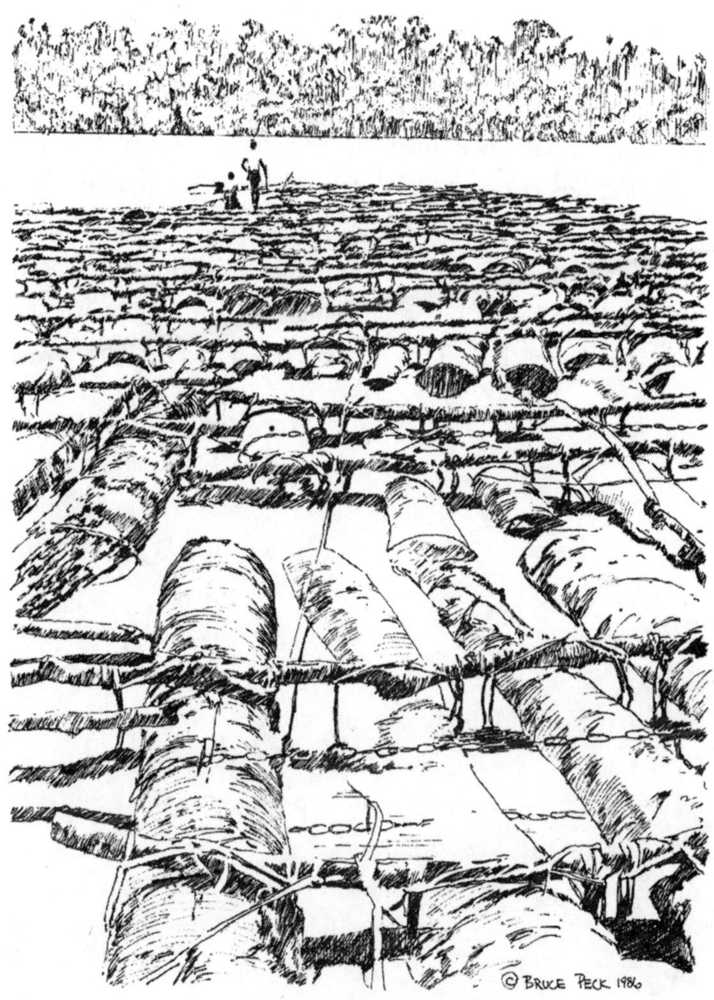

Logged timber, symbolic of the devastation of the Andamans, used to be transported by tying the logs together as rafts.

this initiative, we met and talked to a lot of people, notably some enlightened members of the Rotary Club and a few young scientists from the Central Agricultural Research Institute (CARI) who made us feel a little optimistic about this biodiversity paradise. We felt that these programmes, as well as the growing concern in India and abroad about this biodiversity hub, would have an effect on national policies. But we also sensed that other changes were rolling in, which may drastically change the region. And we were right.

Birds of Paradise

Growing up in the age of postage, many of us had stamp collections and rushed out excitedly when the postman arrived. Baba's *Newsletter for Birdwatchers* had readers and contributors all over the world, and Shama and I got first dibs on stamps (brother Murad was safely away in boarding school). Senders often took the trouble to lick and stick bird stamps on mail to him, so we got to see and find out about exotic birds from exotic countries like Magsaysay, Rhodesia, Siam, Ceylon (now with different names of course). One of these featured the raggiana bird of paradise, that gaudy avian masterpiece, and we read the *Encyclopaedia Britannica*'s lively description of it. The envelope and stamp must have come from Australia, or perhaps Indonesia, both of which owned parts of New Guinea island (which resembles a prehistoric bird!) thanks to the haphazard land-grabbing in the Pacific after World War II. In 1973, the eastern half of the island gained independence from Australia and became the country of Papua New Guinea. The western half, Irian Jaya – the bird's head – remains a province of Indonesia.

Shama and I subsequently looked at many more photographs and paintings of the raggiana, one among the forty or so species of birds of paradise. Apart from their indescribably beautiful feathers and dense rainforest homes, we later learnt about their unique habits, such as the males' comical displays and lekking or group performances. We talked about how amazing it would be to actually see them . . . and this particular dream was to come true!

Birds of paradise didn't get their name owing to their general beauty as a species, or rather specifically the beauty of the male because the females, as in many species of birds, tend to be dull and drab. When flamboyant bird feathers became fashionable adornments on ladies' hats in nineteenth-century Europe, and milliners began importing birds of paradise from parts of Indonesia, New Guinea and Australia, the bird skins were exported after chopping off the legs. The glitterati, fashionable but ignorant, believed that these were legless birds that had descended from heaven/paradise. The spectacular feathers are no longer seen on aristocratic European heads but remain ceremonial adornments on those of tribal chieftains and other tribal bigwigs in Papua New Guinea (PNG) and Irian Jaya.

So at the tail end of 1978 when Rom thrust a telegram in my hand from the United Nation's FAO and asked if I fancied going to PNG for two years, and I'd finished jumping up and down, my wish list began with the raggiana bird of paradise, by then their national bird. Rom's, of course, was a long list of reptiles, with the taipan in the No. 1 spot. Large, fast and highly venomous, herpetologists dream of catching a wild one the way gourmands dream of Kolkata biryani.

In those pre-internet days, you couldn't punch a word into your phone and get heaps of information on every topic under the sun. To find out about the forests and wildlife of PNG, we visited public libraries and bookshops and asked friend and family networks if they knew people who'd been there. It was thin pickings, except for a fascinating article about the cargo cult. This was a post-World War II belief system that broke out among PNG's primitive tribes, in their attempt to explain the white man's wealth and unwillingness to share it. They believed that the strange big birds in the sky (aeroplanes) were the reason for the wealth, and concocted ceremonies and rituals to attract them and their cargo to their villages. There were dances and songs, ceremonial ornaments and piles of yams and tubers for the big birds to feast on. Soon after our arrival in Port Moresby, the city's newspaper, the *Post Courier*, reported an 'outbreak' of the cult near Mendi in the Southern Highlands, with a photo of feather-clad tribals placing taro and sago on an airstrip, waiting for the magic bird to come with gifts for them.

In Madras, we met a couple who had lived in PNG for a few years, and were delighted to be back and out of that

When we reached PNG we found that, as in the Andamans, the ancient cultures that had survived were those of communities that had kept away from outsiders, even resorting to arms to do so.

'punishment posting'! But they gave us a tattered old Pidgin phrase book printed by a Christian mission, which turned out to be very useful because on getting there, we were able to understand and respond to simple everyday chat. Pidgin's basic grammar, simple logic and many words morphed from English, made it an easy language to master (or *masta*). The elbow, for example, is *screw bilong han*, and the knee, *screw bilong lek*. Our favourite was the phrase for helicopter: *mixmaster bilong Jesus*. We became proficient (we thought) and I was able to get prices at Goroka market (*Hamas long dispela?*), ask someone their name (*Wanem nem bilong yu?*), and the crucial direction for the washroom (*Smolhaus i stap we?*).

The Snake Park trustees agreed to keep an eye on things there and at the Croc Bank, which we had started working on soon after our marriage. Some land had been bought and the first mugger pen built. We also had a basic habitation for ourselves that would be extended and improved with time. Seed funds for the Croc Bank had come in the form of wedding presents from family, including our parents, my grandparents, my Sálim Mamoo and later, grants from WWF and other conservation folks. It was a bad time to leave, as things at the Bank were just getting under way, but we would make a couple of interim visits before returning from the PNG assignment in 1980. And we were off, with five-month-old Nikhil, and soon flying over the Coral Sea, sprinkled with emerald islands bordered with snow-white beaches.

At Port Moresby airport, an immigration official responded with an impressed whistle when Rom explained what he was there for. '*Moa yet!*' he exclaimed, pidgin for 'Wow!' It was a good beginning to two wonderful years. Apart from many unique wildlife sightings and experiences, we were in a treasure chest of ancient cultures, though colonization had de-cultured many parts of the country. Colonizers included the British, Dutch and Australians, as well as Christian missionaries from Europe and the United States who put an end to many indigenous practices and skills. By the time of our visit, Bible stories had replaced the traditional beliefs of many tribes, but often with Pontius Pilate replacing Jesus as the hero!

Rom's top wish came true soon after we got there because the government allotted us a house next to the Moitaka Croc Farm, his base, which is prime taipan habitat (something I wasn't thrilled about). Word had spread at Moitaka that the *Masta bilong India emi laik snek tumas tru*, and if anyone came across a snake, they should let him know. And a few mornings later, John Seba ran up the steps of our house to announce that he'd just seen a big *pela snek* on one of the grassy trails leading out of the farm towards a stream. We set off with him.

There was an initial disappointment – no *snek* where John Seba had seen it – but then as we prepared to leave, there was a streak of black lightning heading towards thick vegetation across an open patch of ground. That memory byte is still so fresh in my mind! I was enough of a herp-wife to know Rom would want to pre-empt it from entering the forest and sure enough, he'd sprung across the stream. Sensing danger, the snake whipped into the bushes, but Rom was able to leap forward and grab the tail. I knew it was a taipan and, adrenaline gushing, watched as it lunged at him, mouth open. As Rom was to relate, 'I had dropped the snake hook in the jump and needed it desperately right now; it was either let go and lose the snake or hang on and take a chance. A big chance because there was no taipan antivenom in PNG. Fortunately, after years of watching me in tight spots, Zai had become an experienced assistant and leapt across the stream to retrieve the snake hook. She quickly pressed this into my hand and I nodded my thanks, not taking my eyes off the snake.'

The next stage of the episode is carved even deeper into my memory board. As I stepped back, the snake launched itself towards Rom, who swept his arm back to unbalance it and used the snake hook to block the open-mouth strike. It turned out to be one of the most heart-stopping interactions I've seen between a snake and Rom, and there are many including those with king cobras. But while kings (and most others) just want to escape, taipans often have other plans. This one was long, irritated (understandably), and made repeated thrusts at its attacker. One eye on Rom to make sure he was unbitten, I helped John Seba rig the snake bag in its frame. The contraption, like a butterfly net, makes snake-bagging a safer operation. By this time, the taipan seemed to be getting tired. Phew, I thought.

To return to Rom's words, 'Still keeping my eyes on the snake, I gently swung the snake hook around to where Zai held the short pole. She lowered the open mouth of the dark blue snake bag to the ground and I guided the snake towards it. The taipan, relieved no doubt to find a dark hiding place, began to slide in. I let go. It shot in with a burst. Zai quickly twirled the handle to shut the bag.'

Taipans were indeed common snakes of the open savannah habitat where we lived; Rom (sometimes with my trembling assistance) caught seven in the first year we were there. He even stepped on one inadvertently, and luckily wasn't bitten. We were driving up into the Sogeri mountains one night to visit friends when it crossed the road in front of the Land Cruiser. Rom braked, grabbed a snake bag, jumped out and sprinted barefoot towards where he thought the snake would have reached. But his calculation had been wrong, and he felt something soft and wriggly underfoot, which triggered an impressive gymnastic move. The bagged snake was placed on the back seat, and we set off again. Rom grinned when I kept turning back to make sure all was well behind me, the knot secure and snake inside. I reminded him of the times when snakes had escaped from his 'tight' knots and 'safe' places:

sea snakes from a bucket secured with a cloth and rope; baby king cobras from a terrarium, a large Papuan python (my favourite, because it was so tame) from its cage under our house. His grin faded.

Several Australian herpetologists had worked in PNG during the decade before we got there. They believed the reptiles and amphibians there had declined greatly because of the introduction of the South American cane toad, a creature both poisonous and huge that feeds on young herps. But still, we managed to see quite a few PNG specialities. Our most dramatic herp 'safaris' were to the World War II ruins of Japanese and Allied camps with their ingenious water filtration and laundry systems, bomb shackles, machine-gun barrels and other contraptions. These had become the favoured habitats for snakes, and we visited them on many nights with powerful torches to pick out snaky shapes and eyes. Leaving the Land Cruiser on the road, we'd walk through tall spiky tall grass to one of the hills of crazily balanced rusty biscuit tins or kitchenware. On one of the first visits, Rom spotted the stunning iridescence of the D'Albertis python. He was to join our snake collection at home, in the conveniently constructed window louvres that made perfect snake cages. These pythons make perfect pets and soon become tame and easy to handle. Carpet pythons were another kettle of snake altogether; and Rom often felt the power of their sharp, curved teeth. On one memorable night, he gently hooked one that was resting on a rusty hill.

It thrashed wildly and pooped generously on him as he staggered down the tin slope with it. At these times, I would pronounce myself the photographer and situate myself at a safe distance.

By the time we left Port Moresby, we had five of the nine species of pythons found on New Guinea island. Each of these has some unique characteristic. The star (according to me) was the green tree python, which rolls itself around a branch into a ball. They are ontogenetic, with dramatic colour changes between birth and adulthood. Most start off yellow or orange when they hatch and end up as bright green adults! These beauties are a favoured local *kai-kai*, and it was hard to imagine them being chowed down. We spent good money buying them from markets or vendors passing by our house, and releasing them in the forest bordering the grasslands around us. During the two Hari Krismas feasts we attended at the Moitaka Croc Farm, the menu included flying foxes, sago grubs, snakes and, of course, crocodile. I had to beg the croc keepers to include some pieces of chicken for me, which they did and watched me eat the tame fare with pity. I'd shared rodent curries with the Irular but wasn't able to take this next culinary leap.

However, the FAO hadn't hired Rom to collect pythons, and his crocodile adventures began on Day One when a New

Guinea freshwater croc gave him a bad slash on the arm. When safely medicated and bandaged, the keepers had a good laugh (with him) about the White Masta from India who had come to teach them about *puk puks* and got *kai-kaied* on the first day! We enjoyed their robust humour, often taking the mickey out of their bosses as well: very different from our hierarchical workspaces, with 'underlings' never daring to laugh at a boss's mistake.

Crocodiles play a big role in the religions and cultures of PNG; I use the plural because there are over 600. Each tribe is practically a country unto itself, with its own beliefs, language, livelihood pattern, now watered down considerably by Christian missionary interventions. Of particular interest to us were the crocodile clans that scarify their limbs to resemble croc skin. As in the India of yore, many of their rivers, lakes and other waterbodies are inhabited by two species of crocodiles, the saltie and freshie. In the coming months, during one of his bush trips, Rom would see one of the largest salties ever recorded: over 6 metres long. It took eight or nine people to hold up the skin for a photograph.

Reptile skins were a hot product in European haute couture markets of the 1950s and 1960s when it was highly fashionable to flout a croc skin handbag, or shoes, belt and other accessories. Only the belly skin was used and the favoured species, the most lucrative, was the saltie; a formidable opponent, but the value of the skin was worth risking one's neck for. Its geographic range is extensive: from the Indian subcontinent all the way to the Pacific Islands and Australia. Some of the prize skins of this era were sourced in Australia, by legendary hunters like George Craig, whose adventures are described in the book *To Catch a Crocodile* by Peter Pinney. As their numbers declined, hunters sought fresh, unhunted places where they could find large specimens with valuable belly widths. In India, the new crocodile frontiers included the Andaman and Nicobar Islands. Few people, many crocs.

And the Aussie hunters moved north to the island of New Guinea, one of the last homes of large salties, with vast river systems, lagoons and mangrove swamps. And it got even better because the riverine habitats were inhabited by hunter-tribes who could help with locating, catching and skinning these reptiles for a pittance – sometimes just a few twists of tobacco or some gaudy baubles from the 'civilized' world. The white croc-skin traders made millions. But these populations began to decline as well and in the early 1970s, PNG conservationists and bureaucrats got together to make a plan for the conservation of its two species of crocodilians. The Puk Puk Projek Bilong Papua New Guinea was visualized and started, managed by the FAO and PNG's Wildlife Department. It was based on the idea of sustainable farming, which was the new thing in croc conservation, successful in many countries including Australia, Thailand, the United States and now PNG.

The PNG croc-farming model was simple and pragmatic.

Its foundation was based on three ground truths: large rivers like the Sepik, Fly and their tributaries were home to many hunter-gatherers just entering the cash-economy; croc skins were a valuable export; and a high percentage of hatchling crocs die within the first three years of their lives, mostly from predation.

The plan was that tribal hunters would catch these juvenile crocs (most of which weren't going to make it to adulthood anyway), rear them in village pens made from local materials, and when they reached a certain belly width, sell them to the Wildlife Department, to be processed as skins and exported. Easy-peasy, except for one problem. These were hunters without the innate husbandry skills needed to keep the animals alive, thriving and growing. The answer, again simple and pragmatic, was to transfer the juveniles soon after they were caught to large commercial 'growth' farms where they would be reared to culling size and sold to the government. Three of these 'growth farms' had been looped into the Projek just before our arrival, and were owned by expatriate businessmen – a German pig farmer, Hugo, and two poultry farmers, one in Lae and the other in Moresby. They understood money and profit and knew this was a good deal because the feed (pig and chicken offal) was practically free, and the only costs were the construction of croc pens and keeper salaries. Croc skin prices were high and rising. Let the money roll in!

People working on the Puk Puk Projek, many of them

American, British and Australian volunteers who came through agencies like the Peace Corps and CUSO, had been stationed in croc hotspots like Lake Murray, the largest lake in PNG, and the Sepik and Fly river systems. They lived in basic accommodations, in beautiful places adjoining rare pristine forests. They piloted powerful 'river trucks' to collect and bring back the small crocodiles harvested by nearby villages that were kept in holding pens until the arrival of a Projek plane, usually a Cessna. This would land at a nearby bush strip and transport the puk puks to Port Moresby or Lae, to be picked up by one of the commercial rearing farms.

A neat operation, with benefits for all: money for the hunter-gatherer tribes and the government, and protection for the breeding populations of these important aqua predators, which keep water systems clean. Rom's job was to improve husbandry practices in the village and commercial farms, organize croc pick-ups, and also – the best part – to survey croc habitats to understand the population densities of the two species. Given the unreliable results of eye-shining, especially in hunted areas where crocs are shy, Rom and his team decided to resort to nest-counting from the air and ground. This was a practical idea since both species of PNG crocs construct metre-high mound nests that are easily spotted from a helicopter or boat.

I went along on the croc pick-ups and surveys whenever we could arrange a babysitter for Nikhil. As bad luck would have it, one of these was a nest survey around the Waigani swamp, a croc habitat on the outskirts of Moresby. But it was also the end-stop for sewage outlets from the city. Some experiences are hard to forget and this is one of them. By then, the famous croc biologist Alistair Grahame had joined the Projek on Rom's request to help him with the population census surveys. We were walking along the edge of the swamp towards a nest, trying to avoid looking at the disgusting lumps bobbing along in the 'water', when my foot slipped and I found myself waist deep in it! 'This is where loyalty gets tested,' said Alistair to Rom, who began gingerly plucking at my shirt, pretending to help me. I managed to clamber out on the third or fourth attempt and considerately walked downwind from them to the Land Cruiser, settling as far back on the back seat as I could!

There were much better experiences, however, when Doris, Rom's mother, came to visit and stayed with Nikhil while I accompanied Rom on his 'croc patrols'. These were unforgettable adventures – river surveys on dugouts and river trucks, visits with tribes that hadn't seen outsiders for years, being watched by bow- and arrow-wielding tribes as we went past, croc-catching in muddy, opaque water, all amid the ever-present clouds of mosquitoes. A memorable one was to Boboa Island on Lake Murray, where Jerome Montague, a volunteer from Kentucky, was stationed and hosted us for several days. He welcomed us at the 'airport', a bush strip on which the Cessna bounced from side to side, making the pilot irritable. Before taking off, he lectured the collected crowd on the importance of cutting the landing-strip grass regularly. Some of those PNG bush landings were truly stomach-churning, and it was the village headman's responsibility to ensure the grass was cut and rubble cleared on the strips.

Jerome was even more welcoming after I concocted a rough-and-ready pizza for dinner, a welcome change for him from sago and barramundi fish. The next morning, we were off on his river truck, destination Egiza on the Juni, one of the small river inlets of Lake Murray. The village had 200 crocs in holding pens, waiting to be transported to Boboa in the river truck, then to Moresby by air. Measuring, sexing and weighing would be done in Boboa before they were sent off. I got out my waterproof notepad for data recording.

So much to remember about Egiza and too much to put down here. We arrived well after dark, mooring against an embankment towering over the river, on which a crowd of people stood and watched. More were on the way, all of them with flaming resin torches. They descended to the 'jetty' area and helped us with such enthusiasm and curiosity that I lost my step . . . In Rom's words, 'Zai almost fell into the water. For here was a prize indeed; not only a new face from the outside, but a woman, and of a marvellously exotic colour! Certainly not a white Missus, like the missionary's wife who had come some five years ago; nor a Papuan.' We spent the night in the chief's house, and peering out of the mosquito net at midnight to investigate noises, I saw a group of Egizans peering at me. Not with hostility but curiosity.

When my sister Shama came on a visit, we contacted a British ornithologist who took us to the Varirata National Park to see the raggiana, particularly its display, as this was the breeding season. Imagine our excitement as we watched

The raggiana bird of paradise

a pair high up in the canopy, engaged in their mating ritual! And later, we cooked up a hare-brained scheme to get to the Bayer River Sanctuary in the Highlands, where serious tribal confrontations were ongoing. We were advised to drop the plan, but we didn't, and flew to Mendi and hired a rickety old car in which the owner had forgotten to place a stepney. I drove the jalopy on precarious mountain roads through Chimbu and Huli warriors armed with bows and arrows, and glaring at the two Martians bumping along past them. Two months later, a van with Japanese tourists was attacked, with fatal consequences for some of the travellers. But we managed to get to Bayer, see three species of birds of paradise, and head back down immediately on the advice of the wildlife ranger stationed there. He couldn't believe our stupidity and wanted us to pass that same route – a known 'meeting ground' of warring tribes – before it got dark.

In later years, Rom would visit Irian Jaya, the western, 'head' part of New Guinea island, but by then, our second child Samir had joined the family, so he went alone, and his detailed letters about armed tribes, long jungle treks and mosquitoes neutralized the regret about missing the trip.

The Croc Bank

Unfortunately, while we were having those wonderful adventures in PNG, there were other, less happy events afoot at the Snake Park. Our absence became an opportunity for a few people to create mischief; we ended up paying a heavy price and losing the Snake Park, a project which both of us had imagined would be a lifelong base for us, one which we wanted to develop into a world-class reptile education, research and conservation centre. Because of the move to the central location of the Guindy Deer Sanctuary, it had become financially sustainable, with enough surplus for improvement and development. When Richard and Maisie Fitter of the Fauna and Flora Preservation Society – friends of my father's – visited, they talked at length about the many possibilities of partnerships, both nationally and internationally, and indeed, there was a lot of interest in working with us, from zoos, government, conservation NGOs and individuals. The Snake Park was on the threshold of something big, but this was not to be, thanks to . . . which negative human characteristic? Possibly a combination of many.

We sensed a change in the atmosphere when we returned in 1980. There were some cold shoulders and voices. Initially too excited to notice or care, we divided our time between the Snake Park and the nascent Croc Bank, happy that the trustees' group was 'looking after' the accounts and other boring routines, leaving us time to develop the Bank. It was situated on the Madras–Mahabalipuram road 35 kilometres south of Madras, on land we had found after much cruising around the outskirts of the city. With its high, perennial water table, pleasant scenery and captive tourist flow, it has proved to be an ideal location. Also, the price was suitable for our light pockets (land on this coastal belt was then about four thousand five hundred to five thousand rupees an acre), there was access from the road, and the people of Vadanemmeli village across the road seemed undeterred, even excited, by the thought of having crocs as neighbours. There was 2 acres for sale, running ideally, from the road to the seashore, and thickly planted with casuarina, the local cash crop that is harvested every three or four years. We clinched the deal in 1975, for which Rom had to consume several half-litre Mobil oil tins of toddy with the owners. Immediately after, we formed a trust that later bought over most of the land, leaving us half an acre on the beach. Pieces of adjacent land were acquired as money became available and today the Croc Bank campus covers over 6 acres. The first adult animals at the Bank were the mugger Perayur (from the Marina Aquarium) and Nova (a female from the Central Marine Fisheries Research Institute in Porto Novo); the rest were hatchlings from eggs collected in the wild. Luckily, Perayur and Nova took a shine to one another and produced many clutches of healthy eggs and hatchlings. When we opened to visitors in August 1976, their pen, the centrepiece of the Croc Bank, had thirteen adult mugger, a species that, unlike the saltie, is tolerant of newcomers to the group.

By the time we returned from PNG, the Croc Bank was pulling in enough ticket income to pay for animal feed and salaries. The Coromandel coast was such a different world in those days! Sea turtles nested near our gate, narrow-headed and banded sea snakes often washed up on the beach, there were carpets of intact, collectable shells and jackals trotted away as we walked past rain-fed pools near thickly planted rows of casuarina. Nikhil grew up in two wonderful spaces – the beach, his front yard and the germinating Croc Bank, his backyard, with plenty of unique activities such as helping to catch non-venomous snakes, clipping crocodile scales and measuring turtles. The film 'Nature's Child' documents this unique childhood; and our second son Samir was to have the same.

Both organizations – the Snake Park and Croc Bank – were a perfect match for our skills and interests; the enclosure designing, husbandry and research were Rom's patch, and education and writing (reporting, project and funding proposals, correspondence) mine. Our first book (booklet, rather) – by Romulus and 'Zahi' Whitaker – was an exciting landmark for us. It was called *Endangered Reptiles of India* and sponsored by ITC, to commemorate the panda's birthday, an anniversary of the WWF. On the back cover is a picture I'd taken at the Tuticorin sea turtle market, of an upturned sea turtle with a knife placed on its plastron, ready for butchering (often done while the animal was still alive). The caption was 'Stop Senseless Slaughter of Wildlife'. There were to be many more joint writing projects, including a series published by the National Book Trust and translated into many Indian languages, still in print now, four decades later.

By late 1980, our relationship with the Snake Park trustees had become increasingly uneasy and tense. Some of them strutted around importantly, barking orders and sneering at us and the (many) staff and field biologists who were close to us. And then one day, the bombshell dropped. We learned that patently false accusations had been concocted against Rom, including illegal venom and specimen collection and export. A criminal case had been filed in Saidapet court. One memorable day, the Snake Park's 'Security Officer', hired while we had been away, denied us entry. We returned to the Croc Bank and went for a swim.

Court summons arrived, and case hearings began, with the usual adjournments; Rom spent hours each time in the corridors of Saidapet court, shelling and eating peanuts bought from vendors to pass the time. The famous lawyer Govind Swaminathan, father of our friend Revati, and his Junior Sriram Panchu – now equally famous – represented Rom. As always, our families stepped in to help with advice, money, contacts and moral support. Lawyer friends assured us we had a 99.9 per cent chance of winning the case, but the wheels of justice move slowly and I could sense Rom's patience and energy dwindling. It was a terrible time. Initially, we were told by the lawyers that Rom might be arrested, perhaps while in the conspicuous jeep with its Snake Park logo. They advised him not to drive Nikhil to and from his school. I took over this chore, with four-year-old Nikhil often turning to me during the journey and saying 'Dada is good at driving, no Mama?'

After four years of this, Rom made the decision – against the lawyers' advice and much to my disappointment – to resign from the Snake Park and work in peace at the Croc Bank. We focused on forgetting the past and moving on. We said goodbye to carefully collected and reared specimens, some sent from abroad by friends, our precious library, and the many staff who had become good friends. But wait, one last detail of the 'criminal' episode remains – a wonderful irony. Soon after the prosecutors decided to withdraw the case (following Rom's resignation), they realized the case files had been lost! So Rom was requested to help, and he found himself sitting in Saidapet court, writing out the accusations against himself so they could be vacated by the judge! We loved this story, about how he had to self-accuse and shared it with great gusto once time had softened the memories.

A bunch of crocs isn't everyone's idea of a safe haven, but it was certainly ours. We transferred our conservation aspirations to the Croc Bank, convinced by now about the grim future of these toothy reptiles, survivors of gigantic ecological upheavals for a hundred million years. In spite of the Wildlife (Protection) Act, 1972, poverty and high skin prices continued to incentivize poaching. The salaries and living conditions of the enforcement officials and habitat loss were additional factors. But there were some silver linings too, at least locally. The Tamil Nadu Forest Department had agreed to release 200 mugger a year in the wild, with the precious Government Order having come in 1978. We were excited about creating a safe 'gene pool' of breeders. This rewilding approach is suitable for crocodiles since most of the world's twenty-three species breed well in captivity. Crocodiles are one of the easier animals to capture and transport, and captive-reared reptiles adapt more easily to the wild than do mammals.

Things moved quickly. As in the early days of the Snake Park, friends stepped in to help. Jimmy Yacob, a

Malaysian 'Tunku' from the royal family of Johore, helped with landscaping, water drainage and the construction of enclosures. A nucleus group of thirty-five mugger had been shifted from the Snake Park to their new home and of these, eight females and a male were released into the large 150-metre breeding enclosure, Pen 8, built with a grant from the New York Zoological Society and WWF. Both these organizations have played important roles in the development of the Croc Bank. Funds raised from a 1979 fundraiser snake show along with Kartikeya Sarabhai of the Nehru Foundation for Development in Ahmedabad (where some 75,000 people came to the five-day exhibition) went into building our first enclosures. Our own 'salary' was slim, to say the least, but as always, families pitched in, and our lifestyle was simple.

Other breeding-age mugger were collected from various zoos, colleges, aquariums and wild habitats, with permission and support from the Forest Department. The capture of two females from the Chidambaram Waterworks reservoir remains a vivid memory. It involved night after night of waiting, waiting, and more waiting to find that a croc had almost entered the noose or trap but veered away at the last minute. Once, in pitch darkness on the banks of the reservoir, we were rolled up in our sleeping bags when we heard a thrashing in the bushes where the trap had been set. Waking with a start, we grabbed the nets to throw on the trapped crocodile and sprinted to the spot 5 metres away. And there, in the dim moonlight, was a large paddy bird flapping madly in the bushes. At two in the morning, it wasn't funny.

As the mugger were introduced to their new Vadanemmeli home, the stud male Perayur (Tamil for old man) quickly took charge of the enclosure and swam powerfully up and down the 25-metre-long pond, tail arched out of the water in a territorial display. He dominated the females, now and then extracting a brief show of respect from them in the form of a raised head or rub on the jaw. For the next eight years, he proved an excellent breeder, diligently courting and mating with 5 – and later 7 – females and producing over 1,500 babies. In the summer of 1983, Perayur dug a deep tunnel in a sand bank to escape the heat and suffocated to death when it collapsed on him. To all of us at the Croc Bank, it was like the passing away of an old friend.

Perayur, called Beta in some of our papers, gave us our first glimpse into the fascinating world of crocodile behaviour. This was at a time when few behavioural studies had been carried out on crocodilians except those of Hugh Cott, Tony Pooley and Alistair Grahame on the Nile crocodile in Africa, and Dr Jeff Lang on the American alligator. The Indian species were a blank page except for the fact that the Jaipur Zoo had bred them, and some naturalists, such as K.S. Dharmakumarsinhji and J.C. Daniel, had made observations during the course of other studies. I became especially interested in the habits of the mugger and spent many hours in a hide in Pen 8 during the nesting season.

On one such occasion, I'd been watching Perayur court Alpha, the oldest female of the group, with three attending females keeping guard when one of these disappeared, and ten minutes later, a croc head appeared over the wall of my hide! From then on, I never entered Pen 8 without a stout stick. The information thus collected was the basis of several papers and articles. Results of behavioural research such as this, which adds to the sum total of our knowledge about a species, is in itself worthwhile, but often goes beyond that and contributes to conservation action that influences the ultimate fate of the animal.

The interrelationships among the mugger in Pen 8 turned out to be far more complex than we had imagined. During the mating season, which begins in South India with the northeast monsoon in November, we watched with surprise the gentleness with which these modern-day dinosaurs played out their courtship dramas. In a typical mating sequence, a male approaches his lady, who raises her head in a gesture of submission, and the pair rub the undersides of their jaws together and circle in a solemn, slow display. Sometimes the male submerges and blows bubbles. Mating takes place several minutes after courtship begins.

The mugger proved to be runaway breeders and we quickly ended up with several hundreds of them. Fortunately, crocodiles are surprisingly restrained eaters; their metabolism is slow and energy-conversion rate high, a factor that makes them ideally suited for captive farming. An average adult crocodile, say 2.5 metres long and weighing 50 kilograms, eats only about 3 kilograms of meat a week. Luckily for us, they seem to be on a perpetual slimming diet! A light bulb hung in the hatchling ponds attracts nutritious insect life and it's fun to watch the agile young jump up to catch fluttering moths and termites after dark. After several weeks, this diet is bolstered with *tilapia* fish, common in the vast backwater that borders Vadanemmeli village. Mole crabs, the collection of which provides a little pocket money for our village *thambi*s, are also fed to the crocs.

Initially, adult mugger and salties were fed meat as well as large bandicoot rats brought by the flamboyant Kuruvikaran (bird people), a hunting tribe conspicuous in those days by their green berets and

Rules for hand feeding crocs (as demonstrated by Rom here): keep your finger nails short and your eyes on those jaws!

muzzle loaders slung over the shoulder. The Kuruvikaran are examples of pragmatic tribal adaptation to urban living; they make themselves at home on city pavements and proceed about their business with a fine devil-may-care attitude. They eat practically anything that moves, including jackals, crows, vultures, and even domestic cats! We have seen them roasting the last at their Adyar encampment, expertly turning the meat over a fire of cycle tyres. But the bandicoot supply stopped as the Kuruvikaran moved away, out of Madras, ending their city safaris. Incidentally, people like the Kuruvikaran and the Irular could become wonderful resources for the Swachh Bharat project!

As they were ideal captive crocs, we were able to house large numbers of mugger together with minimal fights and injury. The other two Indian species, the saltwater croc and the gharial, are less adaptable. Salties in particular are problematic because they will not get along amicably, and we learnt early that the policy of divide and rule would have to be applied. The Central Leather Research Institute in Madras was engaged, at the time the Croc Bank was getting under way, in studying the growth rates of five Malayan salties in the context of commercial farming for skins. They were planning to kill them in order to determine the size increase in captivity and were easily convinced by us that this could be done just as effectively by keeping them alive! Their salties came to the Croc Bank on the agreement that regular growth data would be supplied to them. A pair of these began to breed, producing over forty babies each year. The saltie is the only Indian species of crocodile to build a mound nest; this is often a metre-high dome of leaves, vegetation and earth, and the eggs are laid in a conical depression near the top. After laying her eggs, the female protects them like a dragon, which makes the collection of the eggs for incubation a difficult exercise. At the nest site, two keepers with long poles are needed to keep her at bay while a third quickly removes the vegetation covering the eggs and transfers them to a box. For days and sometimes weeks after the eggs have been collected, the female defends her empty nest fiercely.

The saltie is the traditional man-eater of the croc tribe because of its large size and fearless temperament. The largest of these at the Croc Bank was a massive, jowly individual called Jaws III who had to be consigned to solitary confinement because he refused to get on with others of his species; even females were greeted with powerful rejections. At over 300 kilograms, the operation of transferring him to his new residence was fraught with the sort of frightened hilarity well known to croc handlers. At one stage, while he was being released, half the thirty or so people holding him panicked when he made a sudden lunge, leaving the others to their fate, which could have been disastrous. Everyone panicked and ran off, shoving and pushing in their eagerness to vault over the wall. Jaws III made the headlines the next day in the local newspapers and became one of the better-known crocs at the Bank. The other such star was Heyward, the American alligator, who for a dozen years was the only alligator in India. He was a gift from Rom's friend Heyward Clamp, who kept several in his backyard in South Carolina.

Across the road from the saltie enclosure are the gharial, which have the opposite temperament and are calm and easy to approach. Our sons, Nikhil and Samir, would often 'help' the keepers here at feed time as they placed piles of fish near the long, toothy jaws. The gharial feed exclusively on fish, though at the Croc Bank they ate mole crabs as well, in the days when these were plentiful on the beach. We waited eagerly for this rare species to start breeding, and for a long time, only platonic relations and infertile eggs prevailed. Would they breed here, or did they need their natural habitat of deep, cool, moving waters? The male began to grow the prominent *ghara* or pot on his nose, creating even further expectations. Twentieth April 1989 was an exciting day indeed when one of the females was found digging a nest, and later laying eggs! She herself was a 1979 baby and had come from the government's Kukkrail gharial centre. She laid only two eggs; first-layers often have small numbers of eggs. But both were fertile and both hatched.

The tropical climate of South India is well suited to rearing crocodilians. This, and our early breeding successes of several species, caught the attention of the Crocodile Specialist Group (CSG) of the IUCN, and its 1978 meeting was held at the Croc Bank. The members agreed that the Bank should become a breeding centre for all the species, an ambitious scheme, which may never be fully realized. But a beginning was made, with a group of spectacled caimans from Heyward Clamp, Siamese crocodiles from the New York Zoological Society, African dwarf crocodiles from Zoo Negara and offers of other species. The CSG meeting was useful and stimulating. Fred Medem, who was at the helm of crocodile conservation in South America, was there, as were Wayne King and Ted Joanen from the United States, John Lever from Australia, and other croc people. One could never sit down to a meal without a mention of sexing techniques, unformed embryos, gall bladders and such, which I, then in my third or fourth month of pregnancy, found hard to take.

Over half a million tourists visited the Bank annually in the 1970s and 1980s, and the income from ticket sales provided some extras for development and improvement as well. From the start, most staff were hired from the local village, Vadanemmeli; thus the Croc Bank's success reflects directly on the village exterior and the lives of the community. The input of cash from salaries, purchase of animal food and other services has resulted in better housing, healthcare and education.

Apart from supplying mugger for release in wild habitats, the Croc Bank played – and continues to play – a big role as a public education centre. Through signboards, guides and of course the exhibits themselves, visitors learn interesting information, which broadens their understanding of the natural world. As at the Snake Park, we heard about people for whom this direct contact with crocodiles and other reptiles created a new and zestful interest in all wildlife and its conservation.

The greater space and smaller number of visitors at the Croc Bank made it easier to deal with the 'people problem' as compared to the Snake Park. But even so, difficulties often arose, especially on holidays when busloads of brew-happy tourists thought that the ticket was a licence to behave as badly as possible. Most of the ugliest incidents followed a typical pattern; tourists breaking off branches (from carefully tended trees), attacking the crocodiles with this and other ammunition, trying to jump into the enclosures, and assaulting the assistants when asked to stop. A couple of times, the police had to be summoned.

Sometimes, tourists behave strangely. One morning, I was sitting in the office overlooking Pen 8 (the mugger-breeding enclosure) when two legs slithered down the wall on the other side; mysterious, since cleaning time was long over and anyway, none of the staff wear bright red and white checked trousers while raking away croc faeces. I hurried over and found an American tourist taking a leak, with horror dawning in his eyes, because 3 metres away was Nova, clambering up the bank. 'Hey! There's a gator in here!' he yelled, frantically trying to scramble over the wall. He explained that he'd thought it was a toilet! Then there was the Frenchman who got very irate when stopped from leaning down and waving his hand in a rearing enclosure. He even hit the assistant who was trying to save his life. A big crowd collected around Monsieur whose few words of English proved inadequate for an explanation. 'I want only, only, I want only,' he repeated louder and louder. Fortunately, his wife managed to take him away.

Continuing studies at the Croc Bank revealed two facts about the mugger, which have a bearing on their conservation. The first was that the mugger at the Croc Bank did not follow the egg-laying pattern of other species of crocodiles. All crocodiles are supposed to lay one clutch of eggs each season, but the 'mug' had not read the books, and was laying two. This was so abnormal that, at first, we could not explain the extra nest in Pen 8. The next year, there were two 'spares' and so on until one year, seven females laid eleven nests altogether (three laid a single clutch; four were 'double clutchers'). There was considerable discussion about this at the meeting of the Society for the Study of Amphibians and Reptiles on Crocodile Biology at Milwaukee, Wisconsin, in 1980, which Rom and I attended and presented our paper on the mugger. The reason for this aberrant behaviour was conjectured to be the high summer temperature and food abundance at the Croc Bank – the only place in the world where the mugger had been recorded to double-clutch.

The second discovery was even more interesting, with a deeper ecological significance. Scientists had found that the sexes of some freshwater turtles are not determined genetically, but in the egg, by the temperature of the nest. The same had been found to be true for the American alligator and some marine turtles. In 1983, the American crocodile biologist Dr Jeff Lang, from the University of North Dakota, began a study at the Crocodile Bank on the mugger's breeding biology, working at night, when mugger females usually nest, and sleeping during the day. His special interest was sex determination and double-clutching. We'd first met Jeff in PNG, where he was studying the New Guinea freshwater crocodile and the saltie. Later, in 1980, we stayed with him and his anthropologist wife, Gretchen, before the Milwaukee crocodile conference and put ourselves in Jeff's capable hands regarding the presentation of our paper on the biology of the mugger. Writing it had been easy but to make it interesting and stimulating to a scientific audience was another matter. With this, as with numerous other projects, Jeff's help was invaluable.

His study confirmed that gender in mugger is determined by the incubating temperature and in a very cut-and-dried way. Males predominate at high temperatures, females at low. So, you can have controlled situations with fairly simple equipment to 'run off' males, females or a combo of the two. This opportunity to monitor and arrange sex ratios is significant for commercial croc farms.

As was the case in those days in India with practically every group of animals, so little was known about the natural history of crocodiles that new information was turning up every now and then. One year, a nest in Pen 8 was not detected and hatched naturally in the enclosure. The mother crocodile scraped away the earth from the nest hole when the hatchlings beeped from inside the eggs, and gently carried the hatchlings and partly hatched eggs in her jaws to the water. We were watching this behaviour when 'Holy Cow!' exclaimed Jeff. It wasn't a female this time but Makara, the male who'd taken Perayur's place as the group stud. The large lumbering male was helping out with maternal duties! One of the hatchlings had fallen into a depression near the nest and he nudged it with his mouth so it slithered down to the water. That was the first time that a male mugger had been found participating in nest excavation. In South Africa, the naturalist Tony Pooley had photographed a Nile croc male roll unhatched eggs in his mouth, to release hatchlings from the eggshell.

In 1981, the Crocodile Bank started a freshwater turtle research and breeding programme. By that time, Vijaya Jaganathan, who'd worked with us at the Snake Park, had completed the first freshwater turtle surveys with WWF sponsorship and had a collection of almost half of the twenty-six Indian species. Several of these were now breeding at the

Croc Bank under her supervision and care. It soon became obvious that freshwater turtles were another unknown group of reptiles. Turtles are eaten by Adivasi people all over the country, with West Bengal topping the list of states. Hundreds of thousands of turtles were brought into markets there from all over north India for their meat. In 1983, Dr Ed Moll of the University of Illinois spent nine months in India gathering data on the distribution and status of turtles. He made the

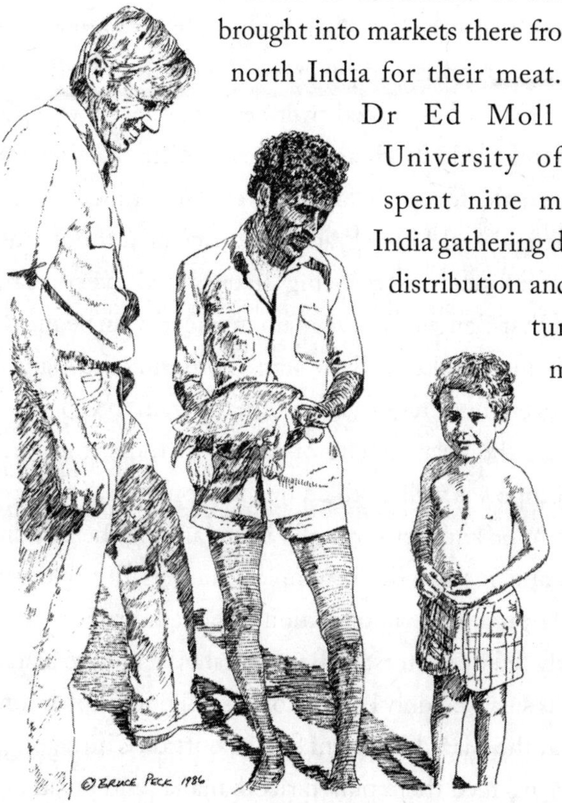

©BRUCE PECK 1986

Turtle man Ed Moll arrived at the Croc Bank at a time when Nikhil, five, was full of insatiable curiosity about reptiles. During the months that he helped Ed, Nikhil learnt a lot about turtles.

Bank his base camp, living between endless train journeys, in a leaky, rat-infested hut in the Croc Bank compound, which he maintained was 'just great', and which Jeff Lang later inherited. Both became expert rat trappers.

Viji and the sea turtle biologist Satish Bhaskar worked with Ed on his turtle surveys and the team put together the first substantive reports and papers on the status of turtles in India. Their methods spanned river netting, interviews with fishermen and turtle catchers, and visits to markets where turtles were sold for meat and as a cure for tuberculosis. In West Bengal and Uttar Pradesh, particularly, thousands of freshwater turtles were being slaughtered every year. Although West Bengal was the main market for turtle meat, they were being caught in all the states bordering the Ganga and transported hundreds of kilometres by train to Calcutta. Turtles share the peculiar fate of snakes in India; they are both worshipped as well as killed by the thousands. They are considered to be another form of Vishnu among the Hindu pantheon, and many Hindu temples, such as the one we visited in Tripura, have a population of sacred turtles which are regularly fed by visitors. In Bangladesh, the unique black softshell has survived only because of the religious protection it receives at the Biazid Gostami Shrine outside Chittagong, where pilgrims feed them puffed rice, bananas and bread on bamboo skewers.

Ed Moll worked mainly in Uttar Pradesh, Bihar, Madhya Pradesh, Andhra Pradesh, Orissa and West Bengal and

One of the strangest turtles in India, the forest cane turtle lives in the damp environment of the tropical rainforest and dives under leaves to escape predators, the way other turtles dive under water.

when he left India, Viji began a study under him on the rare forest cane turtle of the Western Ghats. She rediscovered this species at a point when nothing was known about them other than two captive specimens that had been identified over 70 years ago. She worked on its natural history and that of its eco-counterpart, the Travancore tortoise. During the cane turtle study, Viji lived in a large cave in the Nadukani Reserve Forest in Kerala, which Dr Brian Groombridge, of the Species Monitoring Centre in Cambridge, England, pronounced to be one of the healthiest surviving rainforests in South India.

In June 1984, our secretary Brenda Bhaskar and I set off to visit Viji in her cave dwelling and arrived at the town of Chalakudy early one morning after a sleepless train journey. But the forest officials were not keen on allowing us into Nadukani. 'How do we know you will not take away specimens?' I explained that we only wanted to visit Viji and that, in any case, there was so much poaching going on from every account that taking away a few specimens would not matter; it might even save them from being killed. Of course, our popularity plummeted further but we did get a permit for Nadukani. An autorickshaw took us to Kodali from where we hired a jeep to take us to Anaipandam, a small camp where a group of Kadar Adivasis had been relocated by the government.

Halfway up the two-hour climb from Anaipandam to Viji's camp, it began to rain, drenching us and our knapsacks, which felt like dead bodies. Luckily, we'd run into Chandran from the Kadar tribe, who worked for Viji, or we might never have found our way in the wet darkness of that evening. 'How much more?' we asked him again. 'Just a little,' he answered pointing beyond the sunset. I had just come out of hospital some weeks before this after an appendicitis operation. The steep trek up and later the bounding from rock to slippery rock on grassy hilltops made me wonder if I'd flown the coop too soon. Brenda generously shared my anxiety. 'Walk slowly, or you'll open up again.'

We arrived in inky darkness and soaking wet at Viji's cave home, 50 metres above a stream frequently used by elephants, and kept a wary lookout for them later while bathing in the chilly water. The rocks were smeared with yellow powder, which turned out to be homemade bark soap that Chandran's family used. Later on, we watched his wife, Laila, roast and crush snail shells to fill her lime container. Over a dinner of rice piled with fresh mushrooms, Viji summarized the progress of her study in the tracts of evergreen forest at an elevation of about 600 metres. Here the cane turtle leads a most un-turtle-like existence, scurrying under leaves like a lizard when startled and feeding on fruit, mushrooms and insects. We turned in early to bed, which was a section of the steep cave floor, down which we slid by degrees during the night. At midnight, there were cries, '*Yaanai, yaanai!*' (Elephants, elephants!) and Brenda and I shot up ready to run. But it was only Chandran's aunt having nightmares.

We spent the next day with the Kadars looking for turtles in the forty-two 100-metre grids, which constituted Viji's study area. Just before leaving the camp, we were putting on our damp, steaming shoes when a scorpion careened up Viji's leg. It was quickly apprehended with a twig and deposited on the camp's periphery. Down in the valley, there was soon that familiar cold sensation between the toes and we stopped to pick off leeches with a dab of salt; though we soon gave up to avoid being stationary targets. By midday, Chandran had a cane turtle and a Travancore tortoise; the latter seemed to favour open rocky places. We found one wedged sideways between two boulders and rescued it.

At dusk, a large flock of Malabar hornbills flew noisily overhead while we looked up at a fruiting banyan tree laden with parakeets, scarlet minivets, nuthatches, grey hornbills, orioles and sundry other birds I was unable to identify. At times like this, I wish – but only briefly – that I had availed myself of the numerous attempts made by my father and Sálim Mamoo to knock the names of some of the commoner birds into our heads when we were children.

The only snake we saw that day was a hump-nosed pit viper, then very common in Nadukani. Several of the larger trees supported the dizzying bamboo ladders that the Kadars use during the honey-collecting season. Using the flexible parallel support, they lever themselves skyward after dark, often to 30 metres and more, to collect the honey from large hives of hill bees that is then sold to a local cooperative. There was elephant dung everywhere, and a few weeks after our trip, Dr Groombridge was lucky enough to see a troop of lion-tailed macaques, the rare endemics of south-western India. But already the signs of doom and destruction were evident in Nadukani; it was obviously on the hit list of the timber merchants.

There was no transport for us the next day, so we took a leisurely six hours tramping back to Kodali, the nearest bus stop. Our batteries were recharged every couple of hours when we came to a stream or river; throwing off our knapsacks, we would dive in for a soak.

Another exciting discovery was the presence of *Batagur baska*, alive but not so well, in the Sundarbans. This is the largest Indian hard-shelled turtle and there are reports

After half a century of no reports, Rom and Mohammed Reza Khan of Dhaka University found that the batagur *turtle was alive in the Sundarbans, in both Bangladesh and West Bengal.*

from the turn of the twentieth century about the harvest of millions of these turtles and their eggs on rivers like the Hooghly. But the turtle had been unreported in this region for the last sixty or seventy years. Then in 1981, when Rom was at Dhaka Zoo with Reza Khan of Dhaka University, they saw a large *Batagur* with its distinctive turned-up nose, which the keeper said had come from the Sundarbans. A year later, Rom was surveying crocs in the Bangladesh Sundarbans and met fishermen who were routinely catching the same turtle that they call *kata*. They kept several alive in small ponds near their houses for eventual sale at the market; these had been caught on hooks baited with mangrove fruits. Soon after this, during our surveys on the Indian side of the Sundarbans, Viji found them being caught and kept in the same way.

A generous grant from the Wildlife Preservation Trust International enabled us to begin a systematic study of captive freshwater turtles at the Croc Bank by building a large deep pond now holding many Indian species. The most impressive inhabitants of the pond are the huge softshell turtles, some nearly 35 kilograms in weight. One of these behemoths is a Leith's softshell, gifted to Ed at a temple tank in the hinterland of Andhra Pradesh. This extraordinary gift is a good advertisement for Ed's pleasant nature and winning smile.

During September 1989, two Ganges softshells dug nests and laid twenty-four eggs each. This was a happy event in itself, but more importantly, it told us that the size and design of the pond did cater to the needs of the turtles. Aside from just wanting to find out about the turtle's breeding habits, we had other important reasons for starting this breeding programme. The softshell turtles are true river vultures and help keep our rivers clean. Half-burnt corpses would litter our northern rivers if it wasn't for them. We also found that hard-shelled turtles can devour huge quantities of water weeds, like hyacinth, and hope to prove that turtles can be effective answers to weed-choked waterways. The Government of India's Ganga cleaning project has now included a turtle-rearing component, much to our satisfaction. And one of the most important reasons for perfecting turtle husbandry was to demonstrate that Bengal could be living on home-grown turtles instead of continuing the destruction of its wild populations.

In 1987, we had a short but important visit from American turtle man Mike Ewert. He opened our eyes to a lot of amazing facts about turtle breeding and got us on the way to solving some of our most perplexing turtle questions. For example, why did our Indian flapshell turtle eggs develop almost full-term embryos, then sit and wait for six months before hatching? Once, they'd hatched to the stimulus of a hard rain beating on the roof of the lab in which they were incubating. Mike explained that the embryos know that the time to pop out of the egg is when there is adequate rain to form the ponds and streams they need to live in. If they hatched in the hostile hot season, they probably wouldn't survive for more than two days.

Another question we asked was, why eggs from north Indian species, obviously fertile in the beginning, only developed for a couple of months, before gradually dying. Mike deduced from examining that year's batch of Ganges softshell eggs that the embryos had entered into a state called 'diapause'. This sort of suspended animation could only be broken or stimulated by the normal winter drop in temperature they would experience in their northern home. The way he suggested we solve this problem was to make a modified refrigerator to keep the eggs at 15–20 degrees Celsius for forty to sixty days. This was done by Viji successfully.

Our turtle girl Viji continued to break new ground in turtle studies until we lost her in tragic circumstances later in 1987. For many years, I felt her work on chelonians at the Snake Park and Croc Bank had not been adequately acknowledged. The opportunity to do so came in 2023 when I was invited to write about her in the book *Women in the Wild.* Viji adorns its cover, and her bright eyes foretell a promising future for women field biologists in India, for whom she was, and remains, a wonderful pioneer.

Worshippers and Victims: A Complex Relationship with Snakes

To be involved in the conservation of snakes – as we have been since the early 1970s – it's important to know something about their place in our country's culture; cultures, rather, because there are literally thousands. It was Shama, a scholar of Hinduism, who introduced us to the rich world of reptile mythology in India. During our 'recce' at the Snake Park, she listened carefully to Rom's narratives about the many beliefs surrounding snakes, and would later write about it in our newsletter, *Hamadryad*. She and Rom became good buddies, and he invited her to join us on a snake survey in Pudukottai for the Tamil Nadu Archives soon after we were married. This district, formerly a princely state, turned out to be a Russell's viper paradise, and Rom and the two Irular with us found thirty of these snakes in the first two days. We stayed with Nadu Dorai of the Trichy raja's family, and apart from

Snake stones are symbols of fertility in South India and believed to work miracles.

the snake surveys with Rom and the Irular, we were able to experience the royalty's exquisite cuisine as well as their fighting bulls' performance at the Jallikattu event, sitting under ornate sunshades with gold tassels. At the Perayur temple near Pudukottai, we saw hundreds of *pambu kallu*s or snake stones, brought by women as offerings to beget male children. We also saw the cruel practice of torturing a live owl over a fire to melt its eyes in order to exorcise evil spirits. Unfortunately, by the time we arrived, the bird was almost dead, so there was nothing we could do except to make an unsuccessful attempt to convince the crowd that it was a cruel and useless practice.

I became infected with Shama's interest in these stories and practices, a fascinating fund of living realities because snakes – and serpents, their avatars in mythology – play a major role in Indian belief systems. Hindu, Jain and Buddhist mythologies are populated with powerful serpents, which perform memorable feats. They are a part of the Mahabharata, Puranas and other ancient texts, and their stories are narrated, heard and celebrated in poojas, festivals and other gatherings. Indian myths feature the serpents *bhuj-naag*, Sanskrit for born-of-the Earth, which sport shining gems in their five, seven or nine hoods. Then there are the *naga*s, the Hindi word for cobra. Nagas and naginis, beings that are half human and half serpent, inhabit *patala*, the netherworld. The king of the nagas is Ananta (Aadisesha in the south; also known as Sheshnag), the Everlasting or Immortal One, often used by Vishnu, the Preserver of the Hindu Trinity, to lie on. When Vishnu was incarnated as the child Krishna, Ananta went along with him and protected him from a storm using his several hoods.

Shama wrote about Ananta in one of the *Hamadryad* issues:

> He remains with Vishnu even during the periodic destruction of the world. As soon as the world is washed away, the serpent acts as a raft for Vishnu to float on the

> primeval waters till creation is achieved again. While creation is in existence, it is his hoods that support the world and the heavens, and he himself is coiled on the back of a gigantic tortoise floating on cosmic water. This is why several temples have a small unexpected carving of a tortoise in the centre of the floor . . . and many an unwary tourist has come to grief on this while admiring the temple ceiling.[1]

As the protector of Vishnu, Ananta/Sheshnag is also worshipped, and it is believed that he carries the Earth on his hood.

In terms of reptiles, the cobra is the dominant figure in temple carvings all over India and ranges in form from the many-hooded Ananta to the representation of rivers as nagas. But there's much more. There's Vasuki, the serpent-protector, usually found wrapped around Lord Shiva, also used as the rope to churn the ocean and thus recreate the universe using Mount Meru as the rod. It was no easy task; the seas were stirred and churned until *soma*, the elixir of immortality, floated up to the surface.

The goddesses Nagamma, Renuka, Parameswary, Ambal and others are worshipped in their serpent forms. Some temples have a particular spot where a serpent is believed to reside, and devotees offer milk and eggs here during *sarpa pooja* or serpent worship. At the Snake Park, this offering was a regular event. Interestingly, Vasuki and other nagas have a place in the sermons of Buddha, and their role includes protecting him. Snakes/Serpents are also associated with Kubera, the god of wealth, and are believed to bring luck and wealth, as well as fertility and immortality (including rebirth).

At one time, India used to be practically synonymous with the snake charmer or *sapera* and his *been* or flute. Because of the present wildlife laws, those days are history. In Rajasthan, the Kaalbelia tribe were *sapera*s, and the women performed a special dance called the Kaalbelia dance. Now that they can't use live snakes, they perform for money at tourist hubs, where men play the *been* and women depict the swaying movement of a snake, a performance that needs great strength and flexibility. One famous Kaalbelia dancer, Gulabo, even performed at several international festivals.

Bharatanatyam or Sadir, our classical dance style, depicts many myths related to snakes, and I asked my dancer-friend Lavanya Narain to tell me about them. I take the liberty of using her own succinct words:

> The Bharatanatyam repertoire used to have a special item, called snake dance (*paambu natanam* in Tamil) to be offered in the second half of the performance. Its accompanying song is called *Aadu paambey* which literally means Dance, snake! The dancer mimics the movements of a snake. This song is set to raag *punnagavarali*, which has the word *naga* (snake) incorporated in its name. The

dance movements are acrobatic, and the dancer showcases her fluidity with graceful lifts and twirls.

There are many mudras or hand gestures in Bharathanatyam. One is the *sarpaseersham* which means snake hood, where the fingertips are curled. To depict Vishnu in his reclining form (Ranganatha) on Ananta/ Aadisesha, the dancer introduces the snake, then the bed and Vishnu.

Shiva, often depicted in dance, wears a naga as a garland, and Krishna dances on the head of five-hooded Kaaliya, who had been pestering the cattle and cowherds of Vrindavan, and poisoning the waters of the Yamuna (Krishna did not kill him incidentally, but sent him off to the underworld, Patala Lok, where he lives peacefully with his family). And Ganesha, who also appears in many dance-dramas, wears a snake-belt, to hold together his belly – which represents the cosmos. This serpent is the kundalini or cosmic energy.

These are just a few of the dazzling legends we grow up with. And how they are translated into worship and practice in various parts of the country – different from village to neighbouring village, sometimes – is just as fascinating. My friend Bimla Gour grew up in Mathura and relates that snakes are worshipped there because of Krishna's rescue of Vrindavan by forcing the surrender of Kalia. A prevalent

Mathura myth is that snakes go blind on seeing a pregnant woman. And further, killing a blind snake is a sin. Pragmatic beliefs, which protect both pregnant women as well as snakes from harm! Bimla relates:

> My mother always worshipped snakes on Naag Panchami festival, which falls in July–August, during the rainy season. She would draw dangerous-looking snakes with charcoal on the kitchen wall and pray for the welfare of the children and for a good yield in the fields. *Sapera*s would also visit homes with their snakes, and were offered milk, money and grain. We were asked to touch the snakes for their blessings. Later on, we realized that snakes don't drink milk . . . and anyway, in time the government banned snake catching.

She adds:

> My cousin tells me that some people are born with *sarpa dosha* (snake curse) in their horoscopes. As it creates a lot of hurdles in life, remedies are also prescribed, one of which involves visiting a Shiva temple and chanting his mantra 108 times. The fail-safe remedy is believed to be a visit to the Triambakeshwar temple in Nashik to perform a special pooja. There is usually a long waiting list, so one can book in advance, the American visa sort of thing.

Against this rich tapestry of legends, it is no surprise that there are colourful stories about specific species, especially the ones with odd features. The red sand boa, which has an absurdly blunt tail, is called the two-headed snake and people swear that it travels in one direction for six months, then in the other. Unfortunately, it is also a symbol of wealth in some parts of the country and reportedly sold at exorbitant prices, by weight; with female snakes, the cloaca is sometimes stuffed with ball bearings to increase the weight, leading to a prolonged and painful death. The slate grey common sand boa, because of its blotched, spotty pattern, is said to cause leprosy and the pointy-headed vine snake is called *kann-kuthi pambu* or eye-pecking snake. The bronze-back tree snake is credited with one of the most colourful myths – it is believed that after biting someone, the snake climbs a high tree to wait for the victim's funeral pyre! But the classic Indian snake myth, exploited regularly by the film industry, is the revenge story – kill a cobra and its mate will seek vengeance. And the rustic imagination

The spectacled cobra, one of the Big Four venomous snakes of India. This cobra is worshipped in different ways throughout the country.

carries it further – you must burn the dead snake, as otherwise the image of the killer will remain in its eyes, and thus enable revenge. I recently heard a new version of this one, with a wonderful tech twist. The cobra, before it dies, can click and save the killer's image and 'forward' it to its mate, who then does the revenge part. The digital age comes to snake mythology!

In parts of Karnataka, such as Agumbe in Shivamogga district, the curse connected with cobras involves elaborate and expensive poojas for several days in the distant Kukke Subramanya temple, all done to avoid the deadly *sarpa dosha* being inflicted on the family for generations to come. This is a must if a cobra is killed . . . or even if you see a dead one; and the whole family must participate, first at a local temple and then in Kukke Subramanya. It becomes an expensive business and I've met subsistence-level farmers who had to spend twenty thousand rupees to protect their families, present and future. (Sometimes it can even be a lot more, depending on the advice of the local priest.)

And it's not just snakes. The gecko is revered and features in rock carvings in Kanchipuram and elsewhere. At Konark in Orissa, a stone crocodile emerges from the side of the Sun Temple with a fish in its jaws. River Goddess Ganga rides a crocodile or gharial, as well as a softshelled turtle in the temples of Agra and Varanasi. Lizards are equally the target of naive beliefs; the harmless house gecko has an awesome reputation and is blamed for much illness, and even death. 'Lizard falls in food: wedding guests in hospital' is a typical headline in newspapers and the innocent reptile is a convenient scapegoat for food adulteration. With surprising ignorance, journalists blandly repeat the same story; such as in the *Indian Express* of 18 October 1985: 'About 200 children were admitted to hospital following complaints of vomiting and giddiness after taking noon meal [*sic*]. One child was stated to be in a serious condition. A lizard was reportedly found in the meal.' And more recently, one of many in 2023: '36 students fall sick after lizard found in mid-day meal . . .'[2]

Snakebite, however, is not a myth. India tops the list, with 50,000 or more deaths a year and at least triple that number of morbidities like the loss of a limb, kidney failure or PTSD following snakebite. The majority of victims are poor farmers or farm labourers, often the sole earning members of the family. Rom, and later both of us, have been witness to heart-rending stories and events related to snakebite. In the early days of the Snake Park in Selaiyur outside Madras, victims of snakebite from adjoining villages came for advice and treatment. Even in the unlikely event that antivenom was sought soon after the bite, the hospital was 30 kilometres away, taxis were not to be had, buses were infrequent and the last one left the village at 9.30 p.m. These logistics often made a farce of our slogans, songs and other presentations about snakebite and antivenom – that there are four common dangerous snakes and antivenom is the only cure for snakebite. (Silver lining: lives were also saved by innovative travel to hospital on bullock carts, stretchers and bicycles.)

Some victims came in a state of shock – eyes rolled back, foaming at the mouth – from the bite of a harmless watersnake or rat snake, and the only treatment required was a smart slap and a sound scolding, with an aspirin for good measure. More often, though, it was a serious bite, such as that of a krait. Kraits are nocturnal, and the typical bite happens at night when the person is sleeping on the ground outside their hut. Flicking in their sleep at a movement – a krait out hunting for rats and mice – they are bitten and may die hours later without even knowing what happened. The dramatic, paralysing symptoms of krait bite are usually apparent only at the end, with not enough time to get to the hospital.

One early morning, Rom was woken by a farmer whose daughter had felt something bite her in the night and who, he said, had fainted. 'It's not serious, some tablets will set her right,' he said, adding that she was of a nervous disposition and even a bee sting could send her into a faint. His confidence made Rom's subsequent task doubly difficult; they sped back to his farm on the motorbike and peering into the dark room, Rom saw that she had died. Kraits are insidious killers indeed, and the legend that they suck your breath away while you sleep is an apt one.

The Irular didn't believe in antivenom in those days and preferred to take their own herbal medicines. Rom's friend Natesan/Sureman was one of these hardliners who swore against taking antivenom. He often argued about it with Rom: 'Hey man – I had so many bites and no problem, so why I waste money on those stupid hospital medicines?' His confidence never wavered in spite of Rom's repeatedly saying 'Look, Sureman, that's because not all venomous bites are fatal. Often, very often, not enough venom is injected. But you may just get one of the few bad ones and then . . .?'

And he did. Celebrating a neighbour's wedding rather too merrily, he began to demonstrate his snake-handling prowess. He brought out a cobra from a bag in his hut, got on his bicycle and took the snake for a ride on the handlebar! For a few seconds everything was fine – cheers and claps from the audience – then the thoroughly frightened snake bit him hard on the thumb. By the time he came to the Snake Park, he'd taken large doses of the *nava kunji* herb he swore by, but the first symptoms of paralysis had set in. His eyelids drooped heavily, his speech was slurred, breathing laboured. As a non-medical person, it was illegal for Rom to give him antivenom, but there was no way he could get him to a doctor in time. There was always a stock of antivenom in the house, and Rom's sister Nina boiled a syringe in deathlike silence as they wondered if it wasn't too late to save old Sureman.

As the 20ccs of antivenom began to course through his veins, Natesan sat up and grinned foolishly, reeking of his celebrations. 'I'll stay away from cobras for a while,' he mumbled. 'How about staying off the other poison instead?' Rom asked.

But Rom's suggestion was not taken seriously and Natesan died a few years later of multiple liver complications. For Rom, this was the end of an important friendship. They had become close pals, brought together by their mutual fascination for the jungle. Natesan had been with Rom to every major forest in South India, collecting specimens for the Snake Park. He was also an excellent showman. Tourists loved him and he became a widely photographed star. But Rom wasn't able to get him off booze and had watched his deterioration with regret.

Another Irular who had implicit trust in the community's own snakebite remedies was Chockalingam. He was a famous *vaidyar* or healer and had survived ten cobra bites. Later, however, having seen antivenom at work, he conceded that his treatment may have had a lot to do with the high percentage of dry bites, with no venom injected or too little to cause a fatality. But he exempted his medicine for saw-scaled viper from this statement, saying he had used it for several serious bites with unfailing success. This may sound heretical to the scientific community, but the fact remains that the Irular are scientists in their own right, and their medicines are not to be confused with those of the ubiquitous village quack. Choky's apothecary included a vaccination against saw-scaled viper venom, and he gave his son Kali a monthly swallow of this for six months. His older son Rajendran, also thus immunized, has suffered three serious saw-scaled viper bites and is none the worse for it. (Though, of course, without double-blind clinical trials, Choky's vaccination is just experimental.)

It needs to be said that it isn't just the rural/Adivasi communities that believe in hocus-pocus snakebite remedies. There are many townies even today who swear by snake stones, herbal mixtures, chants and poojas and, not so long ago, by the famous 'telegram or phone call to the station-master'. One example from recent history that comes to mind is that of the naturalist-hunter Kenneth Anderson. He refused antivenom and insisted on this 'proper' treatment when bitten by a cobra. The magic phone call (to a station-master) was made and he survived, as he probably would have anyway, whatever 'treatment' he'd followed, because a large percentage of cobra bites aren't fatal. Surprising 'facts' about snakebite treatment are sprung at us during presentations and workshops, not only in rustic marketplaces but also within hallowed institutions of learning. A few years ago, I was talking about the Croc Bank's work at a university in Vellore. The head of the Zoology Department, no less, brought up the subject of antivenom: 'Madam, it is by no means the only cure . . . My own uncle . . . saw with own eyes . . . I am a science teacher . . .' and so on.

Irrational arguments have one great strength on their side: they don't let the opposition party speak. This is a generic experience, with many such stories related by our snakebite mitigation team. Beliefs in rural areas lean more towards herbal 'remedies', mantras and snake stones, while towns and cities abound in more modern myths, such as cut and suction (which can result in bleeding to death). Then there are the ubiquitous, moneymaking 'snake repellents' such as Snake Maxx, a solar-powered vibrator which is said to repel snakes since they sense surface vibrations. An acquaintance and his family bought one, placed it near a folded tarpaulin sheet, and switched it on. When they came to check a few days later, there was a cobra under the tarp, with the 'repellent' merrily buzzing along! Plenty of opportunities for shrewd entrepreneurs to make good money, thanks to gullible people and their terror of snakes!

In 1972, Rom was contacted by two herpetologists from the Japan Snake Institute, Dr Sawai and Dr Homma. They were studying cobra bites in India and invited Rom to accompany them on their surveys. They interviewed victims and their families, reviewed the (scanty) literature on the subject and visited hospitals and medical personnel. The reality was grim indeed. A shortage of antivenom, its inefficient distribution, insufficient training in the treatment of snakebite, convoluted red tape in hospital admission leading to crucial loss of time, continued viewing of snakebites as criminal cases in some states, medical indifference towards morbidity resulting from bites, insufficient records and recording processes . . . these were just a few of the challenges they found.

This survey with the Japan Snake Institute was something of a turning point in Rom's work in snakebite mitigation. It became more formal, with interactions at the policy level as well. Since 1977, our newsletter *Hamadryad* has been reporting on snakebites from around the country, the first such continuous record of data, information and medical perspectives. That same year, Rom organized the first snakebite prevention and treatment seminar at the Madras Medical College, attended by doctors and paramedics from many parts of the country. In 1978, his field guide *Common Indian Snakes* was published, which plugged the phrase 'Big Four Venomous Snakes of India', often shortened to the Big Four today by clinicians, doctors, NGOs and policymakers. And most important of all, in 1978, he and his team founded the Irula Snake Catchers Industrial Cooperative Society, which remains one of the few suppliers of venoms for antivenom production in India.

But despite these efforts, the number of snakebite deaths remains the same: 50,000 or more every year. Levels of antivenom production and distribution are way below what is required. Snakebite remains one of the many human–animal conflict areas where most victims are our poorest citizens, while others are in charge of making the decisions that affect them.

Rom remains closely engaged with snakebite work fifty years after those initial interventions at the Snake Park. Snakebite Mitigation and Snake Conservation is one of the Croc Bank's most important projects, with Rom at the helm. The team's first coordinator, Ajay Kartik, had all the skills for success in the many facets of the snakebite work: fluency in English, Tamil, Hindi; great social and communication talent, and an impressive knowledge of snakes and their venoms. Working with media experts, we created videos, posters, wall murals, signboards with information on prevention and treatment and the conservation slogan 'If you like snakes, do something about snakebite!' Hundreds of presentations have been done so far, in schools, colleges, town halls and special ones for forest and fire departments, police, and other civic groups. Millions more have been reached via the short educational films.

Over the years, there has been a growing partnership with medical personnel, government departments and officials, and organizations such as Médecins Sans Frontièrs, WHO, the Indian Council for Medical Research, the National Centre for Disease Control, the Directorate General of Health Services, the Ministry of Health and Family Welfare and others.

In 2016, the USV Pharmaceutical Company made a substantial donation to our snakebite project, thanks to its chairperson Leena Tewari's personal interest in snakes. With a focus on education about snakebite prevention and treatment, these funds were used to organize presentations and workshops in the six states with the highest snakebite deaths in the country – Orissa, Bihar, Madhya Pradesh, Tamil Nadu, Jharkhand, Andhra Pradesh. Working with NGO partners in these states, tens of thousands of people have been made aware of our main message regarding snakebite: prevention. This merits a paragraph of its own.

The most practical tips for prevention are: (1) use a torch at night, walk on cleared paths, (2) use footwear, (3) avoid putting your hands and feet in places that might harbour snakes, (4) use mosquito nets. The first aid: no cutting, no tourniquet, keep the patient as calm and still as possible and get to the hospital. But then, sometimes reality rubbishes this advice because hospitals – even big, city hospitals – have not had antivenom, leading to the victim's death. Further, the timings of farmers' tasks, such as turning on and off water pumps and generators, overlap with the activities of venomous snakes such as kraits and Russell's vipers, both nocturnal hunters. The Russell's viper causes about 40 per cent of overall deaths.

Rom has been involved in the production of many films about snakebite and its treatment, all available on YouTube now, the most viewed being 'The 4 Deadliest Snakes of India'. From 2015 until 2021, when he moved to Mysore, we met with Ajay Kartik and the rest of the snakebite team every week to discuss progress and plan future actions. When Ajay left to join the Greens Zoological Rescue and Rehabilitation Centre, Gnaneswar Ch took over as coordinator; both have done wonderful work and their expertise is being used by government committees for the good of this cause, which continues to need urgent attention. The tragic fact that the number of deaths hasn't shifted from the time we started the campaign in the early 1970s indicates that there is much more to be done. Groups like 'The Global Snakebite Initiative (GSI)', of which Rom is the Project Manager for India, can help. This is an international network of scientists, doctors and activists who work together on improving prevention and treatment strategies. As GSI partners through Rom's membership, the Croc Bank has helped drive policies related to snakebite and conducted awareness programmes on prevention and treatment. We also helped with the venom sampling around the country, which resulted in the work being done at the Evolutionary Venomics Lab, Mysore University and Tezpur University. This will eventually enable India to produce an antivenom that is effective throughout the country.

Of the 350 species of snakes in India, 60 are venomous. The Big Four, the spectacled cobra, common krait, Russell's viper, and saw-scaled viper, play a major role in snakebite death statistics. The polyvalent antivenom available in India is effective for these species. But what about the other fifty-six, some of which also cause bites and deaths? The pit vipers, coral snakes, sea snakes and others? Many do not pose a threat because of low venom toxicity, or they're not 'biters' (like sea snakes and banded kraits), or since they live in restricted geographies and habitats. But some, like pit vipers, are being encountered more and more as forests shrink and they move into agricultural lands.

Another challenging aspect of snakebite treatment is the geographical venom variation within the same species of snake! This fascinating fact has become the subject of study among evolutionary biologists around the world and one that impacts effective snakebite treatment. In India, for example, antivenom is made using the Big Four snakes from only two or three districts in Tamil Nadu, supplied to laboratories by the Irular Snake Catchers' Industrial Cooperative Society [ISCICS] (more on that very soon). So, the antivenom made from these regionally specific snakes may not work or prove less effective for the same species in other corners of the country. Doctors who have treated bites in the north report having to use more antivenom, which points to this issue. To make antivenom that is effective throughout the country, it's necessary to use a pool of venoms from different regions.

Why do venoms within the same species differ? As we know, animals evolve to succeed in their habitats (unlike us, who simply destroy them). So, a snake that feeds on frogs, or even a specific species of frog, needs a different venom from one that eats rats or other warm-blooded prey. Therefore, there are myriad toxins, depending on prey, habitat and even age, because in some species, the prey of juvenile snakes differs from that of the adult. Australian brown snakes, for instance, have neurotoxic (nerve-affecting) venom as juveniles, shifting to hemotoxic (blood-focused) as they grow because the diet changes from frogs and lizards to mammals. How cool is that!

Well, not very cool for the clinicians and manufacturers whose task is to produce antivenoms. The manufacturing process of antivenom has certainly changed since Albert Calmette developed it in 1894! This is one of the key messages our snakebite mitigation team harps on at policy-level meetings and workshops. But we are now going beyond the harping. Thanks to the USV grant, we were able to collect venoms in different geographies of the country. Rom, with fellow herpetologists Gerry Martin and Ajay Kartik, travelled to Arunachal Pradesh, Maharashtra, Madhya Pradesh, Andhra Pradesh, Goa, Punjab and West Bengal, trusty liquid nitrogen canister in hand, to collect and bring back venoms of the Big Four, travelling by train to avoid airline regulations. By this time, Rom was in touch with Dr Kartik Sunagar of the Evolutionary Venomics Lab at the Indian Institute of Science in Bangalore, and Kartik began analysing the venoms collected by our team. The lab results were as expected: venoms of the same species differ significantly from region to region, and the presently available antivenom, made only from snakes collected in Tamil Nadu, does not come close to the titre or efficacy required.

Today, Rom is one of the international pilots of the snakebite mitigation ship. Much has happened since he careened around in villages near the original Snake Park, singing a Tamil rhyme he'd invented about antivenom (though he still happily performs it on request).

In 1981, he had helped start the IUCN's Snake Specialist Group, which lasted only a year or so. It has been rejuvenated recently, chaired by Daniel Natusch and at Rom's suggestion a Snakebite Task Force was formed, co-chaired by Gnaneswar. Also, with the help of Simon Pooley from the University of London and other key people, he has lobbied successfully for the IUCN/SSC Human–Wildlife Conflict and Co-existence Specialist Group Task Force to add snakebite to their agenda. He was also part of the pressure group urging WHO to put snakebite back on the list of Neglected Tropical Diseases (NTDs). This came to pass in 2017, and snakebite is now a Category A NTD – an important move as it means upgrading its documentation, policy decisions and funding.

At present, the Croc Bank is helping to extend and upgrade ISCICS to improve the quality of its venoms (and thus that of the antivenom produced by labs it supplies to). One part of the project, the most exciting, is to help the Irular start a serpentarium, preferably near the Croc Bank so we can continue supporting them. This would also mean collecting and using venoms from other parts of the country; this venom cocktail would then resolve the problem of within-species venom differences.

There's so much more to be done! Our Snakebite Mitigation and Snake Conservation project will continue for a long time to come. It's one of our most important contributions to conservation: snakebite prevention and its improved treatment will go a long way towards conserving all snakes because people will feel less afraid and desist from killing every snake they see. And as importantly, it is a vital humanitarian cause. The main victims of snakebite are our farm labourers, whose lives are difficult enough without this add-on.

Sustainable Conservation – From Skins to Venom

A lot has been documented about the snake-knowledge of the Irular – by Rom, myself, our colleagues and the media. During his wanderings with them, Rom gathered unique gems of information about the natural history of snakes in the south – from breeding biology and seasons to feeding habits, habitat preferences and temperament. Once, he and Natesan/Sureman found two female and seven male cobras snuggled up in one burrow during the mating season; another time, they saw watersnakes feeding on mosquito larvae. Sureman could interpret a faint scrape on the ground to arrive at the species, approximate size and sometimes gender. He got tired of Rom's and later my question: 'But how do you know?' The answer was always, 'From the track, of course! Didn't you see?'

The Irular are true detectives! One morning, Sureman showed us the burrow of a *vellai yelli* or gerbil, now a snake-dwelling as per the tracks he was seeing and interpreting. He

Our sons Nikhil and Samir share an iron age dolmen with Irular snakeman Doraiswamy. Coincidentally, many of the settlements of the Irular are situated at these ancient burial sites.

began thumping his crowbar this way and that, following the direction of the burrow. Every now and then he'd stop to examine the (to us) invisible signs and work out which way the tunnel turned. Sureman then walked over to a shrub and snapped off a fresh, green twig and pushed it into the winding tunnel, looking for movement. But there was none. A little more digging and the twig was inserted once again.

This time it gave a convulsive jerk; the snake was at home! He now stopped the horizontal digging and tackled the roof of the burrow. Two or three powerful strokes of the crowbar and there it was, a beautiful cobra, striking out with all the energy and verve of a cornered animal. 'He is a big person,' murmured the Irular, as he sidestepped to avoid the snake's strikes and Rom opened out a snake bag. Using a stick to protect himself, Sureman held the tail and lifted the snake gently into the bag, which Rom quickly knotted. It was a good partnership between these two hippies, one white and the other chocolate-brown, both often shirtless with their hair tied back. Wandering far and wide in the scrub forests of Chengalpattu district, they brought back some wonderful specimens for the Snake Park collection.

After bagging the cobra, Sureman stopped to wash at a muddy pool and spied a yellow head sticking out of a crab hole on the bank. Soon he was in waist-deep water with a struggling chequered keelback watersnake held firmly in one hand while he inspected the other holes for more. Later, as it began to cool down, a chocolate streak zipped by on a nearby tamarind tree. 'I'll shake this person down, be sure to catch him as he falls,' he shouted, clambering up the tree trunk. He shook the lower branch it was resting on, and soon the bronzeback tree snake sailed gracefully into Rom's arms. Most of these snake hunts took place in the picturesque countryside outside Madras, dotted with prehistoric dolmens and ancient burial sites.

Learning snake-hunting techniques from their fathers as soon as they can walk, many of the Irular develop a third eye for snakes, and seasonal microhabitats of various species are pinpointed with amazing accuracy. The ubiquitous land snakes, like the cobra, krait, Russell's viper and the saw-scaled viper, have benefited hugely from the large-scale conversion of forests to agricultural lands in recent years, and it is typically in vegetation bordering fields that they are most abundant. The alternative, seasonal habitats remain: kraits in brick and rubble piles, cobras in evergreen forests, Russell's vipers in cactus hedges and saw-scaled vipers in open, rocky places. But it is the rice field, with its abundance of rodents and plentiful supply of fresh water, that has become the refuge of the commoner species.

The Irular eat several species of rodents which abound in the agricultural areas outside of Chennai, the only instance of their being assisted by the drastic changes in the environment around them. Rodents are more canny than snakes and in hunting them, the Irular must use their cunning against the rat's deviousness. The gerbil builds long tunnels in its burrow, which often extend to several metres, with escape routes to the exits. With this species, you could dig diligently for hours while the alert rodents skip out through hidden exit holes you aren't aware of – the entire floor plan of the burrow can cover over 15 or 20 metres! So the hunter puts down his crowbar and uses an earthen pot, which he fills with dry leaves and twigs, lights it and places the opening over the main burrow hole while he blows from a small opening at the other end. Powerful gusts of smoke surge into the burrow, suffocating the rodents.

Often, of course, snake and rat catching are combined; on seeing a good rat burrow during a snake hunt, a group of Irular will separate, and sometimes the rats are cooked out in the open for the evening meal. We have often participated in such a feast, Rom gnawing away with zest, and me making a feeble pretence at eating.

At the time the *Indian Express* journalist Harry Miller first introduced Rom to the Irular in the late 1960s, and later through the early development of the Snake Park, this Adivasi community was the backbone of the snake-skin industry in South India. Many of them made a living by selling skins to tanneries; twelve rupees per cobra, the same for rat snakes and Russell's vipers, and less for smaller snakes such as chequered keelbacks and sand boas. Pythons had been overhunted and were becoming hard to find. They were also catching common kraits, abundant in the scrub forest around Madras, for the Haffkine Institute's antivenom production unit in Bombay. A good day's catch could bring in thirty or forty rupees, plus very often the incidental benefit of some rodents or mongooses for the pot. A decent living, even though the rapid spread of suburban Madras meant that they had to go further and further afield to find productive hunting areas.

With the move to Madras, Rom came face to face with the colossal size of the snakeskin market for the first time. He and other conservationists like Baba and J.C. Daniel of the BNHS realized that the industry would have to be closed down or closely regulated in spite of damaging the Irular community's interests. They were echoing the fears of herpetologist Malcolm Smith who wrote about the over-exploitation of snakes back in the 1930s in his *Fauna of British India* series. The skin trade's ecological implications were already apparent then, in the massive grain destruction by rodents once snakes, their most efficient predators, were removed from fields and adjoining forests. Though we have only preliminary data on the percentage of rodents in the diet of free-ranging snakes, there's plenty of qualitative evidence from agriculturists to show that removing large rat-eating snakes from an area is a direct invitation to the ravages of rats. One estimate is that these pests destroy a staggering 30–50 per cent of the country's stored and standing grain every year. The director of a group of tea estates in the Nilgiri Hills once visited us to ask if the Snake Park could supply him with rat snakes to release in his 5,000-acre plantation, since the natural predators of rats such as snakes and birds of prey had disappeared following the removal of adjoining forest tracts. His estimated annual loss was staggering. Apart from destroying the roots of tea plants, the prolific rat holes weakened slopes, causing erosion and landslides. A rice farmer from the Cumbum Valley in Madurai district wrote to say that he followed the increasingly common practice of hiring Irular rat catchers every season, paying a bounty of one rupee per rat. He claimed this worked out far cheaper than the damage that the pests caused to his crops. At the governmental level, a rat advisory board was constituted to evaluate and control rodent damage. At the same time, an average of 5 million snakeskins were being exported each year; the Adam tannery in Madras did a brisk business of 5,000 skins a day during the boom period between the early 1950s and 1970s.

In 1976, the Government of India banned the export of snakeskins and put a stop to this wasteful trade. But for the Irular hunter-gatherers, the new legislation was disastrous; they lost their single effective means of earning a livelihood. The psychological implications were as important as the practical. 'I've always thought of myself as a snake catcher, and been proud of it,' said Sureman to Rom. 'Now I must be like everyone else, grubbing around in the city for work, like a bear digging for termites.'

The skin trade ban was actually the last nail in the Irular coffin. Some 60,000 Irular lived in Chengalpattu and neighbouring districts, hunting and gathering food and saleable produce from the forest. But the scrub forests, which had been their hunting grounds, were fast disappearing under the heavy hand of 'development'. Places where they had hunted monitor lizards, mongooses and other game became the city's margins and suburbs. Further, most species that were important food requirements, except rats, were included in the Wildlife (Protection) Act, 1972, a necessary piece of legislation but one which disregarded the question of local protein sources, as well as the conservation status of some. In time, the most common species of softshell turtle, the food of thousands of protein-starved people, was protected under the Wildlife Act, and the penalty for catching, buying or using these prolific turtles is up to six years in jail and a heavy fine.

This dual role – that of befriending and working with the Irular and at the same time campaigning for the closure of the skin trade – was an uncomfortable one for Rom; he was working both for and against their interests, a paradox about which Sureman needled him often. 'Hey man, you give us money with one hand, and take it away with the other!' But he – and many other Irular – realized the ecological necessity for terminating the skin industry.

One day, Sureman and other Irular came to us to ask for help in applying to the government for farmland. But they soon agreed that it wouldn't be a workable proposition; their instincts and traditions are based on mobility and the solution lay elsewhere. Rom began to think about a project that would use their snake-catching skills within the framework of the new laws.

Slowly, things started coming together and the typewriter

– by now an impressive one donated by Godrej – began to clack. Letters and draft proposals went out to friends in the conservation circle including Baba. If an Irular cooperative was formed and registered, and the Big Four venomous snakes were caught by its members and released back into the wild after several venom extractions, it could become a sustainable project encompassing both Adivasi livelihoods and snakebite mitigation. Not only would it resurrect the their occupation and preserve their heritage as hunter-gatherers, it would also play a significant role in the medical world. Antivenom is made by injecting snake venom into horses in increasing doses, then drawing their blood and purifying the serum, which contains the vital antibodies that combat the invasion of venom. The production and distribution of antivenom was far short of the actual needs of the country and most health centres still did not stock it, leading to 50,000 annual deaths. A venom cooperative run by the Irular could save lives by supplying venoms of the Big Four, from which polyvalent antivenom is made. At the same time, the snakes would not be killed, making it a model wildlife management programme.

'Hey Sureman, an Irular venom factory!' said Rom, slapping Natesan on the back. '*Yenna solreenge?*' (What do you say?) Sureman agreed that it was a good idea: good for snakes, good for his people. Unfortunately, he did not live to see the fruits of his long sessions with Rom in the palm leaf office of the Snake Park. A draft of the cooperative's detailed working structure was ready just before he died. Baba helped with this and was supportive of the project. But others in the WWF were reluctant to put their stamp on it. Those were the 'total preservation' days, a necessary stage to be sure in the evolution of wildlife conservation. Rom wrote to the international headquarters of WWF, which he still represented in South India and which had supported his work with donations. Their response was a theoretical approval but a reluctance to be involved with a resource exploitation project. It is very much to their credit that ten years later the Indian chapter of the WWF gave the cooperative a substantial loan, which enabled it to shift its premises from the Snake Park to the Crocodile Bank and get off the ground.

But to backtrack a little, in his reply to WWF International in November 1973, Rom stepped right into the quagmire of the delicate issue of wildlife utilization. He wrote:

> I believe we have brought up a very important policy issue that cannot be quickly dismissed by saying that we (WWF) should not lend our name to schemes of controlled wildlife exploitation. In a sense we have already done that by endorsing institutions like zoos and the Madras Snake Park.
>
> The exploiters of wildlife are in a fairly secure position as long as they have only to deal with confused and vague local wildlife laws and petty officials. Perhaps it

is time that the zoo trade, biological supply trade and the skin trade be gradually pressured into following the recommendations and rulings of the internationally prestigious World Wildlife Fund and the International Union for Conservation of Nature. The best way to know what is going on in this business is to be in it. Who is better suited to evolve and guide a scheme which, while carefully exploiting wildlife, also has a finger on the pulse of the trade than WWF?

If we help establish a biological supply house owned and operated by an Irular Tribal Co-operative and endorsed by our organization, we would soon know which animal species are in demand, where and how they are caught, transported and sold, and in what numbers. Just this one positive aspect from support of a controlled wildlife exploitation scheme might prevent several animal species from reaching endangered status.

The poachers and dealers in rare animal products are always a few steps ahead of us, because of the commercial motivation. The present WWF policy shows a weakness in an organization dedicated to keeping animal species from extinction. At the frightening rate that wild habitat is being destroyed in this country, there is no doubt in any of us that little wildlife can exist outside of sanctuaries. It is a difficult issue, I realize, but I believe that the organization and guidance of wildlife-economy-based tribes is one step toward controlling the trade in Indian wildlife.

Baba, then vice president of WWF-India and one of the vice presidents of the IUCN, wrote to WWF International that 'the sustained exploitation of all natural and wildlife resources is the basic policy of the World Wildlife Fund, and I think that Whitaker has raised an important matter and we should give it serious thought. I support his suggestion that an Irular cooperative be set up.' Baba also wrote to several government officials about Rom's scheme for the cooperative and there was considerable enthusiasm. Dr N.R. Krishnan, Director, Department of Science and Technology, wrote, 'I met Dr B.D. Sharma, Joint Secretary, Tribal Welfare and his assistants in the Ministry of Home Affairs on the 30th June 1977. I handed over to them copies of Romulus's paper. They evinced keen interest in the proposal and felt quite enthused about it . . .'

Venom is one of the most valuable wildlife resources on Earth, many times more valuable than gold, depending on the species. We loved the idea that the Irular, one of the poorest of our Adivasi groups, should produce one of the most pricey products in the country. At that time, a gram of krait venom cost three thousand rupees, ten times the price of gold. About fifty kraits are needed to make one gram. In real terms, that means fifty kraits are potentially worth three thousand rupees. In the skin trade, this number was worth not more than a few hundred. Thus, the venom industry would use far fewer snakes to generate a much greater income for the Irular.

Baba reminded us often that the cooperative should be pursued and established in spite of seemingly endless red tape. He wisely realized that it would have important repercussions in the development of India's conservation policies. So, in 1978 we went ahead and registered it with the Industries and Commerce Department. The Forest Department was approached for permission to catch five thousand snakes per year for venom production, a number that one large tannery could have processed in one day during the skin trade. The project hibernated. As in the early Snake Park days when he was applying for land at Guindy, Rom laid siege at Fort St George, Tamil Nadu's administrative headquarters, knocking on the doors of tribal welfare and forestry officials and being told 'Please come again next week'. During one such visit, a fat cockroach scampered out in surprise when the relevant file was opened and we gave up for a while.

Then we had the good fortune to meet and become friends with Revati Mukerjee, who was to play a key role in the cooperative's establishment. She had given up her job and was looking for something interesting and rewarding to do. We made her the offer of running a problem-ridden cooperative without pay. 'But in two years,' Rom assured her, 'the cooperative will be rolling in the stuff, the Irular driving around in Cadillacs and you can name your price.' The reality was a little different; and in any case, money wasn't what she was looking for.

After several months of chasing around government offices, Revati obtained the necessary permits and licences and the cooperative was in business by mid-1978. Each of the initial sixty Irular members had an identity card and a licence number. Detailed records had to be kept and submitted to the Forest Department on the numbers and species of snakes caught and the amount of venom extracted. This was because all snakes were now protected under the Wildlife Act. One of the conditions on the government order allowing us to function was that 25 per cent of the gross profit from venom sales would be paid as royalty to the Forest Department. This was surprising, to say the least, considering the cooperative is a tribal self-help project and not a commercial business.

The first venom order came from King Institute, Madras, one of the five major producers of antivenom serum in India. We faced the familiar old bugbear: how could we start operating as quickly as possible, with very limited capital? All of us had pooled in our private resources to pay the fifty-rupee membership for each Irular member, besides which there was two thousand rupees in the bank from donations. This was not nearly enough to buy all the equipment we needed. The major expenditure would be cages for the snakes and several carpenters were called in to give estimates, all of which were too high for our budget. Finally, it was the simple clay pot which saved the day. Rom borrowed an idea from the snake catchers of Shirala who keep their snakes in mud pots for the Naag Panchami festival. At two or three rupees each, they were cheap, cool, secure and easy to move around; the perfect snake cages. Wetted down periodically during the hot months and with a water dish in each, the snakes seemed to approve of them.

From the start, functioning from a small room at the Snake Park on borrowed money, the cooperative filled an important gap as supplier of Big Four venoms, and soon its outstanding orders totalled over a kilogram. Several individual donors and companies gave us help without which it would not have been possible to function. Our friends Dino and Sandhya Mazumdar lent generous support, as did Oxfam India, and the British High Commissioner in Delhi donated a sophisticated electronic weighing machine, a vast improvement on the little jeweller's scale that swung wildly with every breath of breeze.

After a year of operating at the Snake Park, the Croc Bank trustees agreed to give the coop a plot of land on a nominal lease. There was a lot more space here and tourists could come and see the snakes for a small fee of fifty paise. The gate collection soon covered the basic day-to-day expenses. Irular snake catchers with licences from the Forest Department would start arriving by bus around 7.30 a.m. with muddy snake bags. They came from Thiruporur, Perungalathur, Chitlapakkam and other Irular settlements.

After a cup of tea and a chat, the process of buying snakes would begin, and Rajendran, the assistant to the manager and himself an Irular, would weigh, measure and inspect each snake. He marked it with a permanent code number by clipping a combination of its belly scales so that every snake was identifiable. Details of where it was caught and any unusual circumstances were noted in a ledger and the snake was placed in a vacant clay pot, with its code number and species marked on it. K 468, for instance, would be the four hundred and sixty-eighth krait caught. In fact, K 468 became famous because it bit Gopal, one of the best snake catchers.

Ramachandran, an Irular cooperative director, readies his hunting implements. He specialized in cobras and Russell's vipers, the main snakes found near his village of Thiruporur.

The ISCICS continues to function, forty-five years later, but is now managed by the Department of Industries and Commerce. Unlike other venom labs, it only keeps snakes in captivity for three weeks. After three extractions of venom over this period, one week apart, the snakes are released back into the wild. 'Release days' are busy ones at the cooperative. Rajendran puts up a 'Closed to Visitors' sign at the gates and he and others start packing the snakes to be released. Often there are well over a hundred to be bagged. On one such memorable day in 1984, at the end of the saw-scaled viper season (the winter months), we joined them in setting 4,000 of these vipers free. It was quite a sight. It's amazing how hundreds of snakes can just disappear in the surrounding jungle in seconds! Nevertheless, we kept our eyes on the ground as we walked back to the jeep.

The smallest of the Big Four, it takes large numbers of saw-scaled vipers to produce a gram of venom.

The recapture of released snakes was an opportunity to collect the first data on the growth rates and migration of wild snakes in India. The co-op keeps careful notes about all the snakes and is scratching the surface of the mysteries of snakes' lives. Rom made sure that such research became an important part of the co-op's operation. As he says, we must learn about the animals we use. Looking closely at snake faeces isn't everybody's idea of fun. But the co-op has checked literally thousands of samples in the last few years and has plenty of evidence to show that all these snakes prey largely on rats and mice.

In the early days, it was Rajendran and Chockalingam, members of the coop living on the premises, who took care of the routine work and conducted venom extractions that visitors could watch. I never tired of watching Choky open one of the clay pots with expert ease and, with a snake hook, gently lift a cobra on to the small central platform in the square pit where the snakes are kept. It is a smooth operation with a minimum of trauma for the snake, which Choky makes graceful. The head is pinned to the ground with the rubber handle of the hook as he steps gently on the tail to give himself the leverage to keep the snake from thrashing and injuring itself. He holds it carefully behind the neck so it can't turn around and bite. This is a crucial stage when most accidents happen; Russell's vipers, for instance, with their long, curved fangs, can bite right through their lower jaw and into the handler's thumb. But Choky was probably one of the best snake handlers in the world and kept every contingency in mind as he played this dangerous game with hundreds of deadly venomous snakes every week.

Thus caught, right hand behind the neck, left hand supporting the tail, the snake is carried to the conical venom

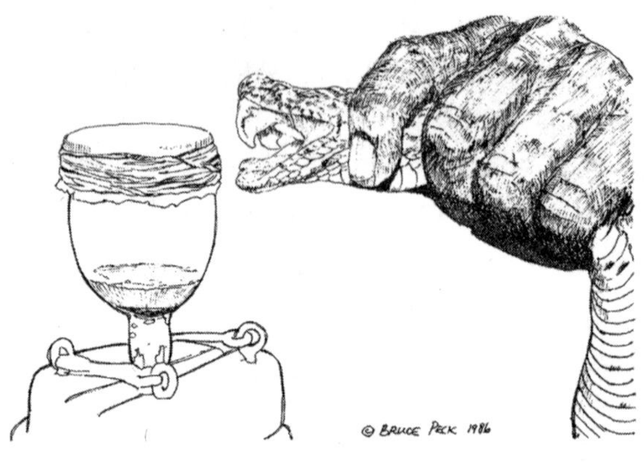

Extracting venom

glass clamped to a stand and with a piece of rubberized cloth stretched tight across the opening. One watches carefully at this stage and visitors hold their breath and comments as the snake's head is brought towards the venom glass. With a sudden forward jab, the jaws clamp onto the rubber sheet. Golden drops of venom, deadly but also life-giving, trickle down the sides of the glass. The quantity of venom varies greatly from snake to snake; one cobra may refuse to yield any venom at all during repeated sessions, while the next will bite energetically and spew a generous quantity. The saw-scaled viper's small size and vibrant energy make it perhaps the hardest species to handle; besides, it takes hundreds of these snakes to make up a gram of venom. One marathon day, Choky extracted venom from 600 'sawskies' and was bitten twice, but luckily with no ill effects.

The liquid venom is frozen and dried under a high vacuum. The powder retains its potency and antigenic properties. Bottled in this form, it is easy to handle and send in the post. Today, ISCICS remains one of the few producers of snake venom in India and our national antivenom production is largely dependent on it.

Rom's experience of working with Bill Haast at the Miami Serpentarium helped the Irular to produce high quality venoms. Haast himself was very supportive of the cooperative and its work. Producing venom involves much more than grabbing a snake and making it bite a container. It's a complicated chemical and the quality depends on the health of the snake, its food and care. Venom that is contaminated, or not properly processed or stored, can't be used to make antivenom. Haast fed his king cobras a high protein mixture with a feeding gun, but at the cooperative, the short duration of the snake's captivity eliminates feeding altogether. They are given water, of course. We also started another arm of ISCICS, which never really took off but which we hope to resurrect – RATS, the rat and termite eradication programme. Rats are undeniably the scourge of our crops, both standing and stored, and pesticides are no solution, apart from creating deadly complications. The Irular approach is based on their knowledge of the rat's natural history: they dig and smoke them out more efficiently than any poison could work. The Oxfam Trust in India supported this programme and provided a jeep for its use as well as for the weekly snake releases. The RATS idea had germinated years ago soon after our marriage, when Rom and I spent a few days at the Central Food Technology Research Institute in Mysore with a group of Irular. The staff of the Institute were impressed with the possibilities of using them as an alternative to pesticides.

We ran some rough-and-ready field trials, and felt it would be possible to eradicate rats by using Irular skills (and with no damage to the environment and wildlife). In nine months in 1986, 56 rat-catching field trials were made and 2,131 rodents caught. The cost of catching each rat was one rupee and sixty-five paise. In this study, calculating the average amount that rats eat and destroy, about 15,000 kilograms of foodgrains were saved, valued at forty-five thousand rupees. The total investment in Irular labour, on the other hand, was thirty-five thousand rupees.

The most destructive rat in rice fields in our area is the lesser mole rat while the bandicoot, house rat and the brown rat operate mostly in godowns and warehouses. These, plus a couple more, destroy a big percentage of India's food resources every year. The true potential of the rat's destructive powers becomes apparent when walking with the Irular in the paddy fields. They often find 5–6 kilograms of rice, paddy or peanuts in just one rat hole; enough to feed a family for two or three days. Surely, RATS has the potential to employ thousands of Irular and other rat-catching Adivasis, and the best part is that rodents aren't on the Wildlife (Protection) Act, 1972; so permits and licences would not be required!

The largest benefit for ISCICS members is the income they earn from catching the Big Four snakes, and the welfare budget that includes money for school fees, uniforms, loans for house repairs and medical expenses. But much more important in the long run, it was through ISCICS that the Irular were drawn into a process of decision-making and planned action, which proved important for their future. Their newfound self-assertion and confidence became apparent at the general body meetings, which were initially silent affairs, at which our suggestions were met with acquiescent nods. It is no longer so. While discussing controversial issues such as snake prices and bonuses, three or four simultaneous arguments would erupt and issues sometimes had to be voted on. But it goes beyond the capacity to decide; the Irular are learning the art of taking decisions that are unfavourable to them personally but beneficial to the collective body of members. For example, one year a few members wanted the price of kraits to be raised. This was possible, but it would trigger a chain reaction that would be disadvantageous to the development of the venom market; it would mean fewer snakes, less venom and the slowing down of business orders. They decided to maintain the same prices.

At one point, a petition was received from three troublemakers who had complained to the Forest Department about the 'mismanagement' of the cooperative. The group later claimed that they had been coerced into signing these allegations and resigning from the cooperative; but their wild accusations had contributed to the closure of the cooperative for six months by the government. The ISCICS had finally gone to court and obtained a stay order on the closure. Anyway, the little renegade group asked to be forgiven and allowed to become members once more. There was a long, heated discussion and we encouraged the members to forgive and forget and take them back, pointing out that it was a victory for the cooperative that they wanted to return. But Rajammal, an expert snake catcher and one of the seven directors of the cooperative, raised her fist and sat up on her haunches in readiness for a fight. 'Okay, *dorai*,' (Okay, sir) she addressed Rom, 'if we do as you say and take them back, and if they get up to the same tricks – then who will be responsible? You?'

There has been great interest in and support for the ISCICS's work, both in India and abroad. This includes donations from many individuals and organizations, including Norad, Oxfam and WWF. But it has been through some bad patches, mostly because of false, jealousy-driven allegations that led to long-drawn-out investigations. The red tape is also formidable, and permits, such as snake-catching licences, sometimes take several months to renew. During this interim period, when they are not allowed to catch snakes, the Irular have little or no income. It's not only the Irular who suffer but also the antivenom industry, which is already hard put to keep up with the national antivenom demand.

Soon after the ISCICS got established, we embarked on another exciting project with the Irular; this time, with the women. In November 1986, while sorting the otherwise mundane daily mail – requests for reprints, information on snakes, bites – we came upon a winner: approval of a grant from the National Wasteland Development Board (NWBD) for an agro-forestry project. We had asked the NWDB to help us with land and jobs for Irular families through a new society, the Irula Tribe Women's Welfare Society (ITWWS). Most Irular women do not catch snakes but are knowledgeable about medicinal plants and their use, as well as germinating and nurturing trees. We felt these could mesh well with the vision of the NWDB, and luckily they thought the same.

The funds came in and then began the period of locating swathes of wasteland in Chengalpattu district and taking tea with village officers, revenue inspectors and tahsildars. Fortunately, the assistant collector at that time, Dr Prasada Rao, was very helpful and interested. Finding land with no squatters or other claimants proved to be difficult but finally, 700 acres were identified in Echoor village, and the paper-pushing began. The idea was to plant it with indigenous, timber and medicinal species, with the advice of expert tree people in Auroville, and settle some landless Irular families there to look after the growing forest. It was an exciting effort – a chance to grow a forest from scratch and to nurture and use a private ecosystem.

But it came to a heart-rending and violent end about a decade later. Local timber merchants must have been eyeing the increasingly valuable timber, and one night, set fire to the thatch huts where the staff and Canadian volunteer Mike Miller were living. They were able to escape, and the land and its assets were taken over by the miscreants in spite of appeals to officials and a police case. Fortunately, this was not the end of our efforts on behalf of Irular women, because a friend of Baba's, Shankar Ranganathan, gave us a donation to buy land for the society, which we did in the village of Thandari. Womankind Worldwide, Action Aid, Kindernothilfe, the Canada Fund and others pitched in, and we soon had a beautiful building, medicinal plant nursery, seed bank and offices buzzing with activity. Village *sangams* or committees and staff work on the key issues within the community, which include land ownership, drinking water, access to welfare schemes and education and violence against women. Rom and I resigned from the Executive Committee of the ITWWS in 2016, feeling that it was time to hand over the reins to the community, and this has been a good decision in spite of some initial chaos as leadership decisions were made. At times I wondered if we'd done the right thing, and there were guilt pangs as I heard stories about verbal battles, petitions, accusations and such. But it has settled down.

The work of the ITWWS and its achievements, although the path was not always easy, is a great source of satisfaction, because it helped Irular women stand up for their rights . . . and hold conversations with government officials in loud, confident, strident voices. The venom unit, rat-catching programme and the ITWWS all help the Irular to take pride in what they have to offer and rebuild the confidence that is a prerequisite for Adivasi people to thrive. And perhaps, in time, these two organizations, the ISCICS and ITWWS, will become prototypes for Adivasis in other parts of the country; and the emphasis will shift from teaching these communities to learning from them. How cool that would be!

Centre for Herpetology

In 1994, in the twentieth year of our marriage, Rom asked for a divorce and if there's such a thing as a heart breaking, then mine did, and I heard it.

I was then teaching at the Kodaikanal International School (KIS), which meant free education for the boys. The principal, Dr Paul Wiebe, gave me a carte blanche on leave to recuperate; I will never forget his generosity and support. My wonderful sons Nikhil (by then in the Gedhai School in the Nilgiris) and Samir, aged sixteen and twelve, made room in their hearts for me in spite of their own pain and loss, and my sister Shama, brother Murad and sister-in-law Irmela, our parents, the school's wonderful counsellor Kristin Kehler and friends like Bimla, Betsy, Evelyn, Jayashree, Pippa, Tikku, Aruna, Jody, kept me going. And many others. Kodai looks after its own.

In 2000 when Samir graduated and left for college, I moved to Bangalore, to teach at The International School, Bangalore. It wasn't a good fit for me; and I moved back to Chennai, to our house adjoining the Croc Bank, to be with Nikhil who had been working there since he'd finished school. I helped out at the Croc Bank for six months, then took the position of principal of Abacus Montessori School for two years, until our beloved Shama – by then a well-known novelist and teacher at the National School of Drama – was diagnosed with pancreatic cancer. I left Abacus to be with her for her last few months. She died in December 2004 and my heart broke again.

I moved to Bangalore to support and be supported by my parents, and worked as principal of a school started by the CNN Trust – Outreach School (named by my mother). But my heart and mind hated city life and hankered for natural landscapes. When KIS asked me to return and set up their Special Needs department in 2006, I accepted and moved back there, making frequent trips to Bangalore on the juddering overnight bus. Being involved with the Palani Hills Conservation Council, and talking to people like Pippa Mukherjee, Bob Stewart and Tanya Balcar, made me feel closer to the conservation world, which helped me continue to write about the environment. By that time I had written nine or ten children's books, mainly on the environment, and today that number has doubled – my contribution to the rapidly exacerbating climate and biodiversity tragedy.

I was by then trustee emeritus of the Croc Bank, as was Rom, and kept in close touch with its work (and many ups and downs) through Nikhil, who had stuck it out in spite of the long absences of Rom and others while they were engaged in fieldwork in the Andamans and elsewhere. I missed him. Samir had completed the Conservation Leadership course in Cambridge, UK, and then been hired by BirdLife International, delighted that his office was in the David Attenborough building. And even better, it had a Sálim Ali auditorium! He would soon marry, and bring lovely Lenke Balint into our family. Lenke also works in the conservation world, and both are increasingly engaged with business conservation partnerships.

During my years at Kodai School, Rom's career and interests had moved into making wildlife films, several of which earned awards and unprecedented viewing. The most well known of these are probably *King Cobra* (Nat Geo), *Snakehunter*, *North America* (Nat Geo) and *One Million Snakebites* (BBC Natural World). His trips to Kodai had become less frequent and his travels to other parts of India (to film) and abroad (for production/editing) more so. Along the way, he also resigned as the Croc Bank's director and its administration was in the hands of several others – initially Harry Andrews, then Patrick Aust, Colin Stevenson, then Gowri Mallapur. Gowri played the dual role of vet and director until she left in December 2014 to start a conservation trust of her own, in Goa.

By that time, having taught for eighteen years, I had decided to switch back to a conservation-centric life. I needed to continue working, having trusted untrustworthy people with my savings, and rashly gone through the (generous) divorce settlement that Rom had given me. Fortunately, part of this was our property in Kodai, which I would later sell and use the money to improve our family home next to the Croc Bank. I was wondering where to apply when a (nice) shocker landed in my Inbox – an email from Rom on behalf of the Croc Bank trustees, asking if I would accept a position at the Madras Crocodile Bank Trust (MCBT). By the time I moved there, the director's seat was vacant, and I was asked to occupy it. I accepted, with fear and joy.

So, by 1 January 2015, I was living near and working closely with Nikhil, who was – and continues to be – a wonderful pal. But those early years weren't easy. The close proximity of Rom and his wife Janaki Lenin, who were living near Chengalpattu, brought surges of self-pity. Then came another surge: of wind and water, as Cyclone Vardah of 2016 ripped through our campus and brought down trees on crocodile pens and buildings. The MCBT's bank balance was sliding gracefully downhill and income – expenditure systems needed tightening; the staff was disgruntled and divided; there was confusion at field stations and projects; the electric network was shocking (literally) and needed replacement; a large hotel (Sheraton Grande) was being constructed cheek-by-jowl with metallic shrieks, booms and bright lights, and our own home was in bad shape and practically uninhabitable (except by staunch Nikhil, who had survived a tree fall within metres of him during a storm, live wires sparking like firecrackers, and a close shave with the tsunami of 2004).

I was excited about being back at the Croc Bank but less than eager about budgets and accounts; luckily, our number-savvy trustee Samit Sawhny agreed to supervise this area. Our entire trustees group is resourceful and supportive, each with their own area of expertise that is generously shared. And one day, while I was (once again) scratching my head about something, I remembered Baba's wise words after the divorce. 'Look for your mainstays. Surprising ones can turn up.' I decided that, whether he liked it or not, Rom remained one of mine, and also the Croc Bank's. We needed his expertise and knowledge, to ensure the progress of our goals: research, conservation, education. In the intervening two decades, he and I had continued to discuss and work together on the multiple issues and crises that surfaced at the ITWWS, ISCICS, Croc Bank and the three field stations, determined that the divorce wouldn't affect the conservation work we had started and developed together. I now suggested that he come to the Croc Bank once a week for an extended talk with us; especially on the Snakebite Mitigation Project. He was happy to do so and soon after this, thanks to the USV grant, we began building a snakebite mitigation team to expand this work. Rom's visits were also a time when he and Nikhil could discuss Croc Bank work, and have father–son chats. In 2021, he and Janaki moved to Hunsur near Mysore, but thanks to the post-COVID online world, he keeps in close touch with the work of the Croc Bank, especially that of our work on snakebite.

His initial visits had some awkward moments but it got easier with time. He agreed to accompany me to meetings at the ITWWS, offices of forest and wildlife bureaucracy, and conversations with funders, filmmakers and others when I felt his presence (especially the selfies!) would make a difference. And it did.

Over time, I began to realize that there was another mainstay; a more quiet, low-key one but someone who often came up with good advice and perspective. Nikhil had been at the Croc Bank for almost twenty years by then, since he graduated from school except for the time at the Charles Darwin University, Australia, where he completed his master's in Wildlife Management. I am happy that I can acknowledge his contribution here, both to the Croc Bank and to me personally.

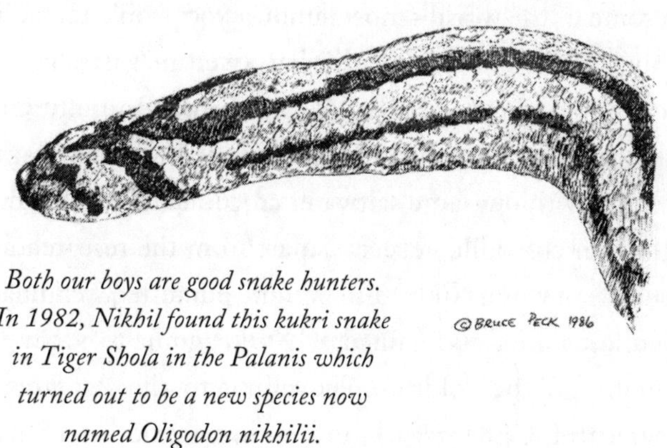

Both our boys are good snake hunters. In 1982, Nikhil found this kukri snake in Tiger Shola in the Palanis which turned out to be a new species now named Oligodon nikhilii.

His work with crocodiles began when he was but a wee lad, when he'd 'help' the staff catch hatchlings to measure growth or for transfer to another pen, and watch and imitate research students candling eggs, recording temperatures and other croc-related tasks. Of course, he'd been whisked off to Papua New Guinea at the age of five months, and spent parts of the next eighteen months in his pram or 'backpack' with us in tepid croc habitats or at the Moitaka Crocodile Farm where Rom worked. Once he was made to do a 'hero pose' in front of a New Guinea crocodile nest (both mother and nest were behind a chain link barrier, so he was not in danger). Another time, sitting in the baby seat on Rom's back, he peered over Dada's shoulder at the cluster of highly venomous banded sea snakes he was (foolishly) holding.

By tenth grade, his career goal was to do a doctorate in crocodile biology and work at the Croc Bank. Both have been accomplished, the bonus being the opportunity to work with some of the world's most famous croc people including catching 'freshies' on the McKinley River in Australia with famous croc man Grahame Webb. He was initially Croc Bank's assistant curator, and during that time had a scary adventure with our large saltwater crocodile Jaws III, which taught him crocodile–respect. Apart from the research and conservation work, Nikhil also became interested in human–crocodile conflict and gained a UNDP grant to study the problem and the solution. Travelling to the Andamans, Maharashtra, Chhattisgarh and elsewhere, he interviewed victims, did training workshops for Forest Departments in restraint and capture, and helped transfer 'nuisance animals'. Those trips also brought in a lot of new experiences and ideas. For instance, at the confluence of the Krishna and Warna rivers in Maharashtra, he saw a 'croc watcher' at work – a good system to warn people who were in the water, usually women washing clothes.

He is also quite the chelonian guy and has collected eleven species of freshwater turtles including four Critically Endangered ones. Under his care, the Croc Bank was the first place where Travancore tortoises bred, and our chelonian rewilding includes twenty-six red-crowned roof turtles released in Uttar Pradesh.

The kachuga, a turtle found in the Ganga, is among the endangered species being bred at the Croc Bank. The male is striking and dons brilliant colours during the breeding season.

My own special interest is education, and soon after I took over, we applied for and received a grant from the Oracle Giving Grant Program, to upgrade the Croc Bank's education programme, including the signboards. I enjoyed learning about this new and different kind of writing and the importance of pictorial communication in our seriously multilingual country. Visitor communication and interaction points are so important for a conservation centre like ours, and this has been a key interest area for me. Over the years, I've planned many new signboards for the Croc Bank as well as passed on my learnings to visiting staff from other zoos.

At the start of the Croc Bank in 1976, we had a tanned mugger skin on display with a 'Please Touch' sign, which was very popular. Unfortunately, the popularity frayed it to bits. It fell apart and had to be removed. I'd thought often that we should replace it, this time protected under glass. When our 5-metre saltie Jaws III died on 13 January 2020, it was a sad day for everyone, especially Nikhil, who had known him since he was the croc equivalent of a tadpole. I had to use all my tact and diplomacy when I phoned him – he was in the field, on the Cauvery – to suggest that we skin Jaws to preserve his legacy and gain a unique exhibit. It felt like asking someone to preserve a beloved friend. But he was able to push aside the sentiment, and another call brought Rom to the Croc Bank. We all stood around as our vet Dr Ruchika made the first cut. Rom called zookeeper friends and herpetologists abroad for advice, which we also got from the internet, as well as the leather research institute where Jaws was originally from. A volunteer was dispatched to the city to buy the salt and chemicals needed to preserve the skin. I provided fans and cold drinks to help deal with the stench. The operation lasted for some eight or nine hours, ending well after dark. Then began the bureaucratic runaround, getting permits from the Forest Department to transport the skin to the city for tanning, and then more paperwork to bring it back, and finally, one day about a year later, the legacy of Jaws was mounted in a handsome glass-fronted cabinet in the interpretation centre.

One of my first, and least fun, tasks when I returned to the Croc Bank as director in 2015 was to close down a swatch of field projects that were going nowhere. The disappointment in their progress was not the most serious problem. Tardiness in submitting accounts and reports from field staff was affecting our relationship with funding agencies and more importantly, our accounts process. From misguided kindness, we had adopted projects in order to help sincere biologists doing important fieldwork. But administering these had become a daymare. With Assistant Director Allwin Jesudasan's competence in accounts, we were able to set things right and terminate the projects, making some enemies in the process.

Today, the Croc Bank has an impressive collection of animals – over forty species of reptiles including fifteen crocodilians. In 1993, the trustees added the tag 'Centre for

Herpetology' to its name, to indicate that its work wasn't just limited to crocodiles but all reptiles. The year after I rejoined, we received komodos from the Bronx Zoo in New York in exchange for some juvenile gharial. Being large animals that tend to be aggressive, it is important to enrich (train) komodos so that husbandry tasks become easier. Using a target stick with a colourful balloony object at one end, Ajay and Nikhil taught them to approach it calmly, and that it was not associated with food! They could thus be moved around for enclosure cleaning, vet care and feeding, with minimum stress.

It's good to see that the Croc Bank has become a resource for other zoos and reptile collections as far afield as Cambodia, where Ajay and Nikhil travelled to train keepers about husbandry procedures for Siamese crocodiles. At the Bank, we have been conducting workshops on croc handling, vet care, snake rescue and snakebite mitigation for many years and our work has inspired a host of young people working in the field of herpetology and conservation in India and elsewhere, many of whom have been a part of the Croc Bank's volunteer and intern programmes.

I was lucky to work with two great assistant directors, both of whom left a significant mark; before Allwin, there was Yamini Bhaskar, who helped to organize our fortieth anniversary at the Radisson Blu hotel in Mamallapuram. Luckily, the Croc Bank has always been able to attract some truly special staff, each of whom has contributed to its growth and development.

Soon after I rejoined, Rom and I decided to open up a conservation officer position; we felt that as one of the oldest conservation organizations in the country, the Croc Bank should be stepping out more in that space, especially given the dismal environmental outlook in our surroundings. When ex-volunteer Ganesh Muthiah applied, we grabbed him. He engaged tirelessly with our greatest challenge, the noise from neighbouring hotels and beach resorts during their loud events for weddings and other functions. This had been a problem practically from the time we started the Croc Bank, because deafening noise has become a part of Indian festivities, the louder the better. But now, we began measuring the decibel levels and found that they were hitting over eighty at times, well within the range of medical damage to humans and animals, with the wedding and other 'events' sometimes lasting way beyond the regulated time of 10 p.m. In response to our posts about this on social media, other zoos came forward verbally with their own, similar, problems with noise, but were reluctant to put anything in writing. If anything, the stress factor for their animal collections is even higher, as they include mammals.

The Noise Pollution (Regulation and Control) Rules, 2000, mandates a maximum of 55 decibels (db), and 85 db can cause hearing loss. Firecrackers routinely exceed 140 db, and weddings and other 'events' often go well over 80–90 db. In February 2020, a bridegroom in Telangana died of a heart attack during his own wedding festivities and the news item reported that 'the high decibel sound of the music played during (the) baraat might have triggered the cardiac arrest'.[1]

We were getting increasingly worried about the safety of the animals and felt more and more certain that it was the high decibels from a nearby 'event' that had caused the death of one of our Cuban crocodiles. An oft-quoted incident connecting noise and crocodile deaths took place in 1989 in South Africa where twenty-six Nile crocodiles died from blasting at a construction site 2 kilometres away.

One of our trustees was instrumental in contacting the Department of Mechanical Engineering at IIT Madras for help with the sound recording, to ensure the accuracy of our equipment and measure the discrepancy between regulations and reality. The IIT team made several visits with their cumbersome, sophisticated equipment and their final report supported our contention that commercial establishments in our area needed to lower their noise levels in the interests of our zoo as well as wildlife, including sea turtles, birds and the small mammals that are holding out here in spite of the rampant development. Ganesh, in spite of having had to resign following his father's death and family responsibilities, continues to help us with this issue; we owe much to this long-term friend of the Croc Bank. In the meantime, the decibel levels have reduced, and some hotels are trying to convince their customers that high decibel levels are not part of the services the hotel can offer. But it's early days, and more work remains to be done.

As Rom and I became comfortable as colleagues, I made more demands on him, and one fine day threw out the question 'Why don't you go and meet him?'

The question was in the context of our 'surplus mugger' issue. We had bred and reared hundreds of mugger for release in the wild, as requested by the Tamil Nadu Forest Department in their G.O. of 8 December 1978, but another order dated 8 June 1994 informed us that the rewilding project had hit a snag and would not be implemented. As a result, we had a serious problem – a problem of plenty – with its attendant needs of expenditure and space. Before the 'stop' signal came, we had supplied 460 mugger to Tamil Nadu and other states for rewilding, but still had way too many.

Rom and I began to focus on this issue back then and approached several private enterprises and state Forest Departments with the offer of donating the surplus stock. We visited and wrote to Forest Department officials in Tamil Nadu, Goa, Maharashtra, Andhra Pradesh and

Chhattisgarh, and provided Rom's detailed description of how to set up and run a croc farm, using it as the core for a conservation and education centre. We hoped that the Tamil Nadu government would take some responsibility for the animals since they had been bred for their rewilding project. This had been stopped because of the lack of suitable crocodile habitats for the release of the captive-bred mugger, thanks to rampant environmental degradation, and also the widespread belief that being fish eaters, crocodiles are detrimental to commercial fisheries. Research has proved that it's actually quite the opposite because they eat predatory fish that feed on the commercially valuable species. Rom would repeat this fact at every meeting.

This initial goal of the Croc Bank – to restock wild areas – had run into another roadblock, because at the same time that the Crocodile Bank was established, the Government of India (with the help of the FAO), set up its own network of breeding and rearing centres that we initially helped stock and which were now producing offspring on a large scale. Several of the staff of the National Crocodile Project, such as Binod Choudhury, Kartick Vasudevan and D. Basu, had been trained by Rom at the Snake Park and in the field and they proudly proclaimed this. We were proud of this too but their success had also seeded our failure (to offload surplus animals).

By the turn of the century, we were getting desperate. Too many mugger, too expensive to maintain. Earlier, during one of its evaluation visits, the Central Zoo Authority (CZA) had mandated that the surplus croc issue had to be resolved, and the Croc Bank had bought some land about an hour's drive away, to move the surplus stock. However, the expenses involved in the upkeep of this satellite facility proved to be beyond our capacity. It was now even more important to resolve the problem because the CZA had asked zoos to create a masterplan for their development and improvement, with some requirements like the percentage of green spaces, visitor facilities, and human–animal barriers. We had optimistically factored in the area where the surplus stock was housed, expecting that they would have found other homes by the time we began implementing the layout of the master plan. But this hadn't happened!

And then there was a faint light at the end of the tunnel. It came from our friend and former assistant curator, Soham Mukherjee: 'Rom, I am trying to reach out to Reliance; Mukesh Ambani's son specifically, as he loves animals and collects tons. They have a private zoo in Jamnagar with an impressive collection of non-native animals.' Things progressed, and we were soon in touch with Anant Ambani's brainchild, the Greens Zoological Rescue and Rehabilitation Centre (GZRRC). On 4 and 5 February 2020, soon after I'd spoken the words 'Why don't you go and meet him', Rom and Allwin were at GZRRC in Jamnagar, and then in Mumbai with Mr Anant Ambani. I got an SMS from Rom: 'Looks promising!' My heart sang and I began calculating the money and space we would save once the mugger were gone.

Thus began what we proudly call the largest croc transfer in the world. Between December 2021 and July 2023, eight road trips were made and 850 mugger transported from the Croc Bank in Chennai to Jamnagar in temperature-controlled trucks. Each trip had an average of sixty mugger in individual boxes, accompanied by a convoy of cars and an ambulance. Nikhil and Rom, the latter living near Mysore by then, had corresponded with herpetologist friends around the world and discussed points connected with crocodile transport, such as whether the mouth should be tied or open (answer: the latter).

Nikhil straddles a crocodile during the great croc transfer to Gujarat.

Typically, the Jamnagar convoy would arrive in the afternoon, and the mugger catching would start early the next morning. Nikhil supervised and was part of the catching team, ensuring the safety of the humans and animals. Our croc capture methods have developed over time, and involve an initial 'lasso', then covering of the eyes (animal, not human), and finally straddling the animal. For the last stage, it is important to get the human number right, so that the weight doesn't damage the animal's spine. For support during the lifting and carrying of the crocodile, a strong ladder works well but there are many other details to be aware of, such as the position of the animal's legs. It's easy to cause an injury, even a fracture, if the limbs are not angled right.

Having watched Rom and other experts handle crocodiles from childhood, Nikhil is now at that level himself and has an intuitive sense of how to approach the capture of a particular animal, given its size, species and the available space. I watched proudly as he worked with the team during these GZRRC operations, one part of me also remembering the terrible day Jaws III had almost ended his life. But as he himself says, it wasn't Jaws' fault, but his own.

It was a proud moment when we heard that the last animal from the last shipment had been released into the last mugger enclosure in Jamnagar. We had pulled it off and transferred the animals 2,000 kilometres with nary an injury. The delight level was increased because Ajay Kartik, our former assistant curator and a gifted animal handler, had moved to GZRRC and we knew 'our' mugger would be well looked after. They even have a heated pool, in case a warm winter dip takes their fancy.

⁓

The best part of my job is the time spent out of the office, such as watching animal handling, feed sessions (especially gharial catching fish) and visiting our field stations. But in the initial years after rejoining, I also invested a lot of time and energy into strengthening the team spirit and work culture, taking advice from friends like Aruna Rajkumar and Renu Gupta, who had worked in human resources management. When Allwin also left to join GZRRC, Pramila Rajan joined us as director in April 2021, and I took on the managing trustee role. With her in the 'hot seat', I was able to take a back step and scrounge some writing time for myself though most of it is done at odd hours in the early morning. In 2023, two books scampered off the press one after the other, a novel called *Termite Fry*, and a revision of the 2003 *Sálim Ali for Schools*, with its name changed to *Sálim Ali for Children.* I realize now how easy it is to write a book, compared to helping the publisher sell it! In the last few months, I've been to multiple lit fests, launches and other events, offline and online. There's a lovely road safety sign on the Kodai Ghat: Don't Zoom to your Doom! I have definitely done that.

On the other hand, how lucky I've been to return to this organization I helped start, work with an amazing team and be able to see hundreds of animals during my morning walk! And at age seventy to have other things to think, worry and obsess about than joint pains and creaky knees! And so lucky too, to have two wonderful sons, one offline, the other online, both committed conservationists who often guide and advise me.

The Field Stations

On my return to the Croc Bank, I was keen to know what was happening at our field stations: the Andaman and Nicobar Environment Team (ANET) on the island of South Andaman, the Agumbe Rainforest Research Station (ARRS) in the Western Ghats and the Gharial Ecology Project (GEP) on the Chambal River.

The seeds of ANET were sown during a conversation Rom and I had with Baba in Kodaikanal, in 1989. Baba shared our concern for this piece of paradise, which was being rapidly decimated by logging, sand mining, encroachment, haphazard development and the misguided attempts to 'civilize' its indigenous communities. The three of us impulsively decided to register a trust, which would give us a base to lobby for the protection of this biodiversity hotspot and to start field surveys, studies and conservation initiatives there. With over twenty endemic species of reptiles in the archipelago, and so little known about them, there was plenty of herp work to be done. The Kodai registrar was surprised that a trust for island protection was being created on a mountaintop but did the needful. It turned out to be a good decision: ANET was the platform for many petitions, campaigns, projects and finally, a fabulous field station. Initially, its physical base was a plot of land in Wandoor, which belonged to Rom, and the little establishment functioned from there between 1989 and 1993. It was managed by Alok Mallick and his sister Rashmi (from the Aurobindo Ashram in Pondicherry) and saw the beginnings of conservation-related research projects. Field biologists like Jayashree Ratnam, earlier a Croc Bank volunteer and today a senior scientist at the National Centre for Biological Sciences in Bangalore made it their base, using Burmese-Karen staff (and their dungies) as guides; they are also jolly companions who contribute to jokes and laughter in the field.

In 1991, ANET acquired its own land, bought by the Croc Bank from donations. Things moved quickly. The beautiful base was designed by Rom and an architect friend, and built with the help of traditional Karen carpenters, many of them related to Allen Vaughan whom I had met on my 1975 trip. It was completed and made functional in 1998, and is a much-photographed conservation hub, which became our office, library and dormitory. Shaded by large local trees, with a krait living nearby and king cobras passing through, it was to become a foothold for researchers, volunteers and visitors from organizations in several countries. Individual cottages were built for researchers around the periphery of the property and were sometimes shared with pit vipers, day geckos and other herps that fancy human dwellings. There were collaborative 'cottage agreements' for partner organizations to build and maintain specific ones. These included the Indian Institute of Science, the National Centre for Biological Sciences and the Dakshin Foundation, whose researchers used ANET's facilities for their studies on marine and rainforest habitats and fauna. Topics ranged from the day gecko to growth patterns of indigenous trees, sea snakes, the shark fin industry and bats. The Croc Bank's own surveys were mostly focused on saltwater crocodiles and sea turtles, especially the giant leatherback, which has nesting sites on Little Andaman Island and Galathea Bay on Great Nicobar. Sea turtle surveys followed Satish Bhaskar's maps of nesting locations and added data on the four species that nest in the islands. ANET's team conducted five years of intensive island-wide surveys, dungy-sailing every year for two to three months to circumnavigate the nesting beaches and record observations.

Most of the funding for the base as well as the initial surveys came from some twenty-five supporters, including the Ministry of Environment, Forest and Climate Change (MoEFCC), Ministry of Human Resources and Development, WWF, the Australian High Commission, the Indo German Social Service Society, the Harvard Museum of Comparative Zoology, the Royal Netherlands Embassy, UNESCO and UNICEF. As with the Croc Bank, friends and family introduced us to the right people. Meeting our policymakers in Delhi was a much more informal and easy process in those days. In time, the administration of ANET was turned over to the Croc Bank.

ANET's backbone was and remains a group of Karens, most of them from Webi in North Andaman. While it was being built, Saw Allan Vaughan (Saw is a Burmese prefix that denotes respect) was employed by the Forest Department but took leave to come and help supervise the work at the base. When it was time for him to return to his job, Saw Pa-Aung brought in Saw John, who had finished school in Port Blair and was fluent in English, useful for communicating with volunteers, visitors and government officials. John turned out to be gold. He, Saw Pa-Aung and Saw Shwether formed ANET's core group, each a brother and adviser to the other Karens who came and went as their jobs allowed. These included Saw Felix, Uncle Pambwint, Saw Agu, Saw Nelson. Collectively, they made ANET what it is today. They played – and continue to play – many roles; as boat builders, field assistants, data recorders and cooks who can make a mean Burmese nappi that sets your mouth on fire. Expert jungle folk, many had also been commercial divers in the Andaman–Nicobar reefs. Wearing homemade goggles and flip-flops (often flattened PET bottles) to avoid coral cuts, they used to supply turbo and trochus shells to the mother-of-pearl industry.

The construction of the main building, which would

become the office and dormitory, began in 1997. About thirty to forty Karens were camped there at any given time, working under the Bengali head carpenter, Polin *maestri*. And there was the wonderful Manish Chandi, who had arrived in 1995 as a WWF Conservation Corps volunteer. For the next twenty-five years, he grew with ANET and vice versa. Apart from his passion for wildlife and conservation, he is also an anthropologist, and his knowledge and understanding of the Nicobarese communities is unsurpassed.

His brief from Rom and Harry was near-impossible: afforest the campus, they told him, and create a water source for it. He managed to do both. Using the help and knowledge of Saw Pa-Aung and Saw Shwether, he planted the 5-acre ANET campus with local trees and shrubs. For the other task, the water source, he set off to where else but Auroville, to learn about rainwater harvesting, filtration, restoration, bunding and also seed and sapling collection and planting, so a nursery could be developed for local plants. The team of three roamed the forest collecting seeds and saplings. But the challenge lay in watering them. They decided to clump them in the hands/plates washing area outside the kitchen so that they could catch the run-off. There was also another, unexpected source: dew that collected on the roof during the pre-summer period and dripped down every morning, keeping the saplings moist and happy.

Initially, water for ANET was brought by intrepid staff members, Mrinal Kanti Bhowmick (Montu) and Shwether on a *sangha* (long pliable cane stick, notched at both ends, on which bundles, buckets and other objects can be hung). Conversations between Manish, Harry and Rom led to a plan to make a waterbody in front of the kitchen, where the land is low lying, and a backhoe was hired to beat the bumps and banks into submission. Surprisingly, the bottom turned out to be white sand, not clay as they had expected. More later, about this mystery!

Then came the creation of the filtration device, which would be a 2-metre hole, a metre in diameter. This was filled with layers of brickbat, coal, sand and gravel, with a mud and clay topping, around a homemade filtration outlet – a small pipe with serrations connected to a half HP motor pump. The water from the pond would seep through the brick–sand–charcoal–gravel combo and then enter the serrated pipe from which the pump pulled water out of the pond. The rains came and the storage tank filled up with close to 7 lakh litres of cool, clear water. Overflow pipes were needed, but money was anything but overflowing. When Manish found some huge pipes bobbing along the sea surface near South Brother Island, he loaded eight into the dungy but had to return six to the ocean because of the rough weather – the protruding pipes were bringing in water and flooding the boat. The remaining two turned out to be useful additions to the water system and are still in place. Manish and the 'planting team' then visited swamps on South Andaman, looking for reeds that would hold the soil and filter out its 'undesirable elements', as per the advice of the Auroville experts.

While digging the pond, Saw Pa-Aung, Saw Pambwint and Manish were also making a well for washing clothes, next to the mangroves bordering the property. They went deep through the dense and sticky mangrove soil and lots of shells and coral bits began to appear. They realized they were digging through an ancient coral reef; more treasure appeared in the form of an ancient, hollow log, practically the diameter of the well. It was mature redwood or padauk (*Pterocarpus dalbergioides*); clearly, a tree that had fallen into the reef. In effect, they were on land that had been a coral reef, aeons ago! This meant that the white sandy soil below the pond was from an old beach, which explained its colour and texture. It was exciting to learn how these landscape changes had occurred, and there were other such geography lessons as the campus developed.

Once the reeds were established, whistling teals arrived and made the pond their home. Wonderful Manish created a hump at the back, to give them a little privacy from prying birdwatchers! It was an exciting day, a year or two later, when pairs of the endemic Andaman teals were first seen on the pond. Meanwhile, the tree planting continued, and Manish managed to convince Saw Pa-Aung not to do this in the Forest Department style, in straight soldierly rows, but to plant randomly and create a forest. Apart from tree saplings, they added lianas, varieties of cane, smaller trees and other undergrowth species. And three years later, birds began to stop by, which was a huge help in the planting. They brought in seeds, and the diversity shot up to a level that mere humans could never have achieved.

So, thanks to this innovative and indefatigable team, ANET acquired a dependable water source, even when others were scrounging around roadside taps in peak summer. Being able to offer water to neighbours at these times created great local friendships and support.

In the 1990s, Harry Andrews, then Croc Bank director, spent long periods at ANET to administer it and carry out surveys. Many puns were made about his 'hairy' adventures and courage in stormy weather aboard Karen dungies in spite of being a non-swimmer! He and Manish Chandi had many 'good times' together, about which Manish promises to write soon. On a 1997 trip to Little Andaman in Saw Santein's dungy, they chugged straight into a cyclone and the vessel rocked and swung and filled with water that required constant bailing. Taking double the usual time, they reached Bumila Creek with all rations drowned in saltwater. 'We ate fruit bats for three days,' says Manish blandly. And adds reassuringly, 'Boiled.'

In later years, my ecologist cousin Rauf Ali of Pondicherry University joined the team whenever he could, giving valuable advice on best practice field research. Many researchers hopped off the ANET springboard and landed in high positions in conservation and research platforms around the world. Rauf's student Jayashree Ratnam, who studied the Andaman day gecko, is one of them. Manjula Tiwari, who worked on our early sea turtle surveys (and kid-sat Nikhil and Samir for us) is now with the prestigious National Oceanographic and Atmospheric Administration, Florida.

The collective bank of ANET memories is vast, and keeps the conversation rolling: adventures in dungies and mangrove stands, king cobra nests in the forest, sea snakes beaching to lay their eggs, phosphorescent coral gardens, Shompen jungle camps and nesting leatherbacks on Great Nicobar, foot surveys into the interior of Little Andaman, snorkelling in Japanese and British shipwrecks and spotting Jarawa in the distance. Rom and the team worked closely with the central and local government in those early years and helped demarcate marine and forest Protected Areas. The Croc Bank and ANET staff hosted and supported field biologists from India and abroad who were engaged in pathbreaking studies. Some years earlier, Rom had spoken to Rajiv and Sonia Gandhi about the Islands when they visited the Snake Park, and the need to preserve this paradise. Whether it was coincident or not, the Gandhis holidayed there soon after that and set in motion a series of conservation policies. We Andaman-lovers felt hopeful. But as often happens, there were too many forces at play, which led to forest and reef decimation on a huge scale, including the construction of the Andaman Trunk Road that goes right through the heart of the Jarawa Reserve. Today, we are facing the grim reality that the Galathea Bay Wildlife Sanctuary has been denotified and the plan is to build a gigantic transhipment port, which will include an airport, township and power plant spanning about 18 per cent of Great Nicobar. Ironically, the island was declared a UNESCO Biosphere Reserve in 2013 and has two national parks and a tribal reserve that encompasses much of the island for the Shompen and the Great Nicobarese. Further, in its National Marine Turtle Action Plan of 2021, the MoEFCC listed Galathea Bay as one of the 'most important marine turtle habitats in India'.[1] So, in terms of conservation in the Islands, it has been one step forward and two back; but one keeps hoping. Given the climate breakdown of the recent past, our conservation policies and priorities may well change.

After my return to the Croc Bank in 2015, I visited ANET a couple of times to see how it was getting on. I sensed that it was no longer the busy hub of herp research and conservation it had been when Rom, Harry and Manish were spending chunks of time there. Moreover, Rom and I had been talking about 'bequeathing' the projects we'd started to younger teams with a similar conservation vision. We began a search for a suitable individual or organization, which ended with ANET becoming the property of the Dakshin

The construction of the Andaman Trunk Road cut through the heart of the Jarawa Reserve.

Foundation, our long-time partners in the Islands, in 2019. Its trustees, Drs Kartik Shanker and Meera Oommen are old friends; Kartik was one of the early 'sea turtlers' who walked the Chennai coast during the ridley nesting season. Our assistant director Allwin came with me on that last trip to ANET to complete the paperwork, a sad couple of days teeming with memories of my trips with Rom and the children and questions about whether we were doing the right thing. I went for a walk to ponder this life question while Allwin played netball with the staff. As I turned a corner, a street dog jumped up and bit me on my back. I decided to take that as a sign: that yes, it was the right decision, and it was time to leave. And now, several years later, I'm even more sure, because the base is buzzing again, with researchers from many corners of the country.

The second field station, the Agumbe Rainforest Research Station (ARRS), is in the Western Ghats, an IUCN Biodiversity Hotspot and one of Rom's heart-spots. It became possible thanks to his mother Doris Norden, who left him a legacy of fourteen thousand dollars at her death in 2004. He was off to Agumbe in a flash, looking for land and got lucky a year later: 4 acres right next to the Someshwara Wildlife Sanctuary, with a stream running alongside the boundary, the whistling thrush, trogon and giant squirrels in residence, and black panther, bison and king cobras in the vicinity. The location, and his growing reputation, were winners with funding agencies, and as with ANET, support came in from several sources, including the prestigious Rolex and Whitley Awards. A skeletal multitasking staff was hired, and researchers, volunteers and visitors started arriving. As at ANET, the infrastructure consists of a central building with outlying cottages.

Gowri Shankar, who later went on to start the Kalinga Centre for Rainforest Ecology, helped Rom build both the campus and its work. He also completed a PhD on king cobras, probably the only one in the country. Soon after, Ajay Giri, a snake rescuer from Maharashtra joined ARRS as a volunteer; he went on to become its education officer and is presently field director. Ajay has become a well-known name and face in the online corridors of herp lovers, and his work has helped build a positive community attitude towards king cobras in Agumbe, which are frequently rescued from homes and gardens, firewood stacks, shops, godowns, road culverts and once even from a car engine! As the king's forest home gets commandeered by human settlements and agriculture, there are more and more 'rescue calls'. Thanks to support from the Deshpande Foundation, Wildlife Conservation Trust, the King Cobra Conservancy and others, this is a free service, with each rescue followed by a talk about the natural history of this flagship species and the importance of conserving it. ARRS's relationship with the community has

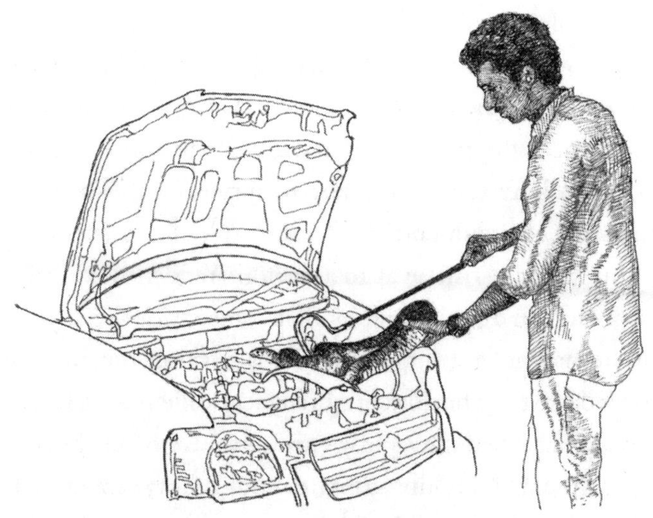

King cobra rescue sites include car engines!

brought about a sea change in their attitude towards kings, and indeed snakes in general. Calls in the early days had an element of panic, which is now missing. 'There's a *kalinga* in the garden, we'll let you know if there's a problem,' is a standard message today. How cool is that! They understand that in spite of being the largest venomous snake in the world, king cobras are not aggressive, and will go along minding their own business if left alone.

In March 2023, while on a three-week visit to ARRS, I was lucky enough to observe ten king cobra rescues; but just as exciting for me were the interviews with neighbouring farming families who had shared their gardens and farms with kings for several days, sometimes weeks, at a time. This level of tolerance towards a potentially dangerous animal had always fascinated me. I asked Ajay to introduce me to some of the families he'd encountered during rescues, so that I could meet the real conservationists, the people who are the reason king cobras continue to survive in this human-dominated environment.

One of these visits was to a farm in Yeddehedlo village. The owner Mr Rajesh, told us that some six or seven years ago, he had seen a large male king basking outside the cowshed, next to a burrow. Frightened, he called ARRS; Ajay arrived and calmed the rapidly growing crowd of neighbours. He told them about king cobra natural history; about male competition for a female, leading to combat. He guessed there must be a female in the burrow, and he was right. Rajesh and his family spotted her the next day and watched from a safe distance as they had been advised to do.

On the fourth day, along came another male! Rajesh was lucky enough to watch the combat. The two males engaged in the famous king cobra combat, with one-third of their body upright, trying to push the rival's head down to the ground, then flopping down to continue the combat horizontally, still entwined, then up again . . . a muscle tussle, with no biting; after all, why waste good venom? (It's needed for catching prey, and in any case, as far as we know, snakes are immune to their own venoms to some degree.) The combat lasted for a couple of hours, and the intruder, the second male, was clearly the loser. He left. But that wasn't the end. Two days later another male arrived, and the combat was repeated, with the same result. Five males were thus dismissed by that first arrival, who then entered the burrow and stayed with the female for three weeks. Once in a while she would join him in a bask outside but remained in the burrow most of that time.

Thanks to the work of ARRS, we have learnt a lot about king cobras, and the Agumbe community has learnt to share the habitat with them – a success in the field of human–animal conflict.

One morning in 2008, Rom and six others gathered around the dining table at ARRS; not to eat, but to examine a large male king cobra stretched out in front of them. He had been anaesthetized in preparation for a surgery, to implant a tiny battery-driven transmitter that would enable a team of volunteers to follow and study him for the duration of the battery's life (about two years). A lot of paperwork had been done to get permission to handle and study this protected species, and enter Protected Areas such as reserve forests and sanctuaries while following the snakes. The Principal Chief Conservator of Forests, Karnataka, had granted ARRS these permissions for four kings, two males and two females. This was a first for king cobra telemetry in India, an exciting moment for ARRS and the Croc Bank. Rom's friend and snake ecologist Dr Matt Goode, from the University of Arizona in Tucson, was also present to ensure the safe implantation of the transmitters. He and his students had been studying rattlesnakes in Arizona using telemetry, which is the ideal study tool for secretive animals like king cobras.

After the implant surgery, it was time for the 'kiss of life', and one lucky person got to bring the snake back to life. Using a Café Coffee Day straw, air was blown into the trachea, and the snake slowly returned to consciousness.

Volunteers signed up to help in the project, young snake lovers from several countries for whom this was the opportunity of a lifetime. Very conveniently, kings sleep at night and spend the day foraging for food (snakes, mostly rat snakes and cobras) or lying still, so the trackers were often able to settle down and have their picnic lunch, or read or catch up with the note-taking, while keeping an eye on their 'trackee' snake. On some days, the snake was active, especially during the male-combat season, and many miles had to be covered, with lunch on the go. They had to be up before their snake was, and, using a receiver, find it. Often, it was still where it had come to rest the night before, or close by. The goal behind the telemetry project, this first phase and then the second one in 2018, was to study the behaviour and movements of king cobras so that appropriate conservation measures could be suggested to the government. Two discoveries emerged from this project – one, that kings had extensive territories, (sometimes as large as 10 square kilometres!), and the second that they were cannibalistic (which had led to the loss of a radio transmitter!)

Our third field station, the Gharial Ecology Project or GEP, lies 2,000 kilometres north of Chennai, in Garhaita village on the Uttar Pradesh stretch of the Chambal River. The GEP has its foundations in conversations over many years between Rom and Jeff (Dr Jeffrey Lang, mentioned earlier), about their concern for the gharial. Conservation was a challenge, because the Chambal River, their last stronghold, spans the states of Uttar Pradesh, Rajasthan and Madhya Pradesh, which meant dialogue with the MoEFCC as well as the Forest Departments of the three states.

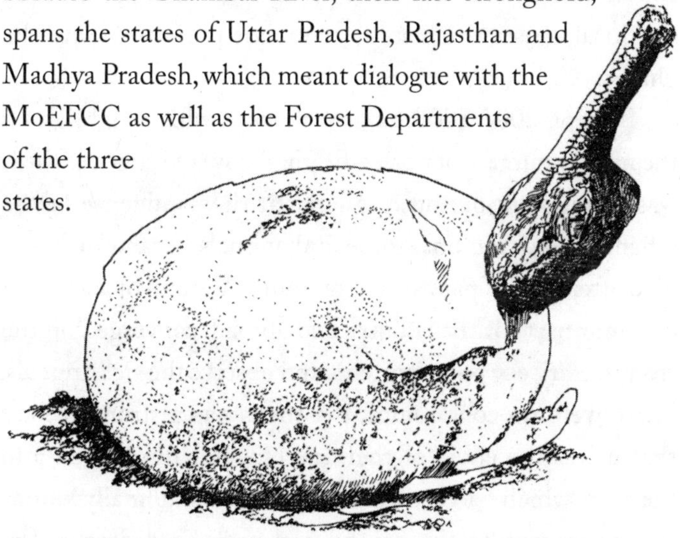

A baby gharial takes its first peep at the world. The focus of the Gharial Ecology Project is the gharial, one of the most endangered reptiles in the world.

The IUCN's Crocodile Specialist Group was also seriously concerned and listed it as one of the most endangered animals in the world.

While in college in Darwin in 2004, Nikhil attended a meeting of the Crocodile Specialist Group, during which the rapidly falling numbers of the gharial, by then declared a Critically Endangered species, was discussed. Its extinction was a very real possibility, and he joined meetings about this with Rom, Jeff, Grahame Webb, Colin Stevenson and other biologists. An informal group, the Gharial Conservation Alliance, was formed to raise funds for the animal's conservation, and they networked with funding agencies and local conservationists to formulate projects to save the gharial.

Then, in 2007/2008, came a shocker, which highlighted the need for urgent action if the gharial was to survive. There was a landmark die-off of gharial at the confluence of the Chambal and Yamuna; some 200 animals became sick and died after days of pain and immobility. A group of vets, from different parts of the country and abroad, converged on the river to carry out post-mortems and observe the sick animals. There were no conclusions, but there was a strong feeling that it was the effect of chemical effluents discharged into the river, which had caused joint inflation and finally kidney failure, leading to the painful and prolonged deaths. The animals, land-bound, were hardly able to move, the limbs swollen to almost double the normal size.

Luckily, the deaths stopped just as suddenly as they had started. The incident led to the Croc Bank establishing the GEP in Garhaita on the Chambal River, again under Jeff's guidance. By this time, our younger son Samir had also joined the Croc Bank, and Jeff and the three Whitaker men contributed to its development.

At the same time, the four of them were lobbying for a tri-state gharial sanctuary across their remaining habitats. Luckily Jairam Ramesh was then the Minister of Environment, and the National Chambal Wildlife Sanctuary came to pass. The GEP team, which now includes the intrepid Jailabdeen A., have a rough-and-ready life, with long hours on boats and makeshift camps as they follow animals using telemetry and observe their behaviour for hours in extreme temperatures.

Given Jeff's expertise and experience, the GEP's surveys are among the most detailed and thorough crocodilian studies in the world. My own favourite GEP discovery is the extent to which the male guards the nests and hatchlings, even taking clusters of them piggyback on river rides! Long may this amazing animal survive, in spite of all the challenges it faces, including the illegal sand mining, which is decimating its nesting grounds.

It's not hard to imagine why visits to the field stations are the best part of my job: wonderful wildlife sightings, with others taking the risks! But there is another element to love – wonderful people, the likes of whom one wouldn't meet elsewhere, such as Saw Agu, who was at the ANET leatherback camp in South Bay, Great Nicobar, when the 2004 tsunami struck. With him was a sea turtle biologist and a group of birdwatchers who were guests at ANET and had gone along with them for some exotic birding on Great Nic. It was the day after Christmas and Saw Agu and the biologist had returned from a night walk close to dawn. They crawled into sleeping bags and fell asleep, exhausted. But their sleep was broken by an extended juddering of the ground. Agu had experienced many earthquakes and knew immediately that this wasn't a normal one. Running to the beach, where the others had also gathered, he noticed the sea's strange recede-and-rush movements. His mind raced to a hill behind them; he knew they had to get there instantly. But the delays caused by the others, who were gathering important possessions to take along, made this impossible. The ocean seeped inland, then rushed into the forest with a roar. They were just about able to climb a large tree and watch the swirling water and debris 5 metres below, as the ocean surged into the forest. Then came the next wave, 15 metres high and towering above them.

Agu's next memory is of being whipped down into the dark, smelly mess of swirling water and debris, and the absence of answering calls from the others as he repeatedly shouted out to them. Bruised and with a broken arm, he struggled free of the tangle of fallen branches around him. The next wave ripped off his clothes and changed the surroundings to one endless seascape, with all landmarks gone. Between dunkings in the filth, he saw a standing tree and crawled towards it so he could cling to it and survey the landscape. But it gave way and fell on him, causing further injuries.

'Keep your head up, breathe,' he kept telling himself as the churning waves and whorls of water dragged him down. Then he saw a raft of floating logs, climbed aboard and lay down to rest his bruised and battered body. Often delirious and fainting from pain, hunger and thirst, he continued to call out whenever he was conscious and had the strength. Night and day became an inseparable stretch of never-ending time. Thirsty and dehydrated, he longed for a sip of water. Then came a blessed shower of rain, but the temperature dropped and his naked body shivered uncontrollably. Two weeks passed this way. Now and then he mustered the dregs of his strength in self-preservation, such as when an Asian water monitor, tongue flicking, examined his body to check if it was carrion. It was a superhuman effort to shake his body, but he knew he had to show the animal that he was alive. It moved away reluctantly.

An added torture were the helicopters on rescue sorties. They flew low but his desperate one-armed waving was invisible among the tangle of broken forest. There were sandflies, which descend at dusk and have surprisingly painful bites for their tiny size. There were other misfortunes; repeated falls into the stinking water and debris, rain . . . then came a life-saving thought, thanks to the depth of his forest-knowledge. He realized that his tree-raft came from a patch of lowland forest near the Galathea, and this gave him an orientation on where the coast lay.

Encouraged, he began to move in that direction, stumbling, falling, sinking, thrashing his way forward with one arm. And then, on 11 January, the sixteenth day of his nightmare, he began seeing different debris, the remains of a human habitation. He realized this must have been Shastri Nagar village, now destroyed by the tsunami. The lone survivor he met – an old acquaintance who couldn't recognize him at first – helped Saw Agu cover his nakedness with a pair of trousers lying in the muck, which they belted with a strand of vine around his now skeletal body.

Surely one of the great stories of survival in the wild. A miracle.

And there was another miracle to come. At the Croc Bank, the manager Harry Andrews had been worried about the ANET team, having seen the news about the tsunami's raging surges in the Islands. He left for Port Blair as soon as he could get a flight, and relating the turtle team's disappearance to the navy's rescue squad, asked if he could join their sorties over Great Nic.

The day he managed to do so was the day when Saw Agu reached Shastri Nagar.

Harry and the pilot circled the mouth of the Galathea and scanned the ravaged landscape for signs of life. The pilot began a descent. In a forest clearing above the water line, he'd seen someone. When he landed, Harry spotted Saw Agu sitting under a coconut tree and they waved to each other; a life moment for both. As they exchanged news came the realization that others at the camp hadn't made it.

~

Saw Agu's story has been an inspiration to me, a metaphor for overcoming what Life chucks at us. As powerful as the courage and stoicism was a conversation I had with him about it.

'Agu, what horrors you lived through!'

'Yes,' he said, 'I was so worried about where the others were, what was happening to them.'

Something to learn from this. Maybe a lot.

Wow, I said to myself a few days later. What a life.

I wasn't thinking of Agu's life, but mine: about how lucky I've been in the places I've seen, the people I've met, and the experiences I've had, thanks to my family and my work with Rom – as his wife and then as a friend.

Endnote

Having grown up and grown old in the NGO world, many friends and acquaintances are from this space and many 'founders' talk about the difficulty of handing over to the next, younger team. I agree with them to some extent because it's hard to see things being done differently from one's original vision. At the same time, I remind myself that different is not necessarily less effective and may well be better, especially in the light of changing circumstances and perspectives in the world. The need for this transition becomes even more obvious to me after I've searched for the spectacles while they're perched on my head, or struggled to open a cupboard with the wrong key, or tried to charge the laptop with the Kindle charger.

So there are twingy moments, but how exciting it is to watch the younger lot in action! We are lucky, Rom and I, that this future team is truly wonderful: each and every one of them, here at the Croc Bank as well as those in the field stations. I try to guide and encourage them in the most productive ways I can think of, remembering the mistakes we ourselves made, and the need to morph with the rapidly changing times. We plan together, and they execute. Their commitment to the Croc Bank leaves me more and more time to write, read, travel and engage with archival, reportage, signboard and publicity texts, ideal for my personal interests and ageing knees.

And sometimes, sitting in my sea-facing office, I reflect on the history of India's conservation movement, beginning with Project Tiger, the Wildlife (Protection) Act of 1972, and Prime Minister Indira Gandhi's passion for wildlife and forests and the need to preserve them. I had a ringside seat at this show and then at Rom's spectacular work in reptile conservation and research. I was fortunate to participate in it as well, from cyclostyling the *Newsletter for Birdwatchers* to welcoming the first visitor to the Croc Bank. What are my thoughts as they wander backwards in time?

Often, they remind me of the difference in how committees and institutions see themselves and their role. In the hoary past, there was a strong commitment to the task at hand, consensus and dialogue, and invisibling oneself, however hard! Self-confidence was good, but self-publicity wasn't. In meetings and workshops, one focused on the issue, and personal friendships and enmities were to be shrugged off. I watched and heard examples of this from Baba, Sálim Mamoo, Anne Wright, Bittu Sahgal, J.C. Daniel, Sir Peter Scott, George Schaller and many others. And, of course,

Rom, who continued to be polite and helpful to the Snake Park coup team (much to my irritation.)

But today, it's a more self-centric space, though even as I write this I realize it may be an unfair statement because I can think of many exceptions; among them, the Croc Bank trustees, who go straight to the heart of the matter despite what may be in their hearts. After our unfortunate choice of Snake Park trustees, Rom and I were more careful about picking people on this group, and they have served us well. My gratitude to them, for their understanding of the mistakes we made, and generosity with their time, thoughts, and social and professional contacts.

The Croc Bank is special because it has been my home for a very long time. Thanks to the divorce settlement I received from Rom, Nikhil and I are in comfortable living spaces in a two-storeyed house on the beach; him downstairs and me 'sitting on his head' upstairs. The sea in front and crocs in the backyard; life could be worse! Samir and Lenke visit when they can, as do other family and friends. And several projects, writing and others, are in my mental pending tray. Whether they actually happen or remain plans is to be seen. But either way, they provide much excitement. Maybe not as much as wandering in the forests of PNG or the Andamans, but close, and certainly more suitable for an elderly adventurer!

Notes

Gaimukh Bundar

1 Patrick Russell, 'An Account of Indian Serpents, Collected on the Coast of Coromandel: Containing Descriptions and Drawings of Each Species, Together with Experiments and Remarks on their Several Poisons', W. Bulmer and Co. Shakespeare-Press; for G. Nicol, 1796. https://www.biodiversitylibrary.org/item/252813#page/7/mode/1up.

Herps in Paradise

1 Census of India, 1931, Vol. 2, Government of India, Central Publication Branch, 1932, p. 119.
2 M.V. Portman, *A History of Our Relations with the Andamanese*, Calcutta Office of the Superintendent of Government Printing, India, 1899.
3 Raghubir Singh, 'The Undefeated: Last Stand of the Andaman Islanders (The Untamed Shores)', *Sunday Times*, 14 September 1975, pp. 34–48.

Worshippers and Victims: A Complex Relationship with Snakes

1 *Hamadryad,* Vol. 3 (3), September 1978.

2 India Today News Desk, '36 Students Fall Sick After Lizard Found in Mid-Day Meal at Govt School in Bihar', *India Today,* 19 May 2023, https://www.indiatoday.in/india/story/bihar-students-ill-sick-lizard-mid-day-meal-stable-condition-saran-district-2381242-2023-05-19.

Centre for Herpetology

1 'In Telangana, Groom Dies of Cardiac Arrest After Dancing', *The Hindu,* 16 February 2020, https://www.thehindu.com/news/national/telangana/in-telangana-groom-dies-of-cardiac-arrest-after-dancing/article30834863.ece.

The Field Stations

1 'National Marine Turtle Action Plan', Government of India, Ministry of Environment, Forest and Climate Change (2021–2026), 2021, https://mangroves.maharashtra.gov.in/Site/SiteInfo/Pdf/NMTAP.pdf.

A Note on the Author

Zai Whitaker grew up in a family of naturalists that included her father Zafar Futehally and granduncle Sálim Ali, India's original Birdman. Not surprisingly, conversations, holidays and outings often centred around birds. Zai has written twenty books including *Andamans Boy*, *Kali and the Rat Snake*, and the recent *Termite Fry*. She has also written extensively about the Irular snake catchers, and started the Irular Women's Society which focuses on Irular women's economic and social empowerment. She lives and works at the Croc Bank outside Chennai, where she is the managing trustee.

About Indian Pitta

Indian Pitta is India's first dedicated book imprint for bird lovers, conservationists and policymakers. Our books about birds and natural history go beyond field/identification guides, to explore the bigger mosaic of habitats, ecosystems and human interactions that touch the lives of birds. Successful conservation programmes, troubling environmental challenges, personal exploration of a landscape, deep dives into the ecology of a species, the quest for a rare species and the sheer joy of birding – these are some of the ideas that you can expect to explore within the pages of our books.